DIVERTICULITIS COOKBOOK 2022

300+ Days of Quick, Budget-Friendly and Flavorful Recipes to Improve
Gut Health, Prevent Flare-Ups and Clean Your Digestive System.
28 Day Meal Plan and Food List

Jane Richmond

TABLE OF CONTENTS

INTRODUCTION

Diverticula are tiny, bulging pouches that can develop in the lining of the digestive tract. They are commonly seen in the bottom portion of the large intestine (colon). Diverticula are most common in people over the age of 40, but they seldom cause issues. Diverticulosis is a medical term for the condition of having diverticula. Diverticulitis occurs when one or more of the pouches becomes inflamed and, in some circumstances, infected. Diverticulitis can result in severe stomach discomfort, fever, nausea, and a significant change in bowel patterns. Diverticular disease was uncommon before the twentieth century. However, it is currently one of the most prevalent health issues in the Western world. Diverticular disease refers to a range of conditions that affect the digestive system.

The most dangerous kind of diverticular disease is diverticulitis. Its symptoms are typically excruciatingly painful. If the symptoms are not managed, they might lead to persistent health concerns. Diverticulitis symptoms range from moderate to severe. These symptoms may begin suddenly or build gradually over several days.

The following symptoms characterize diverticular disease:

- Bloating
- Abdominal discomfort
- Diarrhea
- Constipation

Diverticulitis patients may have the following symptoms:

- Constant abdominal discomfort
- Vomiting and nausea
- Stool with blood
- High fever and chills
- Rectal bleeding

Abdominal discomfort is the most frequent symptom of diverticulitis. North Americans and Europeans often feel discomfort on the left lower side (sigmoid colon), but Asians typically experience it on the right (ascending colon).

If you have any of the symptoms mentioned above, such as blood in your stool or vomiting, it could be a sign of a severe complication from diverticulitis or another illness, so you should see a doctor as soon as possible.

Causes of Diverticulitis

Diverticula is the medical term for the pouches that form in the colon. They develop when weak areas in your gut wall inflate outward.

Diverticulitis can be caused by inflammation and, in certain circumstances, infection of the diverticula. It happens when partly digested food or excrement obstructs the diverticula opening. Diverticular disease has more than one known cause. Numerous environmental and genetic variables, according to research and clinical experience, may influence its development. The severity of your condition determines the treatment for this disease.

The mild type of this disease is usually treated at home. Your doctor may suggest that you make dietary adjustments. In some situations, medicines such as antibiotics may be given. If problems arise due to the condition, you will almost certainly need to seek treatment at a medical facility. Antibiotics or fluids may be administered intravenously as treatment. Depending on the nature of the problem, you may need to have surgery.

Lifestyle habits such as inactivity, smoking, and obesity can exacerbate the condition. Avoiding seeds and nuts is no longer suggested as a preventative measure because there is no scientific proof that these foods contribute to diverticula inflammation.

According to studies, diverticulosis affects up to 35% of persons in the Western world. In rural Africa, fewer than 1% of the population is afflicted, with 4-15% of those affected developing diverticulitis. The condition becomes more frequent as one gets older. Diverticulitis is responsible for thousands of deaths each year. It is the most pervasive anatomic colon condition. In the United States, it costs billions of dollars annually. Diverticulitis is a severe medical disease, and patient education is essential in preventing it. This book is a complete guide to diverticulitis. It provides a thorough explanation of all you need to know about this illness, including:

- What you should know about your digestive system
- Diverticulitis basics (symptoms, complications, clinical diagnosis)
- Diverticulitis diet stages: clear fluids, low-residue diet, and high-fiber diets
- A comprehensive shopping list for the diverticulitis diet
- 120 tried-and-true dishes for your diverticulitis diet plan

With *The Complete Guide to Diverticulitis*, you can take complete control of your digestive health.

Chapter 1

BASICS OF DIVERTICULITIS

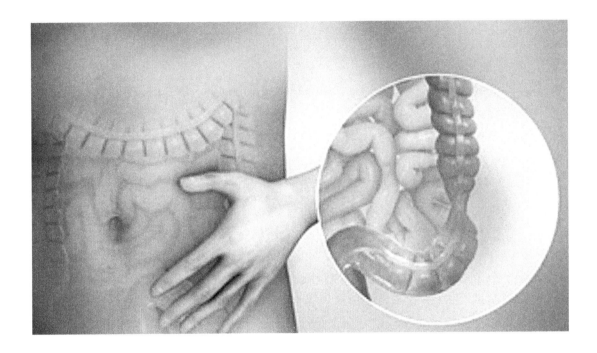

Diverticulitis, more particularly colonic diverticulitis, is a disease of the gastrointestinal tract. Diverticulitis develops when diverticula become inflamed. Diverticula are abnormal pouches that can form in the walls of your big intestine. Diverticulitis symptoms include sudden aches in your lower abdomen, although the discomfort can also persist over days. Diverticulitis can cause constipation, diarrhea, and nausea. If you start noticing blood in your stool or have a fever, the disease may have progressed to a more complex stage. Repeated flare-ups are typical.

Medical research has yet to understand the primary causes of diverticulitis completely. Lack of exercise, obesity, smoking, a family history of the disease, and anti-inflammatory medication usage appear to be risk factors for this disease. A low-fiber diet may also contribute to the condition, although just how is uncertain.

A person may have pouches in their big intestines at times without inflammation. This disease, diverticulosis, is different from diverticulitis. Inflammation occurs 10% to 25% of the time. In some cases, a rash may form, which is the result of a bacterial infection. If your doctor believes you have diverticulitis, they will order diagnostic testing to confirm it. Typically, blood tests, a CT scan, or a colonoscopy are used to make a diagnosis. A gastrointestinal series may also be performed. Irritable bowel syndrome is also among the possible diagnoses.

Diverticulosis may be treated with a prescription for mesalamine.

In the past, health professionals issued warnings to the public, advising us to avoid nuts and seeds as a precautionary measure. It is important to note again that this is no longer suggested because there is no scientific proof that seeds and nuts cause diverticula inflammation. For patients with a moderate case of the disease, doctors typically recommend a liquid diet. Oral antibiotics may also be prescribed if infection is suspected. Severe cases may require hospitalization. Complete bowel rest may also be advised. Probiotics, according to some experts, can be beneficial. Their efficacy, however, is uncertain. Surgery may be recommended if you develop problems from this disease, such as fistula formation, abscess formation, or colon perforation.

The Link Between Diverticulitis and Diverticulosis

The digestive tract is subject to a variety of problems. Some of these illnesses can have symptoms that overlap or are comparable to motility or gastrointestinal function problems. These can also have distinguishing characteristics that set them apart from motility or functional gastrointestinal tract problems.

Diverticulosis

Diverticulosis is characterized by tiny pouches protruding from the walls of the colon. In the United States, one out of every ten persons over the age of 40 has the condition, and more than half of those over 60 have it.

Diverticulosis is not an issue on its own. The pouches are not harmful and do not create any symptoms. However, problems emerge when the diverticula become contaminated, like when feces become stuck in the pouch.

Diverticulitis

Diverticulitis occurs when the pouches become inflamed. Inflammation is caused by an infection. Diverticulitis is a dangerous illness since the condition can lead to further complications. Diverticulitis is present in one out of every five to seven cases of diverticulosis.

Experts feel that a low-fiber diet may contribute to the high prevalence of diverticulosis. Fiber is an essential part of every meal. It softens and bulks up stool, allowing it to pass more quickly through the colon. If you don't consume enough fiber in your diet, your stool will become hard. It will cause pressure in your colon as your muscles try to move stool through the colon. This pressure is what causes the colon's walls to bulge out into pouches.

We've already seen symptoms in the overview, but for thoroughness, let's go over them again.

Most diverticulosis patients are unaware of their condition until their colon is checked for another reason and the pouches are discovered. Nonetheless, some people may have symptoms such as bloating, moderate cramping, or constipation.

If your diverticulosis progresses to diverticulitis, you may experience the following symptoms:

- Fever
- Nausea
- Pain in the abdomen
- Chills
- Constipation or diarrhea
- Vomiting

Diverticulitis and diverticulosis may mimic other diseases such as:

- Appendicitis
- Peptic ulcers
- Ovarian cysts
- Crohn's disease
- Irritable bowel syndrome

That is why your doctor may request tests such as ultrasonography, endoscopy, or x-rays to establish an accurate diagnosis.

Duration to be expected

There is no cure that eliminates diverticula unless the piece of colon is surgically removed. Diverticulosis is a chronic disease. It is, however, treatable with dietary changes.

Diverticulitis symptoms may go away after a few days of treatment. That is also true for diverticulosis. However, you should be aware that these symptoms may persist or increase in the event of complications or severe disease.

People who eat a high-fiber diet have a decreased chance of developing diverticular disease. According to the American Dietetic Association, you should consume 20-35 grams of fiber each day. Fiber from vegetables, fruits, and grains is preferable. Your doctor may also recommend a fiber supplement or uncooked bran. If you want to increase the quantity of fiber you consume daily, do so gradually. Drink plenty of water (at least eight glasses each day) to help relieve bowel pressure. Diverticulosis is rare in physically active people.

If your diverticular is not diseased or irritated, you have diverticulosis. Diverticulosis displays no symptoms in around 80% of patients, according to studies. Without symptoms, there's generally no need for treatment.

On the other hand, diverticulosis may cause symptoms such as bloating and stomach discomfort in some situations. This may be characterized as a symptomatic uncomplicated diverticular disease (SUDD). Diverticulitis affects at least 4% of SUDD patients.

How the Disease Develops

A diverticulum is a protrusion of the mucosa through the wall of your gut. This protrusion occurs along with weak points. The big intestine contains just one entire muscle layer: the inner circular layer. Your small intestine and rectum, on the other hand, have two muscle layers: an outside longitudinal layer and an interior circular one. The longitudinal layer is divided into three ribbons, which are known as the taenia coli. Diverticular disease develops when blood veins in your colon's wall enter the circular layer between the taenia coli.

Diverticulitis develops when the diverticula become infected. This can happen when partly digested food obstructs the entrance of the diverticula.

Diverticula disease does not have a single cause. Several environmental and genetic variables influence its development.

The muscular wall of the colon thickens with age, but the specific causes of this thickening are unknown. It might be related to the increased pressure required by the colon to eliminate fecal material. A low-fiber diet, for example, might result in the production of tiny, hard stools, which are difficult to pass. Small stools, caused by a lack of fiber, may also isolate portions of the colon from the remainder of the colon when the muscle in the segment contracts. Because the increased pressure cannot disperse to other sections of the colon, the pressure in the segments that have been blocked off may become excessive. Over time, colonic pressure produces herniation and pushes the inner intestinal lining outward through weak areas in the muscle walls. Diverticula are the sacs or pouches that form.

A low-fiber diet may contribute significantly to diverticula, according to research and clinical experience, and there is a critical relationship between the amount of dietary fiber consumed and the prevalence of diverticula throughout worldwide populations. Most diverticular disease patients have fairly thick colonic walls where the diverticula develop. Colon muscles contract vigorously as well. These abnormalities could contribute to the development of diverticula.

Signs And Symptoms

Diverticulitis symptoms arise when the diverticula become inflamed. Among these signs are:

Constant abdominal discomfort on the left side. It may appear on the right side in some situations.

One of the most frequent symptoms of diverticulitis is pain in the lower abdomen. Nausea, diarrhea, constipation, and fever may also occur.

Diverticulosis can occasionally produce bleeding, which is typically painless. When you have bowel movements, the bleeding in diverticulosis is bright red or maroon in color.

Seek medical attention if you notice any bleeding or pain in your abdomen. Diverticulitis can quickly escalate into an emergency if it is not treated promptly. When the contents of your colon begin to seep into your abdominal cavity through a perforation, it becomes an emergency (a tear). Diverticulitis bleeding can stop on its own. However, it can be severe at times.

Your doctor may prescribe antibiotics for minor bouts of infection. If you are bleeding, unable to drink fluids, or have severe pains or other symptoms, you may need to be admitted to the hospital.

People with diverticulitis who are bleeding may require a colonoscopy while in the hospital. The colonoscopy will allow the doctor to pinpoint the source of the bleeding. If there is no bleeding, you should undergo a colonoscopy after the flare-up has gone, assuming you haven't had one recently. Colon cancer frequently mimics diverticulitis, and it is a disease that must be treated as soon as it is diagnosed.

Diarrhea, constipation, nausea, bloating, and, in rare cases, cramps are all signs of diverticula disease. Vomiting is an uncommon complication of diverticulitis. When pressure is present in your abdomen, your stomach muscles stiffen up. It is a muscle defensive reflex action. If they suddenly let go, the pain intensifies.

Risk Factors

Diverticula develop in vulnerable regions of the gut, as we have discovered. Typically, the sigmoid colon acts as the origin. The sigmoid colon is positioned in front of the rectum and measures around 40-45 cm in length. The contents of your gut cause the strain on that muscle wall.

Genetics is another risk factor to consider. Because of the nature of their DNA, certain people are predisposed to developing this disease. Other risk factors include weak connective tissue and altered or troublesome wavelike motions of the intestinal wall. Diverticulitis is also more likely in persons who are older or overweight.

Diverticulitis is influenced by lifestyle, although the extent of this impact has yet to be identified. Constipation and firm stools might result from a low-fiber diet. A fiber-deficient diet can increase one's risk of diverticular disease. Excessive consumption of red meat, smoking, and not going to the bathroom regularly (having regular movement) can also raise the risk.

The research to completely understand how the diverticula become inflamed and the variables that make this condition more probable is currently underway. Inflammation is more common in areas of the colon with poor blood supply and where hard lumps of feces develop in the diverticula.

Complications are prevalent in patients with compromised immune systems from conditions such as severe renal disease or an organ transplant. Prolonged use of some medicines, such as nonsteroidal anti-inflammatory drugs, acetylsalicylic acid, opiates, and steroids, increases the chance of more severe consequences.

Diverticulitis-Related Complications

Diverticulitis complications can range from mild to severe. This disease might be difficult to diagnose at times. Diverticulitis is treatable with supportive medical care and antibiotics. Complications such as abscesses, perforations, intestinal blockages, bleeding, fistulas, phlebitis, and phlegmon necessitate extensive treatment. Prompt diagnosis and treatment lower a person's risk of death.

ABSCESS

An abscess is inflammatory pus-filled tissue. An abscess can form in any region of the body (both inside and outside). In most cases, they develop on the skin's surface.

An abscess in the belly or colon may occur in the digestive system.

The abdominal abscess can occur at the anterior abdominal wall, towards the rear of the abdomen, or around abdominal organs such as the kidneys, pancreas, and liver. Abscesses in the belly can occur for no apparent reason. However, they are frequently associated with an underlying illness or event, such as bowel rupture, diverticulitis, intra-abdominal surgery, or an abdominal injury.

Bacteria that enter the abdomen because of abdominal rupture, penetrating trauma, or intra-abdominal surgery can contribute to abdominal abscesses. Crohn's disease, appendicitis, and ulcerative colitis are examples of disorders that can contribute to the condition as well. Additional causes may be present depending on the location of the abdominal abscess.

Abscesses can also form between the spine and the abdominal cavity. These abscesses are known as "retroperitoneal abscesses" in medicine. The retroperitoneum is the gap between the spine and the abdominal cavity.

Diverticulitis can result in an abscess. Your doctor will have to remove the fluid if an abscess develops. They will accomplish this by inserting a needle into the pus-filled region. Surgery may be unavoidable in some cases. A portion of the colon may also need to be removed surgically. When an infection spreads to the abdomen, the disease is known as peritonitis. Surgery will be necessary to clear the cavity and remove the damaged section of the colon. Peritonitis can be deadly if comprehensive treatment is not received.

PERFORATION

A perforation is a hole that can develop in the gastrointestinal system. Diverticulitis and appendicitis are two of the most common causes of gastrointestinal perforation. They might also be the result of trauma, such as a gunshot wound or a knife wound. Perforation of the gallbladder is also possible. The symptoms of a perforated gallbladder are similar to those of a perforated gastrointestinal tract.

Peritonitis can result after a gastrointestinal perforation. Peritonitis is an inflammation and infection of the peritoneum, which is the membrane that lines the abdominal cavity.

If any of the following enter your abdominal cavity, you are at risk of developing peritonitis:

- Bile
- Bacteria
- Stool
- Stomach acid
- Food that has been partially digested

Gastrointestinal perforation is a medical emergency that requires immediate medical attention. It is a potentially fatal condition. Early diagnosis and treatment might enhance your chances of recovery.

Gastrointestinal perforation or diverticulitis perforation is also known as intestine perforation or intestinal perforation.

The following are common signs of a perforated gastrointestinal tract:

- Chills
- Severe stomachache
- Nausea
- Fever
- Vomiting

Your will be in pain if your gastrointestinal system is ruptured and peritonitis develops. When you move, or when the painful area is palpated, the pain intensifies. When the sufferer lies motionless, they experience a sense of relaxation. The abdomen may protrude further than it should and may feel rigid.

Peritonitis symptoms are similar to perforation symptoms. They are as follows:

- Dizziness
- Fatigue
- Tachycardia
- Shortness of breath
- Changes in digestive patterns

Abdominal or chest x-rays will be ordered to identify gastrointestinal perforation. The goal is to see if there is any air in your abdomen. You may also be asked to have a CT scan to determine the location of the hole better. Your doctor will also order laboratory tests that will help:

- Identify symptoms of illness, such as a high white blood cell count
- assess your Hb level
- test for electrolytes
- evaluate liver and kidney function
- assess blood acidity and alkalinity

PERITONITIS

When your peritoneum becomes inflamed, you have peritonitis. The peritoneum is the tissue that covers and supports the organs in your belly. A bacterial or fungal infection is generally the cause of peritonitis (as in the case of diverticulitis).

If left untreated, peritonitis can spread into the blood stream, resulting in organ failure and death. If you detect any symptoms of peritonitis, such as severe stomach pain, get medical care immediately..

Peritonitis symptoms include:

- Nausea
- Severe stomach pain
- Abdominal soreness or distention
- Fluid in the belly
- Fever
- Chills
- Vomiting
- Difficulty passing gas or having a bowel movement

Peritonitis is caused by diverticulitis as a secondary condition.

Other factors include:

- Pancreatitis
- Abdominal trauma
- Pelvic inflammatory illness

Non-infectious causes can include irritating fluids such as bile and blood, as well as the presence of foreign substances in your gut.

If you have any of the signs of peritonitis, please contact your doctor as soon as possible.

Peritonitis can lead to life-threatening consequences such as septic shock and sepsis. As a result, prompt identification and treatment are critical.

Your doctor will analyze your medical history and the symptoms you are experiencing before performing a physical examination, which will include an evaluation of any soreness and sensitivity in your abdomen.

Peritonitis can be diagnosed using the following tests:

- Urine and blood tests
- Exploratory surgery
- CT scans, X-rays, and other imaging tests

Your doctor may also perform a paracentesis. A tiny needle is used to remove fluid from your abdomen during this operation. The fluid is then tested for infection in a laboratory. Paracentesis can also aid in differentiating between original spontaneous peritonitis and subsequent pancreatitis-related peritonitis.

If peritonitis is diagnosed, you will be admitted to a hospital. Antifungal medicines or intravenous antibiotics will be administered promptly to treat the infection. If organ failure occurs as a result of the disease, other therapies will be administered. Blood pressure medicines, intravenous fluids, and nutrition per serving assistance are examples of supportive treatments.

If your peritonitis is caused by peritoneal dialysis, you will be given medicines injected directly into the peritoneal tissue. Clinical trials have demonstrated that this approach outperforms many other medications.

You may require emergency surgery if your peritonitis is caused by diverticulitis, appendicitis, or a stomach ulcer. Any infected tissue, such as an abscess or a ruptured appendix, will be surgically removed. The same is true for any additional peritoneal tissue damaged by the illness.

After you've been admitted to the hospital, you'll be closely watched for indications of septic shock or sepsis. If you present symptoms, you may be promptly transported to an intensive care unit.

Rectal Bleeding (Diverticular Bleeding)

Diverticular bleeding occurs when there is bleeding from the rectum as a result of diverticulitis. It occurs when the pouches in the colon's wall bleed.

A considerable amount of blood can be present in your stool if you have diverticular bleeding. The bleeding usually begins suddenly and can end abruptly. You will not experience any discomfort in your belly while bleeding.

If you have a lot of blood in your stool, you should visit your doctor as soon as possible. Patients may become faint or light-headed if they lose so much blood.

What factors contribute to diverticular bleeding?

Until now, medical research has not explained why diverticula develops in the colon's wall. Some experts believe that the pouches form when high pressure within the colon presses against weak regions in the colon's wall.

When you consume a high fiber diet (also known as roughage), your body produces thick stool that moves quickly through the colon. Conversely, if you consume a low-fiber diet, your colon will have to apply more effort than usual to pass a tiny, hard stool. A low-fiber diet can lengthen the time fecal matter remains in the gut. That, of course, contributes to the high pressure.

The increased pressure acting on weak areas in your colon may help develop these pouches (diverticulosis). Blood arteries flow through these weak areas to deliver oxygen and nutrients to the inner wall.

Diverticular bleeding occurs when the blood artery is supplying the pouch bursts. The most common sign of diverticular bleeding is acute rectal bleeding. Clots of blood can be bright or dark crimson. When you're bleeding, you won't feel any discomfort, and the bleeding will generally stop on its own.

Diagnosis

Diagnosis is accomplished by eliminating other possible sources of the bleeding. You will be subjected to a physical examination. Your doctor will also review your medical history and do further testing. You might have an imaging test, such as angiography, to pinpoint the source of the bleeding. A colonoscopy is used to check your colon to determine the source of the bleeding.

The technetium-labeled red blood cell bleeding scan is another test that can pinpoint the cause of bleeding. A small amount of blood will be taken for this test, and technetium will be added. Technetium is a radioactive element. Following the addition of technetium, blood will be reinjected into your bloodstream and tracked back to the site of bleeding.

Diverticular bleeding usually goes away on its own. However, if it persists, you will need to treat it and restore the lost blood if the amount lost is significant. Under certain circumstances, the patient may need to be hospitalized. Blood transfusions, intravenous fluid delivery, pharmaceutical injections, and, in some instances, surgery can all be used as treatment.

The best approach to avoid diverticula formation is to eat a high-fiber diet and drink enough fluids. However, if diverticulosis is already present, diet will not help prevent bleeding.

If you use aspirin regularly (more than four days per week), you are at a higher risk of developing diverticular bleeding.

Intestinal Obstruction

Bowel obstruction is another term for intestinal obstruction. The obstruction (blockage) stops the intestine's contents from moving through the gastrointestinal system. This obstruction may be caused by factors both inside and outside of the gastrointestinal system. A growth or a tumor can fill and restrict the intestine's route. A tissue or a neighboring organ may compress, squeeze, or twist a piece of the colon outside the gut.

Intestinal obstruction can occur in either the big intestine (colon) or small intestine. In addition, intestinal obstruction might be total or partial, which impacts the ease with which intestinal contents may flow through the region of the blockage.

Diverticular illness is one of the most common causes of intestinal obstruction. In reality, diverticular illness can be a complication of intestinal obstruction.

In the big bowel, the diverticula are tiny balloon-shaped pouches. Diverticulitis is caused by an infection of these pouches, as previously explained. Scars in the colon wall may develop as the infection is resolved.

Colon stricture is a scar that forms around the colon. As the colon stricture tightens and matures, the gut gradually narrows, culminating in a blocked colon.

Adhesions can also create intestinal blockages. Adhesions are vital, fibrous connective tissues. They're a kind of scar. They often appear outside of a damaged intestine. They may also form outside pelvic organs as a result of healing from an infection or surgery. Gynecological procedures and surgery involving the colon or the appendix are risk factors for adhesions. Adhesions may not initially create any symptoms. These scar tissues may be stretched into tethers over time as a result of intestinal motility.

Adhesions can cause intestinal obstruction if they form a constricting band, squeezing a section of the intestine closed from the outside. They can also connect to neighboring intestine loops, producing a structure that prevents the passage of intestinal contents. Adhesions are a major cause of intestinal obstruction in the United States, accounting for about 70% of all cases.

Among the other reasons for intestinal obstruction are:

- Hernia
- Tumors
- Colorectal cancer
- Volvulus

How can you tell if you have an obstructed intestine?

The patient will suffer the following symptoms if the small intestine is obstructed:

- Pain in the abdomen (that feels like cramps) that generally occurs at 5–10-minute intervals and, in some cases, centers around the navel or between rib cage and navel
- Vomiting and nausea
- Impossibility of passing gas through the rectum
- Abdominal bloating, sometimes accompanied by abdominal pain
- During cramping bouts, you may experience rapid breathing and pulse

Prominent bowel obstruction symptoms include:

- Bloating in the abdomen
- Pain in the abdomen that may be mild, vague, severe, or sharp (the source of the obstruction determines the severity of the pain)
- Constipation
- Rectal bleeding (if a colon tumor causes the obstruction)
- Diarrhea is caused by liquid stool leaking around a partial obstruction.

Your doctor will perform a physical examination of your abdomen to determine intestinal obstruction. In addition, they will feel the interior of your rectum. X-rays can assist in confirming the obstruction. The liquid and gas bowel contents above the region of obstruction may be seen with an abdominal x-ray. However, there will be no material viewable below the barrier. If you've been vomiting for a time, your doctor will want you to be tested for electrolyte loss or dehydration.

Chapter 2

DIET STAGES OF DIVERTICULITIS

What you eat and drink might have an impact on your diverticulitis symptoms. In this chapter, you will find out which meals you should consume and which you should avoid. You'll also learn how your diet should change depending on whether you're having symptoms or not.

The Liquid Diet

As the name indicates, a clear liquid diet is a diet that consists solely of clear liquids. These liquids contain broth, water, juices without pulp, and plain gelatin. The fluids may be colored but if you can still see through it, it is considered a clear liquid.

Foods that are totally or partially liquid even at room temperature are included in a clear liquid diet. It is important to note that you cannot add solid meals to a clear liquid diet.

How Does It Work?

When a patient needs to undergo specific medical procedures affecting the gastrointestinal tract, such as colonoscopies, the doctor will prescribe a clear liquid diet.

Some digestive problems, such as diarrhea, diverticulitis, and Crohn's disease, may be relieved by a clear liquid diet. This diet is also ordered following some types of surgery. Why? This diet is easy for your digestive system to digest, and because it is mainly liquid, it helps to clear out your digestive tract.

The objective of a clear liquid diet is to keep you hydrated while providing enough vitamins and minerals to sustain your health. A clear liquid diet also keeps your intestines and stomach in good working order.

As a diverticulitis sufferer, you should include the following clear liquids in your diet:

- Broth without fat
- Clear nutritious drinks such as Ensure, Enlive, and others
- Clear soups
- Coca-Cola, Pepsi, Sprite, and other sparkling carbonated beverages
- hard candies (peppermint rounds or lemon drops)
- Honey
- Jell-O
- Juices that include no pulp (like white grape and apple cranberry)
- Lemonade without the pulp
- No cream or milk in your coffee
- Sports beverages
- Tea without milk or cream
- Water

Avoid any liquid meals that are not on this list. If you're having a colonoscopy or other associated tests, your doctor may advise you to avoid drinks that are purple or red.

A meal plan for a clear liquid diet is provided as an example.

Breakfast

- One bowl of gelatin
- One glass of fruit juice without pulp
- A cup of tea or coffee without dairy
- Sugar or honey

Snack

- One glass of pulp-free fruit juice
- One bowl of gelatin

Lunch

- One glass of fruit juice (no pulp)
- A cup of water
- One bowl of gelatin
- 1 cup chicken broth

Snack

- A popsicle with no pulp
- Honey or sugar
- A cup of tea or coffee without dairy

Dinner

- A cup of broth
- Sugar or honey
- A cup of tea or coffee devoid of dairy
- A bowl of gelatin

The clear-liquid diet, like everything else, has advantages and disadvantages. Here's all you need to know about it:

The Pros and Cons of a Clear Liquid Diet

Pros

- A clear liquid diet aids in rapid recovery following surgery, a medical test, or any other medical treatment.
- It is not difficult to understand.
- It is inexpensive.

Cons

- When you confine yourself to a clear liquid diet, you can feel hungry and weary since it lacks density.
- After a short while, you might find it to be a boring, mundane diet.

Before starting a clear liquid diet, there are a few things you should know:

- If your doctor has prescribed a clear liquid diet before a colonoscopy, avoid purple or red-colored drinks. They have the potential to interfere with imaging results. If this isn't required, your doctor will let you know.
- If you were diagnosed with diabetes, you should notify your doctor. A clear liquid diet for diabetes should provide up to 200g of carbs distributed throughout the day for effective blood sugar management. Get control of your blood sugar levels and return to solid foods as soon as possible.

Remember that a clear liquid diet lacks some nutrients and calories and should not be utilized for an extended period. When adopting the clear-liquid diet or any other diet plan, always follow your doctor's recommendations.

The Juicing Diet

Juicing diets and juice fasts have grown in popularity in recent years. Many people have touted juicing's weight-loss advantages. A juicing diet consists solely of juices or other clear liquids, such as tea and water. People on a juice fast consume nothing but juices.

In terms of diverticulitis, the juicing diet is nearly identical to the clear liquid diet. Here's all you need to know about the juicing diet.

Juice diets are often referred to as juice fasts or juice cleanses. Juicing diets aid in the recovery of nutrients in the body.

Extracting juices from vegetables and whole fruits is what the term "juicing" refers to. The only thing missing from the juice is the fiber found in the pulp. Fiber is an essential component of a balanced diet. However, if you drink too much of it, it may induce stomach problems.

Minerals, phytonutrients, and vitamins present in vegetables and fruits are abundant in pure juice. When you juice, you are giving your digestive tract a break. You also allow your digestive system to absorb a lot of nutrients. Others believe that juicing boosts the immune system by eliminating toxins from the body and aids in weight reduction.

What is the juicing diet, and how does it work?

It's important to choose the correct ingredients for your recipes before turning on your juicer. Organic fruits and vegetables are preferred because they are free of pesticides and other toxins. The only thing left is for you to select how long you want to fast.

Joe Cross, the man from *Fat, Sick & Dead*, has put together a 3-day reboot juice fast. Cross stated in his documentary that he dropped 100 pounds after a juice fast. The juices in his regimen are made up of 80% vegetables and 20% fruits.

Remember to drink a lot of water throughout the day in addition to your juices when juicing.

Blending foods of similar hues together can provide a wide variety of nutrients and still look pretty! As an example:

- Some beets will be present in the red liquid.
- Orange juice may include sweet potatoes.
- Yellow juice can contain yellow bell peppers, pineapple, and other fruits.
- In many situations, green juices are a mix of cucumber, kale, and celery.
- Purple juices contain a lot of blueberries or purple grapes.

Juicing may have various unintended consequences, such as:

- Dizziness
- Fatigue
- Diarrhea
- Constipation

These adverse effects usually clear up by themselves as your body adjusts to the diet. However, if you develop any of the following symptoms, you should immediately discontinue your diet and contact your doctor:

- Vomiting
- Fainting
- Extreme vertigo
- Low blood pressure
- Diarrhea
- Before starting a juice fast, think about your safety

Before beginning a juice fast, keep in mind that most doctors do not advocate it. Reasons are as follows:

- Juice diets are high in minerals and vitamins but low in protein. Protein is a critical macronutrient. It is used by your body to develop and maintain muscle. When you confine yourself to a juice diet, you can lose good muscle weight.
- Juices contain a lot of sugar, far more than you may expect. Sugar can contribute to weight gain. Not only that, but because the juice is low in fat and protein, you may have significant blood sugar fluctuations.
- Too much juice prepared from green leafy plants such as spinach, kale, or collards can create health issues. These veggies are high in goitrogens. The body's absorption of iodine is influenced by goitrogen. You may suffer from delayed thyroid function if you consume too much goitrogen.

When specific substances are included in your diet, food safety should be addressed carefully. Before consuming raw, unpasteurized juices, consult your dietician or doctor. Apart from those suffering from diverticulitis, the following categories of people must obtain permission from their doctor before going on a juice fast:

- Pregnant women
- Infants and toddlers
- Individuals with a weakened or impaired immune system
- Senior citizens

Before juicing, all fruits and vegetables should be washed thoroughly. You'll prevent germs and a slew of other toxins from entering your body by doing so.

Don't drink too much juice in one sitting; only juice what you can finish. Bacteria thrive in fresh juices. If there are any leftovers, please keep them in a clean, airtight container. The juice should be kept in the fridge. Anything that hasn't been consumed within 24 hours should be thrown away.

Be careful to clean all your juicing equipment after each usage. Most juicers gather pulp from processed vegetables and fruits. Bacteria can thrive in the nooks and crannies of juicers. Wash and scrub your juicer well.

Low-Fiber, Low-Residue Diet

Patients with ulcerative colitis, diverticulitis, intestinal inflammation, or Crohn's disease may benefit from low-fiber, low-residue diets. You can also follow these diets if you have bowel constriction before or after a surgical procedure. Stool moves slowly along the intestines when eating a low-residue, low-fiber diet. It also reduces the amount of fecal matter produced in the intestines. It reduces clogging by doing so.

Plants are the most abundant source of dietary fiber. Humans are unable to digest fiber. The term "residue" refers to the fiber and other components that remain in the colon after digestion. A low-fiber diet does not include more than 15 grams of fiber per day. It also excludes meals that bulk up feces. A low-residue diet is essentially a low-fiber diet with certain limitations.

If you eat the proper foods, you can still benefit from getting the recommended dietary allowances from low-residue and low-fiber diets. However, long-term usage of a low-residue or low-fiber diet might result in folic acid or vitamin C deficiency.

Recommendations for a low-fiber diet

1) Consume refined cereals, white bread, and rice-based foods. Foods prepared with seeds, nuts, bran, or whole grain flour are not included.
2) Choose vegetables and fruits that are prepared or canned.
3) Consume cooked, ground, or tender meats. Dried peas and beans should be avoided.

Recommendations for a low-residue diet

1. Follow the low-fiber guidelines.
2. Exclude prune juice from your diet.
3. Do not consume more than 2 cups of milk or milk products per day.

Chapter 3

CLEAR FLUIDS (BREAKFAST)

1. Celery Apple Juice

Preparation Time: 5 minutes
Cooking Time: 0 minutes
Servings: 2

Ingredients:

- 12 celery stalks, peeled and chopped
- 3 Apple, peeled, cored, seeded, and sliced
- 1-inch ginger root, peeled and chopped
- 1/4 lemon juice
- 2 cups water

Directions:

1. Set all the ingredients into your blender and pulse.
2. Set a fine-mesh strainer in a bowl. Before transferring your juice into the strainer.
3. Gently press the pulp to extract all possible liquid, then discard it.
4. Serve over ice. Enjoy!

Nutrition Per Serving:

- Calories: 116
- Fat: 0.7 g
- Carbs: 28.2 g
- Sodium: 95 mg
- Protein: 1.5 g

2. Homemade Banana Apple Juice

Preparation Time: 10 minutes

Cooking Time: 0 minutes

Servings: 2

Ingredients:

- 2 bananas, peeled and sliced
- 1/2 apple, peeled, cored, and chopped
- 1 tablespoon honey
- 1 ½ cup water

Directions:

1. Set all the ingredients into your blender and pulse.
2. Set a fine-mesh strainer in a bowl. Before transferring your juice into the strainer.
3. Gently press the pulp to extract all possible liquid, then discard it.
4. Serve over ice. Enjoy!

Nutrition Per Serving:

- Calories: 137
- Fat: 0.4 g
- Carbs: 35.8 g
- Sodium: 7 mg
- Protein: 1.2 g

3. Sweet Detox Juice

Preparation Time: 10 minutes

Cooking Time: 0 minutes

Servings: 2

Ingredients:

- 2 cups baby spinach, chopped
- 1 handful parsley, chopped
- 1 green apple, peeled, cored, seeded, and sliced
- 1 large English cucumber, seeded and chopped
- 1-inch ginger, peeled
- 1 lemon, juiced

Directions:

1. Set all the ingredients into your blender and pulse.
2. Set a fine-mesh strainer in a bowl. Before transferring your juice into the strainer.
3. Gently press the pulp to extract all possible liquid, then discard it.
4. Serve over ice. Enjoy!

Nutrition Per Serving:

- Calories: 122
- Fat: 0.8 g
- Carbs: 26.3g g
- Fiber: 7.2 g
- Protein: 4.6 g

4. Pineapple Ginger Juice

Preparation Time: 35 minutes
Cooking Time: 0 minutes
Servings: 7 cups

Ingredients:

- 10 cups pineapple, chopped
- 6 cups water
- 3 Fuji apples, chopped
- 4-inch ginger root, peeled and chopped
- 1/4 cup lemon juice
- 1/4 cup sugar

Directions:

1. Set all the ingredients into your blender and pulse.
2. Set a fine-mesh strainer in a bowl. Before transferring your juice into the strainer.
3. Gently press the pulp to extract all possible liquid, then discard it.
4. Serve over ice. Enjoy!

Nutrition Per Serving:

- Calories: 166
- Fat: 0.4 g
- Carbs: 42.9 g
- Fiber: 4 g
- Protein: 1.6 g

5. Carrot Orange Juice

Preparation Time: 15 minutes
Cooking Time: 0 minutes
Servings: 2

Ingredients:

- 1 medium yellow tomato, cut into wedges
- 1 orange, peeled and quartered
- 1 apple, peeled, cored, and chopped
- 4 jumbo carrots, peeled and chopped
- 2 cups water

Directions:

1. Set all the ingredients into your blender and pulse.
2. Set a fine-mesh strainer in a bowl. Before transferring your juice into the strainer.
3. Gently press the pulp to extract all possible liquid, then discard it.
4. Serve over ice. Enjoy!

Nutrition Per Serving:

- Calories: 145
- Fat: 0.5 g
- Carbs: 35.1 g
- Sodium: 152 mg
- Protein: 3.9 g

6. Strawberry Apple Juice

Preparation Time: 5 minutes
Cooking Time: 0 minutes
Servings: 8-10 ounces

Ingredients:

- 2 cups strawberries (tops removed)
- 1 red apple, peeled, seeded, cored, and chopped
- 1 tablespoon chia seeds
- 1 cup water

Directions:

1. Set all the ingredients into your blender and pulse.
2. Set a fine-mesh strainer in a bowl. Before transferring your juice into the strainer.
3. Gently press the pulp to extract all possible liquid, then discard it.
4. Add in your chia seeds, then leave to sit for at least 5 minutes.
5. Serve over ice. Enjoy!

Nutrition Per Serving:

- Calories: 245
- Fat: 5 g
- Carbs: 52 g
- Fiber: 7 g
- Protein: 4 g

7. Autumn Energizer Juice

Preparation Time: 10 minutes
Cooking Time: 0 minutes
Servings: 2

Ingredients:

- 2 pears, peeled, seeded, and chopped
- 2 Ambrosia apples, peeled, cored, and chopped
- 2 Granny Smith apples, peeled, cored, chopped
- 2 mandarins, juiced
- 2 cups sweet potato, peeled and chopped
- 1-pint cape gooseberries
- 2 inches ginger root, peeled

Directions:

1. Set all the ingredients into your blender and pulse.
2. Set a fine-mesh strainer in a bowl. Before transferring your juice into the strainer.
3. Gently press the pulp to extract all possible liquid, then discard it.
4. Serve over ice. Enjoy!

Nutrition Per Serving:

- Calories: 170
- Fat: 3 g
- Carbs: 33 g
- Fiber: 9 g
- Protein: 4 g

8. Asian Inspired Wonton Broth

Preparation Time: 5 minutes
Cooking Time: 1 hour 30 minutes
Servings: 2

Ingredients:

- 1 chicken thigh, skin on
- 1 carrot, coarsely chopped
- 1 celery stalk, coarsely chopped
- 1 small onion, quartered
- 3 dime-sized ginger pieces
- 2 tablespoons kosher salt
- 1/4 teaspoon turmeric
- 1/8 teaspoon MSG (don't leave it out)
- 5 white peppercorns (can be substituted with black)
- 1-liter water

Directions:

1. Transfer all the ingredients to your stockpot. Top with enough water to cover, then allow to come to a boil on high heat slowly.
2. Switch to low heat and simmer for at least 1 hour and 30 minutes.
3. Set and pour the mixture through a fine-mesh strainer into a large bowl.
4. Taste and season with salt.
5. Serve hot.

Nutrition Per Serving:

- Calories: 181
- Fat: 7 g
- Carbs: 14 g
- Fiber: 1 g
- Protein: 14 g

9. Apple-Cinnamon Tea

Preparation Time: 5 minutes
Cooking Time: 15 minutes
Servings: 4

Ingredients:

- 1 cup chopped apples, Honey Crisp, Fuji, Granny Smith, or Gala
- 3 cinnamon sticks
- 1-quart water
- 2 bags Earl Grey tea (caffeinated or decaffeinated)
- 1/3 cup honey, plus more if desired

Directions:

1. In a large saucepan over high heat, set the apples, cinnamon sticks, and water. Bring to a boil. Set the heat to medium and stir for 15 minutes.
2. Remove from the heat and add the Earl Grey tea bags. Steep for 10 minutes.
3. Using a slotted spoon, detach the tea bags, apples, and cinnamon sticks. Attach the honey and stir until it dissolves. Taste and add more honey, if desired. Serve hot.

Nutrition Per Serving:

- Calories: 101
- Fat: 1 g
- Carbs: 27 g
- Fiber: 1 g
- Protein: 1 g
- Sodium: 6 mg

10. Blueberry Green Tea

Preparation Time: 5 minutes
Cooking Time: 5 minutes
Servings: 4

Ingredients:

- 1/2 cup fresh or frozen blueberries
- 1-quart water
- 2 bags of green tea (caffeinated or decaffeinated)
- 1/3 cup honey, plus more if desired

Directions:

1. In a saucepan over high heat, place the blueberries and water and bring to a boil. Set the heat to low and stir for 5 minutes.
2. Detach from the heat and add the green tea bags. Steep for 10 minutes.
3. Using a slotted spoon, set the tea bags and blueberries. Attach the honey and stir until it dissolves. Taste and add more honey, if desired. Serve hot.

Nutrition Per Serving:

- Calories: 95.67
- Fat: 0 g
- Carbs: 26 g
- Fiber: 0.5 g
- Protein: 0.22 g
- Sodium: 3.86 mg

11. Citrus Sports Drink

Preparation Time: 5 minutes
Cooking Time: 0 minutes
Servings: 8

Ingredients:

- 4 cups coconut water
- 4 large oranges juice (about 1 ½ cup), strained
- 2 tablespoons lemon juice, strained
- 2 tablespoons honey or maple syrup
- 1 teaspoon sea salt

Directions:

1. Place the coconut water, orange juice, lemon juice, honey, and salt in a jug or pitcher.
2. Stir until the salt is dissolved.
3. Serve cold.

Nutrition Per Serving:

- Calories: 59
- Fat: 1 g
- Carbs: 14 g
- Fiber: 1 g
- Protein: 1 g
- Sodium: 304 mg

12. Beef Bone Broth

Preparation Time: 10 minutes
Cooking Time: 12 hours
Servings: 8

Ingredients:

- 2 pounds beef bones
- 1 onion, chopped in quarters
- 2 celery stalks, chopped in half
- 2 carrots, chopped in half
- 3 whole garlic cloves
- 2 bay leaves
- 1 tablespoon salt
- Filtered water (enough to cover bones)

Directions:

1. Transfer the bones and vegetables to your stockpot. Top with enough water to cover,

then allow to come to a boil on high heat slowly.

2. Switch to low heat and simmer for at least 2 hours and up to 12 hours.

3. Set and pour the mixture through a fine-mesh strainer into a large bowl. Taste and season with salt.

4. Serve hot.

Nutrition Per Serving:

- Calories: 145
- Fat: 8.47 g
- Total Carbs: 3.17 g
- Sodium: 1.5 g
- Protein: 13.22 g

13. Ginger, Mushroom and Cauliflower Broth

Preparation Time: 10 minutes
Cooking Time: 50 minutes
Servings: 3

Ingredients:

- 1 large yellow onion
- 1 cup celery stalks, chopped
- 2 carrots, diced or cubed
- 10 French beans
- 1 ginger root, peeled, diced, or grated
- 1-2 stalks celery leaves or coriander leaves
- 1 ½ cup mushrooms, sliced
- 8 florets cauliflower
- 1 teaspoon garlic, chopped
- 1 tablespoon oil
- 1 stalk of spring onion greens or scallions

- 1/2 teaspoon crushed pepper or ground pepper

Directions:

1. Transfer all the ingredients to your stockpot. Top with enough water to cover, then allow to come to a boil on high heat slowly.

2. Switch to low heat and simmer for at least 50 minutes.

3. Set and pour the mixture through a fine-mesh strainer into a large bowl. Taste and season with salt.

4. Serve hot. Enjoy!

Nutrition Per Serving:

- Calories: 141
- Fat: 5 g
- Carbs: 22 g
- Fiber: 7 g
- Protein: 5 g

14. Fish Broth

Preparation Time: 15 minutes
Cooking Time: 45 minutes
Servings: 3

Ingredients:

- 1 large onion, chopped
- 1 large carrot chopped
- 1 fennel bulb and fronds, chopped (optional)
- 3 celery stalks, chopped
- Salt as per taste
- 2-5 pounds fish bones and heads

- 1 handful of dried mushrooms (optional)
- 2-4 bay leaves
- 1-star anise pod (optional)
- 1-2 teaspoons thyme, dried or fresh
- 3-4 pieces dried kombu kelp (optional)

Directions:

1. Transfer the bones and vegetables to your stockpot. Top with enough water to cover, then allow to come to a boil on high heat slowly.
2. Set to low heat and simmer for 45 minutes.
3. Set and pour the mixture through a fine-mesh strainer into a large bowl. Taste and season with salt.
4. Serve hot. Enjoy!

Nutrition Per Serving:

- Calories: 33.17
- Fat: 0.9 g
- Carbs: 6 g
- Fiber: 1 g
- Protein: 1 g

15. Clear Pumpkin Broth

Preparation Time: 15 minutes
Cooking Time: 30 minutes
Servings: 6

Ingredients:

- 6 cups water
- 2 tablespoons ginger, minced
- 2 cups potatoes, peeled and diced
- 3 cups kabocha, peeled and diced

- 1 carrot, peeled and diced
- 1 onion, diced
- 1/2 cup scallions, chopped

Directions:

1. Transfer the bones and vegetables to your stockpot. Top with enough water to cover, then allow to come to a boil on high heat slowly.
2. Switch to low heat and simmer for at least 30 minutes.
3. Set and pour the mixture through a fine-mesh strainer into a large bowl. Taste and season with salt.
4. Serve hot. Enjoy!

Nutrition Per Serving:

- Calories: 71.02
- Fat: 0.25 g
- Total Carbs: 16.1 g
- Sodium: 30 mg
- Protein: 1.84 g

16. Pork Stock

Preparation Time: 15 minutes
Cooking Time: 12 hours
Servings: 8

Ingredients:

- 2 Pounds pork bones, roasted
- 1 onion, chopped in quarters
- 2 celery stalks, chopped in half
- 2 carrots, chopped in half
- 3 whole garlic cloves
- 2 bay leaves

- 1 tablespoon salt
- Filtered water (enough to cover bones)

- 1/4 cup apple cider vinegar
- Filtered water (enough to cover bones)

Directions:

1. Transfer the bones and vegetables to your stockpot. Top with enough water to cover, then allow to come to a boil on high heat slowly.
2. Set to low heat and simmer for 12 hours.
3. Set and pour the mixture through a fine-mesh strainer into a large bowl. Taste and season with salt.
4. Serve hot. Enjoy!

Directions:

1. Transfer all the ingredients to your slow cooker. Top with enough water to cover, then allow to come to a boil on high heat slowly.
2. Switch to low heat and simmer for at least 24 hours.
3. Set and pour the mixture through a fine-mesh strainer into a large bowl. Taste and season with salt.
4. Serve hot. Enjoy!

Nutrition Per Serving:

- Calories: 69
- Fat: 4 g
- Carbs: 1 g
- Fiber: 0.1 g
- Protein: 6 g

Nutrition Per Serving:

- Calories: 65
- Fat: 2 g
- Carbs: 7 g
- Fiber: 4 g
- Protein: 6 g

17. Slow Cooker Pork Bone Broth

Preparation Time: 15 minutes
Cooking Time: 24 hours
Servings: 12

Ingredients:

- 2 pounds pork bones, roasted
- 1/2 onion, chopped
- 2 medium carrots, chopped
- 1 stalk celery, chopped
- 2 whole garlic cloves
- 1 bay leaf
- 1 tablespoon sea salt
- 1 teaspoon peppercorns

18. Homemade Orange Gelatin

Preparation Time: 4 hours 10 minutes
Cooking Time: 3 minutes
Servings: 4

Ingredients:

- 8 large oranges juice (about 3 cups), strained and divided
- 2 tablespoons unflavored gelatin
- 2 tablespoons honey or maple syrup

Directions:

1. In a large bowl, pour in 1/2 cup of orange juice and sprinkle with gelatin. Whisk well and let sit until the gelatin begins to set but is not relatively smooth.
2. In a saucepan over low heat, pour in the remaining 2 ½ cups of orange juice and cook until just before boiling, 2-3 minutes.
3. Remove from the heat and pour the hot juice into the gelatin mixture. Attach the honey or maple syrup and stir until the gelatin is dissolved.
4. Pour into an 8 x 8 inches baking dish and transfer to the refrigerator.
5. Cool for 4 hours to set. Serve cold.

Nutrition Per Serving:

- Calories: 153
- Fat: 1 g
- Carbs: 27.4 g
- Fiber: 1 g
- Protein: 9.76 g
- Sodium: 14 mg

19. Raspberry Lemonade Ice Pops

Preparation Time: 4 hours 10 minutes
Cooking Time: 0 minutes
Servings: 4 ice pops

Ingredients:

- 3 cups frozen raspberries
- 1 teaspoon lemon juice, strained
- 1/4 cup coconut water
- 1/4 cup honey or maple syrup

Directions:

1. In a blender, puree the raspberries, lemon juice, and coconut water until smooth.
2. Set the mixture through a fine-mesh strainer into a bowl to remove the seeds. Stir in the honey until well mixed.
3. Divide the mixture equally among four popsicle molds and freeze until solid, 3-4 hours.

Nutrition Per Serving:

- Calories: 121
- Fat: 0.7 g
- Carbs: 30.4 g
- Fiber: 7 g
- Protein: 1.43 g
- Sodium: 17 mg

20. Homemade No Pulp Orange Juice

Preparation Time: 5 minutes
Cooking Time: 0 minutes
Servings: 1 ½ cup

Ingredients:

- 4 oranges

Directions:

1. Lightly squeeze the oranges on a hard surface to soften the exterior. Slice each in half.
2. Squeeze each orange over a fine-mesh strainer.
3. Gently press the pulp to extract all possible liquid.
4. Serve over ice. Enjoy!

Nutrition Per Serving:

- Calories: 50
- Fat: 0.2 g
- Carbs: 11.5 g
- Protein: 0.8 g

21. Apple Orange Juice

Preparation Time: 5 minutes
Cooking Time: 0 minutes
Servings: 2

Ingredients:

- 1 Gala apple, peeled, cored, and sliced
- 2 oranges, peeled, halved, and seeded
- 2 teaspoons honey (optional)
- 3/4 cup water

Directions:

1. Squeeze each orange over a fine-mesh strainer.
2. Gently press the pulp to extract as much liquid as possible.
3. Add in the apple, water, and orange juice in your blender and pulse.
4. Set a fine-mesh strainer in a bowl. Before transferring your juice into the strainer.
5. Once again, gently press the pulp to remove all possible liquid, then discard it.
6. Stir in your honey, then serve over ice.

Nutrition Per Serving:

- Calories: 86.24
- Fat: 1 g
- Carbs: 20 g

- Fiber: 1 g
- Protein: 1.05 g

22. Pineapple Mint Juice

Preparation Time: 5 minutes.
Cooking Time: 0 minutes
Servings: 4

Ingredients:

- 3 cups pineapple, cored, sliced, and chunks
- 10-12 mint leaves, or to taste
- 2 tablespoons sugar, or to taste (optional)
- 1 ½ cup water
- 1 cup ice cubes

Directions:

1. Set all the ingredients into your blender and pulse.
2. Set a fine-mesh strainer in a bowl. Before transferring your juice into the strainer.
3. Gently press the pulp to extract all possible liquid, then discard it.
4. Serve over ice. Enjoy!

Nutrition Per Serving:

- Calories: 63
- Fat: 1 g
- Carbs: 15.48 g
- Fiber: 2 g
- Protein: 0.73 g

23. Mushroom, Cauliflower and Cabbage Broth

Preparation Time: 10 minutes
Cooking Time: 50 minutes
Servings: 2

Ingredients:

- 1 large yellow onion
- 1 cup celery stalks, chopped
- 2 carrots, diced or cubed
- 10 French beans
- 1/2 cabbage, diced
- 1-2 stalks celery leaves
- 1 ½ cup mushrooms, sliced
- 8 florets cauliflower
- 1 teaspoon garlic, chopped
- 1 teaspoon ginger, chopped
- 1 tablespoon oil
- 1 scallion stalk
- 1/2 teaspoon pepper, crushed

Directions:

1. Transfer all the ingredients to your stockpot. Top with enough water to cover, then allow to come to a boil on high heat slowly.
2. Switch to low heat and simmer for 50 minutes.
3. Set and pour the mixture through a fine-mesh strainer into a large bowl. Mash the vegetables well to extract all their juices.
4. Taste and season with salt. Enjoy.

Nutrition Per Serving:

- Calories: 141
- Fat: 5 g
- Carbs: 22 g
- Fiber: 7 g
- Protein: 5 g

24. Indian Inspired Vegetable Stock

Preparation Time: 10 minutes
Cooking Time: 11 minutes
Servings: 3

Ingredients:

- 3/4 cup onions, roughly chopped
- 3/4 cup carrot, roughly chopped
- 3/4 cup tomatoes, roughly chopped
- 3/4 cup potatoes, roughly chopped
- 1 teaspoon turmeric
- Salt to taste

Directions:

1. Transfer all the ingredients to your stockpot. Top with enough water to cover, then allow to come to a boil on high heat slowly.
2. Switch to low heat and simmer for 11 minutes.
3. Set and pour the mixture through a fine-mesh strainer into a large bowl. Taste and season with salt.
4. Serve hot. Enjoy!

Nutrition Per Serving:

- Calories: 103
- Fat: 0.2mg
- Carbs: 23.3 g
- Fiber: 3.1 g
- Protein: 2.2 g

Chapter 4

CLEAR FLUIDS (LUNCH)

25. Favorite Summer Lemonade

Preparation Time: 15 minutes

Cooking Time: 0 minutes

Servings: 8

Ingredients:

- 8 cups filtered water
- 1/2 cup fresh lemon juice
- 1/4 teaspoon pure stevia extract
- Ice cubes, as required

Directions:

1. In a pitcher, place the water, lemon juice, and stevia. Mix well.
2. Through a cheesecloth-lined sieve, strain the lemonade in another pitcher.
3. Refrigerate for 30-40 minutes.
4. Set ice cubes in serving glasses and fill with lemonade.
5. Serve chilled.

Nutrition Per Serving:

- Calories: 4
- Carbs: 1.14 g
- Protein: 0.1 g
- Fat: 0.041 g
- Sugar: 0.3 g
- Sodium: 4.9 mg
- Fiber: 0.1 g

26. Ultimate Fruity Punch

Preparation Time: 15 minutes
Cooking Time: 0 minutes
Servings: 12

Ingredients:

- 3 cups fresh pineapple juice
- 2 cups fresh orange juice
- 1 cup fresh ruby red grapefruit juice
- 1/4 cup fresh lime juice
- 2 cups seedless watermelon, cut into bite-sized chunks
- 2 cups fresh pineapple, cut into bite-sized chunks
- 2 oranges, peeled and cut into wedges
- 2 limes, quartered
- 1 lemon, sliced
- 2 (12 ounces) cans of diet lemon-lime soda
- Crushed ice, as required

Directions:

1. In a large pitcher, add all ingredients except for soda cans and ice. Stir to combine.

2. Set aside for 30 minutes.
3. Through a cheesecloth-lined sieve, strain the punch into another large pitcher.
4. Set the glasses with ice and top with about 3/4 of the mixture.
5. Add a splash of the soda and serve.

Nutrition Per Serving:

- Calories: 95
- Carbs: 22.4 g
- Protein: 1.3 g
- Fat: 0.3 g
- Sugar: 17.3 g
- Sodium: 8.81 mg
- Fiber: 1.49 g

27. Thirst Quencher Sports Drink

Preparation Time: 15 minutes
Cooking Time: 0 minutes
Servings: 8

Ingredients:

- 7 cups spring water
- 1 cup fresh apple juice
- 2-3 teaspoons fresh lime juice
- 2 tablespoons honey
- 1/4 teaspoon sea salt

Directions:

1. In a large pitcher, add all ingredients and stir to combine.
2. Through a cheesecloth-lined sieve, strain the punch into another large pitcher.
3. Refrigerate to chill before serving.

Nutrition Per Serving:

- Calories: 30
- Carbs: 7.8 g
- Protein: 0.1 g
- Fat: 0 g
- Sugar: 7.3 g
- Sodium: 60 mg
- Fiber: 0.1 g

28. Refreshing Sports Drink

Preparation Time: 15 minutes
Cooking Time: 0 minutes
Servings: 9

Ingredients:

- 8 cups fresh cold water, divided
- 3/4 cup fresh orange juice
- 1/4 cup fresh lemon juice
- 1/4 cup fresh limes juice
- 3 tablespoons honey
- 1/2 teaspoon salt

Directions:

1. In a large pitcher, add all ingredients and stir to combine.
2. Through a cheesecloth-lined sieve, strain the punch into another large pitcher.
3. Refrigerate to chill before serving.

Nutrition Per Serving:

- Calories: 33
- Carbs: 8.1 g
- Protein: 0.2 g
- Fat: 0.1 g
- Sugar: 7.6 g
- Sodium: 130 mg
- Fiber: 0.2 g

29. Perfect Sunny Day Tea

Preparation Time: 15 minutes
Cooking Time: 3 minutes
Servings: 6

Ingredients:

- 5 cups filtered water
- 5 green tea bags
- 1/4 cup fresh lemon juice, strained
- 1/4 cup fresh lime juice, strained
- 1/4 cup honey
- Ice cubes, as required

Directions:

1. In a medium pan, add 2 cups of water and bring to a boil.
2. Set in the tea bags and turn off the heat.
3. Immediately, cover the pan and steep for 3-4 minutes.
4. With a large spoon, gently press the tea bags against the pan to extract the tea completely.
5. Detach the tea bags from the pan and discard them.
6. Set honey and stir until dissolved.
7. In a large pitcher, place the tea, lemon, and lime juice and stir to combine.
8. Add the remaining cold water and stir to combine.
9. Refrigerate to chill before serving.

10. Attach ice cubes in serving glasses and fill with tea.
11. Serve chilled.

Nutrition Per Serving:

- Calories: 46
- Carbs: 12 g
- Protein: 0.1 g
- Fat: 0.1 g
- Sugar: 11.8 g
- Sodium: 3 mg
- Fiber: 0.1 g

30. Nutritious Green Tea

Preparation Time: 15 minutes
Cooking Time: 4 minutes
Servings: 4

Ingredients:

- 4 cups filtered water
- Four orange peel strips
- Four lemon peel strips
- Four green tea bags
- Two teaspoons honey

Directions:

1. In a medium pan, add the water, orange, and lemon peel strips over medium-high heat and bring to a boil.
2. Set the heat to low and stir, uncovered, for about 10 minutes.
3. With a slotted spoon, remove the orange and lemon peel strips and discard them.
4. Attach the tea bags and turn off the heat.

5. Immediately, cover the pan and steep for 3 minutes.
6. With a large spoon, gently press the tea bags against the pan to extract the tea completely.
7. Detach the tea bags from the pan and discard them.
8. Add honey and stir until dissolved.
9. Strain the tea in mugs and serve immediately.

Nutrition Per Serving:

- Calories: 11
- Carbs: 3 g
- Protein: 0 g
- Fat: 0 g
- Sugar: 2.9 g
- Sodium: 0 mg
- Fiber: 0.1 g

31. Simple Black Tea

Preparation Time: 10 minutes
Cooking Time: 3 minutes
Servings: 2

Ingredients:

- 2 cups filtered water
- 1/2 teaspoon black tea leaves
- 1 teaspoon honey

Directions:

1. In a pan, add the water and bring to a boil.
2. Stir in the tea leaves and turn off the heat.
3. Immediately, cover the pan and steep for 3 minutes.

4. Add honey and stir until dissolved.
5. Strain the tea in mugs and serve immediately.

Nutrition Per Serving:

- Calories: 11
- Carbs: 2.9 g
- Protein: 0 g
- Fat: 0 g
- Sugar: 2.9 g
- Sodium: 123 mg
- Fiber: 0 g

32. Lemony Black Tea

Preparation Time: 10 minutes
Cooking Time: 3 minutes
Servings: 6

Ingredients:

- 1 tablespoon of black tea leaves
- 1 lemon, sliced thinly
- 1 cinnamon stick
- 6 cups boiling water

Directions:

1. In a large teapot, place the tea leaves, lemon slices, and cinnamon stick.
2. Pour hot water over the ingredients and immediately cover the teapot.
3. Set aside for about 5 minutes to steep.
4. Strain the tea in mugs and serve immediately.

Nutrition Per Serving:

- Calories: 4
- Carbs: 0.82 g
- Protein: 0.1 g
- Fat: 0 g
- Sugar: 0.1 g
- Sodium: 5 mg
- Fiber: 0.6 g

33. Metabolism Booster Coffee

Preparation Time: 5 minutes
Cooking Time: 4 minutes
Servings: 1

Ingredients:

- 1/4 teaspoon coffee powder
- 1 ¼ cup filtered water
- 1 teaspoon fresh lemon juice
- 1 teaspoon honey

Directions:

1. In a small pan, attach the water and coffee powder. Bring it to a boil.
2. Cook for about 1 minute.
3. Detach from the heat and pour into a serving mug.
4. Add the honey and lemon juice, then stir until dissolved
5. Serve hot.

Nutrition Per Serving:

- Calories: 23
- Carbs: 6 g
- Protein: 0.1 g

- Fat: 0 g
- Sugar: 5.9 g
- Sodium: 1 mg
- Fiber: 0 g

34. Healthier Apple Juice

Preparation Time: 5 minutes
Cooking Time: 0 minutes
Servings: 2

Ingredients:

- 8 medium apples, cored and quartered

Directions:

1. Add the apples into a juicer and extract the juice according to the manufacturer's method.
2. Through a cheesecloth-lined sieve, strain the juice and transfer it into two glasses.
3. Serve immediately.

Nutrition Per Serving:

- Calories: 306
- Carbs: 81.7 g
- Protein: 1.7 g
- Fat: 0.8 g
- Sugar: 64 g
- Sodium: 0 mg
- Fiber: 8.33 g

35. Citrus Apple Juice

Preparation Time: 5 minutes
Cooking Time: 0 minutes
Servings: 2

Ingredients:

- 5 large apples, cored and chopped
- 1 small lemon
- 1 cup fresh orange juice

Directions:

1. Attach all the ingredients in a blender and pulse until well combined.
2. Through a cheesecloth-lined sieve, strain the juice and transfer it into two glasses.
3. Serve immediately.

Nutrition Per Serving:

- Calories: 292
- Carbs: 76g
- Protein: 2.4g
- Fat: 0.9g
- Sugar: 60.1g
- Sodium: 1.4mg
- Fiber: 6.8g

36. Richly Fruity Juice

Preparation Time: 15 minutes
Cooking Time: 10 minutes
Servings: 2

Ingredients:

- 5 large green apples, cored and sliced

- 2 cups seedless white grapes
- 2 teaspoons fresh lime juice

Directions:

1. Set all ingredients into a juicer and extract the juice according to the manufacturer's method.
2. Through a cheesecloth-lined sieve, strain the juice and transfer it into two glasses.
3. Serve immediately.

Nutrition Per Serving:

- Calories: 390
- Carbs: 94.5 g
- Protein: 3.2 g
- Fat: 1.3 g
- Sugar: 70 g
- Sodium: 8 mg
- Fiber: 15.3 g

37. Delish Grape Juice

Preparation Time: 15 minutes
Cooking Time: 0 minutes
Servings: 3

Ingredients:

- 2 cups white seedless grapes
- 1 ½ cup filtered water
- 6-8 ice cubes

Directions:

1. Attach all the ingredients in a blender and pulse until well combined.

2. Through a cheesecloth-lined sieve, strain the juice and transfer it into three glasses.
3. Serve immediately.

Nutrition Per Serving:

- Calories: 41
- Carbs: 10.5 g
- Protein: 0.4 g
- Fat: 0.2 g
- Sugar: 10 g
- Sodium: 1 mg
- Fiber: 10 g

38. Lemony Grape Juice

Preparation Time: 15 minutes
Cooking Time: 0 minutes
Servings: 3

Ingredients:

- 4 cups seedless white grapes
- 2 tablespoons fresh lemon juice

Directions:

1. Attach all the ingredients in a blender and pulse until well combined.
2. Through a cheesecloth-lined sieve, strain the juice and transfer it into three glasses.
3. Serve immediately.

Nutrition Per Serving:

- Calories: 141
- Carbs: 37 g
- Protein: 1.49 g
- Fat: 0.35 g

- Sugar: 31.4 g
- Sodium: 4 mg
- Fiber: 1.81 g

39. Holiday Special Juice

Preparation Time: 15 minutes

Cooking Time: 0 minutes

Servings: 4

Ingredients:

- 4 cups fresh cranberries
- 1 tablespoon fresh lemon juice
- 2 cups filtered water
- 1 teaspoon raw honey

Directions:

1. Attach all the ingredients in a blender and pulse until well combined.
2. Through a cheesecloth-lined sieve, strain the juice and transfer it into four glasses.
3. Serve immediately.

Nutrition Per Serving:

- Calories: 66
- Carbs: 11.5 g
- Protein: 0 g
- Fat: 0 g
- Sugar: 5.5 g
- Sodium: 1 mg
- Fiber: 4 g

40. Vitamin C Rich Juice

Preparation Time: 15 minutes
Cooking Time: 0 minutes
Servings: 2

Ingredients:

- 8 oranges, peeled and sectioned

Directions:

1. Add the orange sections into a juicer and extract the juice according to the manufacturer's method.
2. Through a cheesecloth-lined sieve, strain the juice and transfer it into two glasses.
3. Serve immediately.

Nutrition Per Serving:

- Calories: 172
- Carbs: 43.1 g
- Protein: 3.45 g
- Fat: 0.4 g
- Sugar: 34 g
- Sodium: 0 mg
- Fiber: 8.8 g

41. Incredible Fresh Juice

Preparation Time: 15 minutes
Cooking Time: 0 minutes
Servings: 4

Ingredients:

- 2 pounds carrots, trimmed and scrubbed
- 6 small oranges, peeled and sectioned

Directions:

1. According to the manufacturer's method, add the carrots and orange sections into a juicer and extract the juice.
2. Through a cheesecloth-lined sieve, strain the juice and transfer it into four glasses.
3. Serve immediately.

Nutrition Per Serving:

- Calories: 130
- Carbs: 31 g
- Protein: 2.2 g
- Fat: 0.6 g
- Sugar: 18 g
- Sodium: 139 mg
- Fiber: 8 g

42. Best Homemade Broth

Preparation Time: 15 minutes
Cooking Time: 2 hours 5 minutes
Servings: 8

Ingredients:

- 1 (3 pounds) chicken, cut into pieces
- 5 medium carrots
- 4 celery stalks with leaves
- 6 fresh thyme sprigs
- 6 fresh parsley sprigs
- Salt to taste
- 9 cups cold water

Directions:

1. In a large pan, attach all the ingredients over medium-high heat and bring to a boil.
2. Set the heat to medium-low and stir, covered for about 2 hours, occasionally skimming the foam from the surface.
3. Through a fine-mesh sieve, strain the broth into a large bowl.
4. Serve hot.

Nutrition Per Serving:

- Calories: 256
- Carbs: 4.3 g
- Protein: 21.1 g
- Fat: 16 g
- Sugar: 1.8 g
- Sodium: 219 mg
- Fiber: 1.2 g

43. Clean Testing Broth

Preparation Time: 5 hours 50 minutes
Cooking Time: 15 minutes
Servings: 10

Ingredients:

- 4 pounds chicken bones
- Salt to taste
- 10 cups filtered water
- 2 tablespoons apple cider vinegar
- 1 lemon, quartered
- 3 bay leaves
- 3 teaspoons ground turmeric
- 2 tablespoons peppercorns

Directions:

1. Preheat the oven to 400°F.
2. Arrange the bones onto a large baking sheet and sprinkle with salt.
3. Roast for about 45 minutes.
4. Detach from the oven and transfer the bones into a large pan.
5. Add the remaining ingredients and stir to combine.
6. Put the pan over medium-high heat and bring to a boil.
7. Set the heat to low and stir, covered for about 4-5 hours, occasionally skimming the foam from the surface.
8. Through a fine-mesh sieve, strain the broth into a large bowl.
9. Serve hot.

Nutrition Per Serving:

- Calories: 355
- Carbs: 2.17 g
- Protein: 46 g
- Fat: 15 g
- Sugar: 0.4 g
- Sodium: 167 mg
- Fiber: 0.7 g

44. Healing Broth

Preparation Time: 10 hours 25 minutes
Cooking Time: 15 minutes
Servings: 12

Ingredients:

- 3 tablespoons extra-virgin olive oil
- 2 ½ pounds chicken bones
- 4 celery stalks, chopped roughly
- 3 large carrots, peeled and chopped roughly
- 1 bay leaf
- 1 tablespoon black peppercorns
- 2 whole cloves
- 1 tablespoon apple cider vinegar
- Warm water, as required

Directions:

1. Heat the oil over medium-high heat in a Dutch oven and sear the bones for about 3-5 minutes or until browned.
2. With a slotted spoon, transfer the bones into a bowl.
3. In the same pan, add the celery stalks and carrots. Cook for about 15 minutes, stirring occasionally.
4. Add browned bones, bay leaf, black peppercorns, cloves, and vinegar. Stir to combine.
5. Add enough warm water to cover the bones mixture entirely and bring to a gentle boil.
6. Set the heat to low and stir, covered for about 8-10 hours, occasionally skimming the foam from the surface.
7. Through a fine-mesh sieve, strain the broth into a large bowl.
8. Serve hot.

Nutrition Per Serving:

- Calories: 223.9
- Carbs: 2.76 g
- Protein: 24.44 g
- Fat: 11.9 g

- Sugar: 0.9 g
- Sodium: 67.72 mg
- Fiber: 1.02 g

45. Veggie Lover's Broth

Preparation Time: 2 hours 5 minutes
Cooking Time: 15 minutes
Servings: 10

Ingredients:

- 4 carrots, peeled and chopped roughly
- 4 celery stalks, chopped roughly
- 3 parsnips, peeled and chopped roughly
- 2 large potatoes, peeled and chopped roughly
- 1 medium beet, trimmed and chopped roughly
- 1 large bunch of fresh parsley
- 1 (1 inch) piece fresh ginger, sliced
- Filtered water, as required

Directions:

1. In a pan, add all the ingredients over medium-high heat.
2. Add enough water to cover the veggie mixture and bring to a boil.
3. Set the heat to low and simmer, covered for about 2-3 hours.
4. Through a fine-mesh sieve, strain the broth into a large bowl.
5. Serve hot.

Nutrition Per Serving:

- Calories: 76
- Carbs: 17 g

- Protein: 2 g
- Fat: 0.2 g
- Sugar: 3.04 g
- Sodium: 39 mg
- Fiber: 3.4 g

46. Brain Healthy Broth

Preparation Time: 12 hours 5 minutes
Cooking Time: 10 minutes
Servings: 6

Ingredients:

- 12 cups filtered water
- 2 pounds non-oily fish heads and bones
- 1/4 cup apple cider vinegar
- Sea salt to taste

Directions:

1. In a large pan, attach all the ingredients over medium-high heat.
2. Add enough water to cover the veggie mixture and bring to a boil.
3. Set the heat to low and simmer, covered for about 10-12 hours, occasionally skimming the foam from the surface.
4. Through a fine-mesh sieve, strain the broth into a large bowl.
5. Serve hot.

Nutrition Per Serving:

- Calories: 151
- Carbs: 0.09 g
- Protein: 27.5 g
- Fat: 4.22 g
- Sugar: 0 g

- Sodium: 190.8 mg
- Fiber: 0 g

- Sugar: 1.2 g
- Sodium: 234 mg
- Fiber: 0.7 g

47. Minerals Rich Broth

Preparation Time: 15 minutes
Cooking Time: 2 hours 25 minutes
Servings: 8

Ingredients:

- 5-7 pounds non-oily fish carcasses and heads
- 2 tablespoons olive oil
- 3 carrots, scrubbed and chopped roughly
- 2 celery stalks, chopped roughly

Directions:

1. In a pan, heat the oil over medium-low heat and cook the carrots and celery for about 20 minutes, stirring occasionally.
2. Add the fish bones and enough water to cover by 1-inch and stir to combine.
3. Set the heat to medium-high and bring to a boil.
4. Set the heat to low, cover for about 1-2 hours, occasionally skimming the foam from the surface.
5. Through a fine-mesh sieve, strain the broth into a large bowl.
6. Serve hot.

Nutrition Per Serving:

- Calories: 113
- Carbs: 2.5 g
- Protein: 13.7 g
- Fat: 5.2 g

48. Holiday Favorite Gelatin

Preparation Time: 15 minutes
Servings: 6

Ingredients:

- 1 tbsp. grass-fed gelatin powder
- 1¾ cup fresh apple juice, warmed
- ¼ cup boiling water
- 1-2 drops fresh lemon juice

Directions:

1. In a medium bowl, pour in the tbsp of gelatin powder.
2. Add just enough warm apple juice to cover the gelatin and stir well.
3. Set aside for about 2-3 minutes or until it forms a thick syrup.
4. Add ¼ cup of the boiling water and stir until gelatin is dissolved completely.
5. Add the remaining juice and lemon juice and stir well.
6. Transfer the mixture into a parchment paper-lined baking dish and refrigerate for 2 hours or until the top is firm before serving.

Nutrition Per Serving:

- Calories: 36.2
- Carbohydrates: 8.16g
- Protein: 1g
- Fat: 0g

- Sugar: 7g
- Sodium: 5.24mg
- Fiber: 0g

49. Zesty Gelatin

Preparation Time: 15 minutes
Cooking Time: 5 minutes
Servings: 4

Ingredients:

- 1 tbsp. grass-fed gelatin powder
- ¾ cup filtered cold water, divided
- ¼ cup honey
- 1¼ cup fresh grapefruit juice
- Pinch of salt

Directions:

1. In a bowl, soak the gelatin in ¼ cup of cold water. Set aside.
2. In a small pan, add the remaining ½ cup of water and honey over medium heat and bring to a boil.
3. Simmer for about 3 minutes or until honey is dissolved completely.
4. Remove from the heat and stir in the soaked gelatin until dissolved completely.
5. Set aside at room temperature to cool completely.
6. After cooling, stir in the grapefruit juice and salt.
7. Transfer the mixture into serving bowls and refrigerate for about 4 hours or until set.

Nutrition Per Serving:

- Calories per serving: 98
- Carbohydrates: 23.3g
- Protein: 3.3g
- Fat: 0.08g
- Sugar: 22.4g
- Sodium: 43mg
- Fiber: 0.8g

50. 2-Ingredients Gelatin

Preparation Time: 10 minutes
Cooking Time: 0 minutes
Servings: 4

Ingredients:

- 1 tbsp. grass-fed tangerine gelatin powder
- 2¼ cup boiling water

Directions:

1. In a large bowl, add the gelatin and boiling water and stir until dissolved completely.
2. Divide in serving bowls and refrigerate until set entirely before serving.

Nutrition Per Serving:

- Calories: 5.87
- Carbohydrates: 0g
- Protein: 1.5g
- Fat: 0g
- Sugar: 0g
- Sodium: 6.1mg
- Fiber: 0g

51. Great Lemon Gelatin

Preparation Time: 10 minutes
Cooking Time: 0 minutes
Servings: 8

Ingredients:

- 3 tbsp. grass-fed gelatin powder
- 3 cup cold water, divided
- 1½ cup boiling water
- 1 cup plus 2 tbsp. fresh lemon juice
- 2 tsp. stevia extract

Directions:

1. In a bowl, soak the gelatin in 1½ cup of cold water. Set aside for about 5 minutes.
2. Add boiling water and stir until gelatin is dissolved.
3. Add the remaining cold water, lemon juice, and stevia extract and stir until dissolved completely.
4. Divide the mixture into two baking dishes and refrigerate until set before serving.

Nutrition Per Serving:

- Calories: 15.4
- Carbohydrates: 3.36g
- Protein: 2.35g
- Fat: 0.07g
- Sugar: 0.76g
- Sodium: 8.15mg
- Fiber: 0.09g

52. Weight Watcher's Gelatin

Preparation Time: 10 minutes
Cooking Time: 0 minutes
Servings: 8

Ingredients:

- 1 tbsp. grass-fed gelatin powder
- ¼ cup cold filtered water
- ¼ cup hot water
- 1 cup fresh grape juice

Directions:

1. In a bowl, soak the gelatin in cold water. Set aside for about 5 minutes.
2. Add the hot water and mix well. Set aside for about 1-2 minutes.
3. Add the grape juice and mix well.
4. Divide in serving bowls and refrigerate until set completely before serving.

Nutrition Per Serving:

- Calories: 17.47
- Carbohydrates: 3.7g
- Protein: 0.69g
- Fat: 0g
- Sugar: 3.58g
- Sodium: 2.87mg
- Fiber: 0g

53. Beautifully Colored Gelatin

Preparation Time: 10 minutes
Cooking Time: 5 minutes
Servings: 10

Ingredients:

- 2 tbsp. grass-fed gelatin powder
- 4 cup fresh peach juice, divided
- 2 tbsp. honey

Directions:

1. In a bowl, soak the gelatin in ½ cup of juice. Set aside for about 5 minutes.
2. In a medium pan, add the remaining juice over medium heat and bring to a gentle boil.
3. Remove from the heat and stir in honey.
4. Add the gelatin mixture and stir until dissolved.
5. Transfer the mixture into a large baking dish and refrigerate until set completely before serving.

Nutrition Per Serving:

- Calories: 81.3
- Carbohydrates: 18.6g
- Protein: 1.6g
- Fat: 0g
- Sugar: 18.6g
- Sodium: 4.9mg
- Fiber: 0g

54. Aromatic Cinnamon Gelatin

Preparation Time: 10 minutes
Cooking Time: 5 minutes
Servings: 2

Ingredients:

- 1 cup water
- 1 cinnamon stick
- 2 tsp. grass-fed gelatin powder
- 2 tbsp. honey

Directions:

1. In a small pan, add the water over medium heat and bring to a boil.
2. Add in the cinnamon stick and turn off the heat.
3. Immediately, cover the pan and steep for 3 minutes.
4. Add the gelatin and beat until well combined.
5. Transfer the mixture into a baking dish and set it aside to cool for about 2 hours.
6. Refrigerate to set before serving.

Nutrition Per Serving:

- Calories: 79
- Carbohydrates: 18.1g
- Protein: 2.18g
- Fat: 0g
- Sugar: 17.3g
- Sodium: 8.12mg
- Fiber: 1.64g

Chapter 5

CLEAR FLUIDS (DINNER)

55. Vegetable Stock

Preparation Time: 10 minutes
Cooking Time: 40 minutes
Servings: 8

Ingredients:

- 2 large carrots
- 1 large onion
- 2 large stalks of celery

- 8 ounces white mushrooms
- 5 whole garlic cloves
- 2 cups parsley leaves
- 2 bay leaves
- 2 teaspoons whole black peppercorns
- 2 teaspoons kosher salt
- 10 cups water

Directions:

1. Place all the ingredients in your pot. Secure the lid.
2. Pressure cook and adjust the time to 40 minutes.
3. Set the broth using a fine-mesh strainer and transfer it into a storage container.

Nutrition Per Serving:

- Calories: 31.3
- Fat: 0.3 g
- Protein: 1.9 g
- Sodium: 501 mg
- Fiber: 1.9 g
- Carbs: 6.4 g
- Sugar: 2.3 g

56. Chicken Vegetable Soup

Preparation Time: 23 minutes
Cooking Time: 15 minutes
Servings: 8

Ingredients:

- 2 tablespoons avocado oil
- 1 small yellow onion, peeled and chopped
- 2 large carrots, peeled and chopped
- 2 large stalks of celery having end removed and sliced
- 3 garlic cloves, minced
- 1 teaspoon dried thyme
- 1 teaspoon salt
- 8 cups chicken stock
- 3 boneless, skinless, frozen chicken breasts

Directions:

1. Heat the oil for 1 minute. Add the onion, carrots, and celery and sauté for 8 minutes.
2. Add the garlic, thyme, and salt, then sauté for another 30 seconds. Press the Cancel button.
3. Add the stock and frozen chicken breasts to the pot. Secure the lid.
4. Pressure cook and adjust the time to 6 minutes.
5. Allow cooling into bowls to serve.

Nutrition Per Serving:

- Calories: 276.5
- Fat: 14.2 g
- Protein: 24.18 g
- Sodium: 707 mg
- Fiber: 0.8 g
- Carbs: 12 g
- Sugar: 5 g

57. Carrot Ginger Soup

Preparation Time: 20 minutes
Cooking Time: 21 minutes
Servings: 4

Ingredients:

- 1 tablespoon avocado oil
- 1 large yellow onion, peeled and chopped
- 1 pound carrots, peeled and chopped
- 1 tablespoon fresh ginger, peeled and minced
- 1 ½ teaspoon salt
- 3 cups vegetable broth

Directions:

1. Add the oil to the inner pot, allowing it to heat for 1 minute.
2. Attach the onion, carrots, ginger, and salt, then sauté for 5 minutes. Press the Cancel button.
3. Add the broth and secure the lid. Adjust the time to 15 minutes.
4. Allow the soup to cool a few minutes, and then transfer it to a large blender. Merge on high until smooth and then serve.

Nutrition Per Serving:

- Calories: 94.4
- Fat: 4 g
- Protein: 1.67 g
- Sodium: 1475 mg
- Fiber: 4 g
- Carbs: 14.4 g
- Sugar: 5.8 g

58. Chicken Bone Broth

Preparation Time: 10 minutes
Cooking Time: 90 minutes
Servings: 8

Ingredients:

- 3-4 pounds bones (from 1 chicken)
- 4 cups water
- 2 large carrots, cut into chunks
- 2 large stalks of celery
- 1 large onion
- 2 cups fresh rosemary sprigs
- 3 fresh thyme sprigs
- 2 tablespoons apple cider vinegar

- 1 teaspoon kosher salt

Directions:

1. Put all the ingredients in your pot and allow to sit for 30 minutes.
2. Pressure cook and adjust the time to 90 minutes.
3. Set the release naturally until the float valve drops and then unlock the lid.
4. Strain the broth and transfer it into a storage container. The broth can be refrigerated for 3-5 days or frozen for up to 6 months.

Nutrition Per Serving:

- Calories: 224.29
- Carbs: 5.35 g
- Protein: 19.9 g
- Fat: 13.16 g
- Sugar: 1.6 g
- Sodium: 503.8 mg
- Fiber: 2.12 g

59. Homemade Beef Stock

Preparation Time: 10 minutes
Cooking Time: 2-12 hours
Servings: 6

Ingredients:

- 2 pounds beef bones (preferably with marrow)
- 5 celery stalks, chopped
- 4 carrots, chopped
- 1 white or Spanish onion, chopped
- 2 garlic cloves, crushed

- 2 bay leaves
- 1 teaspoon dried thyme
- 1 teaspoon dried sage
- 1 teaspoon black peppercorns
- Salt

Directions:

1. Preheat the oven to 425°F.
2. On a baking sheet, spread out the beef bones, celery, carrots, onion, garlic, and bay leaves. Sprinkle the thyme, sage, and peppercorns over the top.
3. Roast until the vegetables and bones have a rich brown color.
4. Transfer the roasted bones and vegetables to a large stockpot. Cover with water and slowly bring to a boil over high heat.
5. Set the heat to medium-low for at least 2 hours and up to 12 hours.
6. Pour the mixture through a fine-mesh strainer into a large bowl.
7. Taste and season with salt. Serve hot.

Nutrition Per Serving:

- Calories: 205.68
- Fat: 11.4 g
- Carbs: 6.97 g
- Fiber: 2.16 g
- Protein: 17.9 g
- Sodium: 401.2 mg

60. Three-Ingredient Sugar-Free Gelatin

Preparation Time: 5 minutes
Cooking Time: 0 minutes
Servings: 6-8

Ingredients:

- 1/4 cup room temperature water
- 1/4 cup hot water
- 1 tablespoon gelatin
- 1 cup orange juice, unsweetened

Directions:

1. Combine your gelatin and room temperature water, stirring until fully dissolved.
2. Stir in hot water, then leave to rest for about 2 minutes.
3. Add in the juice and stir until combined.
4. Transfer to serving size containers, then place on a tray in the refrigerator to set for about 4 hours.
5. Enjoy!

Nutrition Per Serving:

- Calories: 17
- Fat: 0 g
- Carbs: 3.2 g
- Fiber: 0 g
- Protein: 0.9 g

61. Cranberry-Kombucha Jell-O

Preparation Time: 5 minutes
Cooking Time: 0 minutes
Servings: 6

Ingredients:

- 1/4 cup room temperature water
- 1/4 cup hot water
- 1 tablespoon gelatin
- 1 cup cranberry kombucha, unsweetened

Directions:

1. Combine your gelatin and room temperature water, stirring until fully dissolved.
2. Stir in hot water, then leave to rest for about 2 minutes.
3. Add in the kombucha and stir until combined.
4. Transfer to serving size containers, then place on a tray in the refrigerator to set for about 4 hours.
5. Enjoy!

Nutrition Per Serving:

- Calories: 13
- Fat: 0 g
- Carbs: 2.17 g
- Fiber: 0 g
- Protein: 1 g

62. Strawberry Gummies

Preparation Time: 5 minutes
Cooking Time: 5 minutes
Servings: 20-40 mini gummies

Ingredients:

- 1 cup strawberries, hulled and chopped
- 3/4 cup water
- 2 tablespoons gelatin

Directions:

1. Bring your water and berries to a boil on high heat. Detach from the heat as soon as the mixture begins to boil.
2. Transfer to the blender and pulse. Add in your gelatin, then blend once more.
3. Pour the mixture into a gummy silicone mold.
4. Place on a tray in the refrigerator to set for about 4 hours.
5. Enjoy!

Nutrition Per Serving:

- Calories: 4.8
- Fat: 0 g
- Carbs: 0.5 g
- Fiber: 0.1 g
- Protein: 0.6 g

63. Fruity Jell-O Stars

Preparation Time: 15 minutes
Cooking Time: 5 minutes
Servings: 4

Ingredients:

- 1 tablespoon gelatin, powdered
- 3/4 cup boiling water
- 3 ½ cups fruit
- 1 tablespoon honey
- 1 teaspoon lemon juice

Directions:

1. Attach all your ingredients into a blender and pulse.
2. Add in the gelatin, then blend once more.
3. Pour the mixture into a gummy silicone mold.
4. Place on a tray in the refrigerator to set for about 4 hours.
5. Enjoy!

Nutrition Per Serving:

- Calories: 50.46
- Fat: 0 g
- Carbs: 11.8 g
- Fiber: 0.9 g
- Protein: 1.8 g

64. Sugar-Free Cinnamon Jelly

Preparation Time: 5 minutes
Cooking Time: 0 minutes
Servings: 2

Ingredients:

- 1 cup hot cinnamon tea
- 1 cup room temperature water
- 2 teaspoons gelatin
- 1/3 cup sweetener

Directions:

1. Combine your gelatin and room temperature water, stirring until fully dissolved.
2. Stir in hot tea, then leave to rest for about 2 minutes.
3. Add in the sweetener and stir until combined.
4. Transfer to serving size containers, then place on a tray in the refrigerator to set for about 4 hours.
5. Enjoy!

Nutrition Per Serving:

- Calories: 112.65
- Fat: 0 g
- Carbs: 28.45 g
- Fiber: 0 g
- Protein: 2 g

65. Homey Clear Chicken Broth

Preparation Time: 10 minutes
Cooking Time: 2-12 hours
Servings: 6 cups

Ingredients:

- 2 pounds chicken neck
- 2 celery ribs with leaves, cut into chunks
- 2 medium carrots, cut into chunks
- 2 medium onions, quartered
- 2 bay leaves
- 2 quarts cold water
- Salt

Directions:

1. Transfer the bones and vegetables to your stockpot. Top with enough water to cover, then allow to come to a boil on high heat slowly.
2. Switch to low heat and simmer for at least 2 hours and up to 12 hours.
3. Set and pour the mixture through a fine-mesh strainer into a large bowl.
4. Taste and season with salt.
5. Serve hot.

Nutrition Per Serving:

- Calories: 308.2
- Fat: 25.34 g
- Carbs: 5.25 g
- Fiber: 1.3 g
- Protein: 14.16 g

66. Oxtail Bone Broth

Preparation Time: 15 minutes
Cooking Time: 12 hours
Servings: 8 cups

Ingredients:

- 2 pounds Oxtail
- 1 Onion, chopped in quarters
- 2 celery stalks, chopped in half
- 2 carrots, chopped in half
- 3 whole garlic cloves
- 2 bay leaves
- 1 tablespoon salt
- Filtered water (enough to cover bones)

Directions:

1. Transfer the bones and vegetables to your stockpot. Top with enough water to cover, then allow to come to a boil on high heat slowly.
2. Switch to low heat and simmer for at least 2 hours and up to 12 hours.
3. Set and pour the mixture through a fine-mesh strainer into a large bowl.
4. Taste and season with salt.
5. Serve hot.

Nutrition Per Serving:

- Calories: 197.22
- Fat: 10.8 g
- Carbs: 3.17 g
- Fiber: 0.79 g
- Protein: 20.87 g

67. Chicken Bone Broth with Ginger and Lemon

Preparation Time: 10 minutes
Cooking Time: 90 minutes
Servings: 8

Ingredients:

- 3-4 pounds bones (from 1 chicken)
- 8 cups water
- 2 large carrots, cut into chunks
- 2 large stalks of celery
- 1 large onion
- 3 fresh rosemary sprigs
- 3 fresh thyme sprigs
- 2 tablespoons apple cider vinegar
- 1 teaspoon kosher salt
- 1 (1/2 inches) piece fresh ginger, sliced (peeling not necessary)
- 1 large lemon, cut into quarters

Directions:

1. Put all the ingredients in your pot and allow to sit for 30 minutes.
2. Pressure cook and adjust the time to 90 minutes.
3. Set the broth using a fine-mesh strainer and transfer it into a storage container.
4. It can be refrigerated for five days or frozen for six months.

Nutrition Per Serving:

- Calories: 215.85
- Fat: 12.7 g
- Protein: 19.7 g
- Sodium: 504 mg
- Fiber: 1.1 g
- Carbs: 4.2 g
- Sugar: 1.7 g

68. Turkey Sweet Potato Hash

Preparation Time: 10 minutes
Cooking Time: 12 minutes
Servings: 4

Ingredients:

- 1 ½ tablespoon avocado oil
- 1 medium yellow onion, peeled and diced
- 2 garlic cloves, minced
- 1 medium sweet potato, cut into cubes (peeling not necessary)
- 1/2 pound lean ground turkey
- 1/2 teaspoon salt
- 1 teaspoon Italian seasoning blend

Directions:

1. Attach the oil and allow it to heat for 1 minute.
2. Add the onion and cook until softened, about 5 minutes.
3. Attach the garlic and cook for an additional 30 seconds.
4. Add the sweet potato, turkey, salt, and Italian seasoning and cook for another 5 minutes.

Nutrition Per Serving:

- Calories: 198
- Fat: 12.2 g
- Protein: 10.5 g
- Sodium: 348 mg

- Fiber: 1.8 g
- Carbs: 11.7 g
- Sugar: 1.9 g

69. Chicken Tenders with Honey Mustard Sauce

Preparation Time: 5 minutes
Cooking Time: 10 minutes
Servings: 4

Ingredients:

- 1 pound chicken tenders
- 1 tablespoon fresh thyme leaves
- 1/2 teaspoon salt
- 1/4 teaspoon black pepper
- 1 tablespoon avocado oil
- 1 cup chicken stock
- 1/4 cup Dijon mustard
- 1/4 cup raw honey

Directions:

1. Dry the chicken tenders with a towel and then season them with thyme, salt, and pepper.
2. Attach the oil and let it heat for 2 minutes. Add the chicken tenders and seer them until brown on both sides, about 1 minute per side. Press the Cancel button.
3. Remove the chicken tenders and set them aside. Add the stock to the pot. Use a spoon to scrape up any small bits from the bottom of the pot.
4. Set the steam rack in the inner pot and place the chicken tenders directly on the rack.

5. While the chicken is cooking, prepare the sauce.
6. In a bowl, combine the Dijon mustard and honey, then stir to combine.
7. Serve the chicken tenders with the honey mustard sauce.

Nutrition Per Serving:

- Calories: 275
- Fat: 9 g
- Protein: 28.3 g
- Sodium: 465.2 mg
- Fiber: 0.3 g
- Carbs: 20 g
- Sugar: 17.1 g

70. Chicken Breasts with Cabbage and Mushrooms

Preparation Time: 10 minutes
Cooking Time: 18 minutes
Servings: 4

Ingredients:

- 2 tablespoons avocado oil
- 1 pound sliced Baby Bella mushrooms
- 1 ½ teaspoon salt, divided
- 2 garlic cloves, minced
- 8 cups chopped green cabbage
- 1 ½ teaspoon dried thyme
- 1/2 cup chicken stock
- 1 ½ pound boneless, skinless chicken breasts

Directions:

1. Add the oil. Allow it to heat for 1 minute.
2. Attach the mushrooms and 1/4 teaspoon of salt. Sauté until they have cooked down and released their liquid, about 10 minutes.
3. Add the garlic and sauté for another 30 seconds. Press the Cancel button.
4. Attach the cabbage, 1/4 teaspoon of salt, thyme, and the stock to the inner pot. Stir to combine.
5. Dry the chicken breasts and sprinkle both sides with the remaining salt. Place on top of the cabbage mixture.
6. Transfer to plates and spoon the juices on top.

Nutrition Per Serving:

- Calories: 338.07
- Fat: 11.8 g
- Protein: 44 g
- Sodium: 1405 mg
- Fiber: 5.3 g
- Carbs: 14.2 g
- Sugar: 6.58 g

71. Duck with Bok Choy

Preparation Time: 15 minutes
Cooking Time: 12 minutes
Servings: 6

Ingredients:

- 2 tablespoons coconut oil
- 1 onion, sliced thinly
- 2 teaspoons fresh ginger, grated finely
- 2 minced garlic cloves
- 1 tablespoon fresh orange zest, grated finely
- 1/4 cup chicken broth
- 2/3 cup fresh orange juice
- 1 roasted duck, meat picked
- 3 pounds Bok choy leaves
- 1 orange, peeled, seeded, and segmented

Directions:

1. In a sizable skillet, melt the coconut oil on medium heat. Attach the onion, sauté for around 3 minutes. Add ginger and garlic, then sauté for about 1-2 minutes.
2. Stir in the orange zest, broth, and orange juice.
3. Add the duck meat and cook for around 3 minutes.
4. Transfer the meat pieces to a plate. Add the Bok choy and cook for about 3-4 minutes.
5. Divide the Bok choy mixture into serving plates and top with duck meat.
6. Serve with the garnishing of orange segments.

Nutrition Per Serving:

- Calories: 520.3
- Fat: 23.13 g
- Fiber: 2.3 g
- Carbs: 10.2 g
- Protein: 67.9 g

72. Beef with Mushroom and Broccoli

Preparation Time: 60 minutes
Cooking Time: 12 minutes
Servings: 4

Ingredients:

For Beef Marinade:

- 1 garlic clove, minced
- 1 piece fresh ginger, minced
- Salt and freshly ground black pepper
- 3 tablespoons white wine vinegar
- 3/4 cup beef broth
- 1 pound flank steak, trimmed and sliced into thin strips

For Vegetables:

- 2 tablespoons coconut oil
- 2 garlic cloves
- 3 cups broccoli rabe
- 4 ounces shiitake mushrooms
- 8 ounces cremini mushrooms

Directions:

For the marinade:

1. In a substantial bowl, mix all ingredients except the beef. Add it and coat with the marinade generously. Refrigerate to soak for around 1/4 hour.
2. In a substantial skillet, warm oil on medium-high heat.
3. Detach the beef from the bowl, reserving the marinade.

For the Vegetables:

1. Attach the beef and garlic and cook for about 3-4 minutes or till browned.
2. In the same skillet, add the reserved marinade, broccoli, and mushrooms. Cook for approximately 3-4 minutes.
3. Set in the beef and cook for about 3-4 minutes.

Nutrition Per Serving:

- Calories: 258.78
- Carbs: 5.8 g
- Cholesterol: 71 mg
- Fat: 13.5 g
- Protein: 28.5 g
- Fiber: 2.24 g

73. Beef with Zucchini Noodles

Preparation Time: 15 minutes
Cooking Time: 9 minutes
Servings: 4

Ingredients:

- 1 teaspoon fresh ginger, grated
- 2 medium garlic cloves, minced
- 1/4 cup coconut aminos
- 2 tablespoons fresh lime juice
- 1 ½ pound NY strip steak, trimmed and sliced thinly
- 2 medium zucchini, spiralized with blade C
- Salt to taste
- 3 tablespoons essential olive oil
- 2 medium scallions, sliced
- 1 teaspoon red pepper flakes, crushed

- 2 tablespoons fresh cilantro, chopped

Directions:

1. In a big bowl, merge ginger, garlic, coconut aminos, and lime juice. Add the beef and coat with the marinade generously. Refrigerate to soak for approximately 10 minutes.
2. Set zucchini noodles over a large paper towel and sprinkle with salt.
3. Keep aside for around 10 minutes.
4. Heat oil on medium-high heat in a big skillet. Attach the scallions, and red pepper flakes, then sauté for about 1 minute.
5. Attach the beef with the marinade and stir fry for around 3-4 minutes or till browned.
6. Stir in the fresh cilantro, then add the zucchini and cook for approximately 3-4 minutes.
7. Serve hot.

Nutrition Per Serving:

- Calories: 350.8
- Carbs: 11.9 g
- Cholesterol: 94 mg
- Fat: 15.68 g
- Protein: 40.71 g
- Fiber. 1.34 g

74. Spiced Ground Beef

Preparation Time: 10 minutes
Cooking Time: 22 minutes
Servings: 5

Ingredients:

- 2 tablespoons coconut oil
- 2 whole cloves
- 2 whole cardamoms
- 1 (2 inches) piece cinnamon stick
- 2 bay leaves
- 1 teaspoon cumin seeds
- 2 onions, chopped
- Salt to taste
- 1/2 tablespoon garlic paste
- 1/2 tablespoon fresh ginger paste
- 1 pound lean ground beef
- 1 ½ teaspoon fennel seeds powder
- 1 teaspoon ground cumin
- 1 ½ teaspoon red chili powder
- 1/8 teaspoon ground turmeric
- Freshly ground black pepper, to taste
- 1 cup coconut milk
- 1/4 cup water
- 1/4 cup fresh cilantro, chopped

Directions:

1. In a sizable pan, warm oil on medium heat. Mix cloves, cardamoms, cinnamon sticks, bay leaves, and cumin seeds; cook for 20 seconds.
2. Attach the onion, and 2 pinches of salt, then sauté for about 3-4 minutes.
3. Add the garlic-ginger paste and stir fry for about 2 minutes.

4. Attach the beef and cook for about 4-5 minutes, entering pieces using the spoon. Stir in spices and cook.

5. Set in the coconut milk and water; cook for about 7-8 minutes. Flavor with salt and take away from the heat.

6. Serve hot using the garnishing of cilantro.

Nutrition Per Serving:

- Calories: 255.8
- Protein: 20.15 g
- Fat: 26.56 g
- Carbs: 10.6 g

75. Ground Beef with Veggies

Preparation Time: 60 minutes
Cooking Time: 22 minutes
Servings: 4

Ingredients:

- 1-2 tablespoons coconut oil
- 1 red onion,
- 2 red jalapeño peppers
- 2 minced garlic cloves
- 1 pound lean ground beef
- 1 small head broccoli, chopped
- 1/2 head cauliflower
- 3 carrots, peeled and sliced
- 3 celery ribs
- Chopped fresh thyme to taste
- Dried sage to taste
- Ground turmeric, to taste
- Salt and freshly ground black pepper

Directions:

1. In a large skillet, dissolve the coconut oil on medium heat.

2. Stir in the onion, jalapeño peppers, and garlic. Sauté for about 5 minutes.

3. Attach the beef and cook for around 4-5 minutes, entering pieces using the spoon.

4. Add the remaining ingredients and cook, occasionally stirring for about 8-10 minutes.

5. Serve hot.

Nutrition Per Serving:

- Calories: 282
- Cholesterol: 74.15 mg
- Carbs: 10.9 g
- Fat: 15.19 g
- Sugar: 4.3 g
- Fiber: 3.8 g

76. Ground Beef with Greens and Tomatoes

Preparation Time: 15 minutes
Cooking Time: 15 minutes
Servings: 4

Ingredients:

- 1 tablespoon organic olive oil
- 1/2 white onion, chopped
- 2 garlic cloves, finely chopped
- 1 jalapeño pepper, finely chopped
- 1 pound lean ground beef
- 1 teaspoon ground coriander
- 1 teaspoon ground cumin

- 1/2 teaspoon ground turmeric
- 1/2 teaspoon ground ginger
- 1/2 teaspoon ground cinnamon
- 1/2 teaspoon ground fennel seeds
- Salt and freshly ground black pepper
- 8 fresh cherry tomatoes, quartered
- 8 collard green leaves, stemmed and chopped
- 1 teaspoon fresh lemon juice

Directions:

1. In a big skillet, warm oil on medium heat.
2. Add the onion and sauté for approximately 4 minutes.
3. Stir in the garlic and jalapeño pepper. Sauté for around 1 minute.
4. Attach the beef and spices; cook for approximately 6 minutes, breaking into pieces while using a spoon.
5. Set in tomatoes and greens. Cook, stirring gently for about 4 minutes.
6. Whisk in lemon juice and take away from the heat.

Nutrition Per Serving:

- Calories: 312
- Fat: 15.28 g
- Carbs: 20.46 g
- Fiber: 5.38 g
- Protein: 25.33 g

Chapter 6

CLEAR FLUIDS (SNACK)

77. Roasted Carrot Sticks in a Honey Garlic Marinade

Preparation Time: 10 minutes
Cooking Time: 25-30 minutes
Servings: 4

Ingredients:

- 1 bunch carrots, halved lengthways
- 2 garlic cloves, minced
- 1 tablespoon honey
- 1 tablespoon lemon juice (alternatively apple cider vinegar)
- 40 g butter
- 3 tablespoons parsley, chopped

Directions:

1. Place the halved carrots on baking paper.
2. For the marinade, first, melt the butter. Add the garlic, honey, and lemon/vinegar, mix well.

3. Set over the carrots so that they are all covered with the marinade.
4. Bake in the oven at 180ºc for about 25-30 minutes. Turn regularly.
5. Garnish with parsley and serve with herb quark or yogurt.

Nutrition Per Serving:

- Calories: 109.9
- Fat: 8.26 g
- Carbs: 9.54 g
- Fiber: 1.39 g
- Protein: 0.7 g

78. Apple and Pistachio Salad on Spinach

Preparation Time: 10 minutes
Cooking Time: 5 minutes
Servings: 4

Ingredients:

- 1 ½ tablespoon butter
- 1 pack baby spinach
- 1 apple, diced small
- 1 teaspoon ginger, grated
- 60 g pistachios
- 1 tablespoon mustard
- 40 g Ricotta cheese
- 1 tablespoon honey
- 1 tablespoon lemon juice
- Salt and pepper

Directions:

1. Dissolve the butter in the pan, add the apple pieces, honey, ginger, and mustard. Fry over medium heat until the apples are lightly caramelized for (about 3-5 minutes).
2. Wash the spinach and divide between 2 bowls. Place the apples on the salad, garnish with Ricotta, and season with a bit of lemon juice, pistachios, salt, and pepper as desired.

Nutrition Per Serving:

- Calories: 187.25
- Fat: 12.45 g
- Carbs: 16.7 g
- Fiber: 3.46 g
- Protein: 5.6 g
- Sodium: 287.84 mg

79. Tomato Cashew Pesto

Preparation Time: 10 minutes
Cooking Time: 0 minutes
Servings: 4

Ingredients:

- 95 g dried tomatoes
- 50 g cashew nuts
- 2 garlic cloves, minced
- 5 tablespoons extra-virgin olive oil
- 1 tablespoon oregano
- Parmesan cheese (optional)
- Salt and pepper

Directions:

1. Puree the garlic, tomatoes, oregano, oil, and cashews with a hand blender until the mixture is even.
2. Mix with whole-wheat pasta and serve. Flavor to taste with salt and pepper, then garnish with Parmesan.

Nutrition Per Serving:

- Calories: 294.6
- Fat: 24.32 g
- Carbs: 16.7 g
- Fiber: 2.1 g
- Protein: 3.34 g

80. Sweet Potato Aioli

Preparation Time: 10 minutes
Cooking Time: 35 minutes
Servings: 4

Ingredients:

- 1 sweet potato
- 3 tablespoons olive oil
- 1 tablespoon mayonnaise
- 2-3 garlic cloves
- 1 tablespoon parsley, chopped

Directions:

1. Bake the sweet potato until it is soft (about 35 minutes at 200ºC).
2. Set out of the oven, let cool down briefly, peel and mix with 1 tablespoon of mayonnaise, oil, garlic, and parsley (use a hand blender).

Nutrition Per Serving:

- Calories: 159.57
- Carbs: 9.7 g
- Protein: 0.84 g
- Fat: 13.38 g
- Sugar: 1.9 g
- Sodium: 42.55 mg

81. Eggplant Paste

Preparation Time: 10 minutes

Cooking Time: 25 minutes

Servings: 4

Ingredients:

- 1 eggplant
- 2 tablespoons tahini
- 2 garlic cloves
- 1 tablespoon lemon juice
- A pinch of turmeric
- 30 g black olives
- 1 tablespoon olive oil
- 1 tablespoon parsley, chopped
- Salt and pepper

Directions:

1. Grill the eggplant in the oven at 190ºC for at least 20 minutes (until it is soft!).
2. Let cool and remove the skin. Set the eggplant in a container and use a fork to mash the meat into a paste.
3. Add the tahini, garlic, turmeric, olives, olive oil, and lemon juice; mix well—season to taste with salt and pepper.
4. Garnish with parsley.

Nutrition Per Serving:

- Calories: 136
- Carbs: 10 g
- Protein: 3.09 g
- Fat: 10.4 g
- Sugar: 4 g
- Sodium: 295 mg

82. Catalan Style Spinach

Preparation Time: 10 minutes
Cooking Time: 5 minutes
Servings: 4

Ingredients:

- 200 g fresh spinach
- 2 garlic cloves
- 2 tablespoons cashew nuts
- 3 tablespoons raisins
- 2-3 tablespoons extra-virgin olive oil

Directions:

1. Warm the oil and fry the garlic over medium heat.
2. After 1-2 minutes, add the cashews and raisins. Fry for another minute.
3. Add the spinach (do not boil!), stir well.
4. Serve with Goat cheese and whole meal baguette.

Nutrition Per Serving:

- Calories: 122.2
- Fat: 9.3 g
- Carbs: 9.2 g
- Fiber: 1.5 g

- Protein: 2.38 g
- Sodium: 40.9 mg

83. Energy Balls

Preparation Time: 10 minutes
Cooking Time: 0 minutes
Servings: 4

Ingredients:

- 120 g oat bran
- 80 ml honey
- 120 g coconut flakes (health food store, drugstore)
- 60 g choice nuts, ground
- 60 g chia seeds, ground
- 40 g dark chocolate, finely chopped
- 1 teaspoon yeast flakes
- 1 teaspoon sea salt

Directions:

1. Mix all ingredients well in a container. Let the chia seeds soak for a moment.
2. Set small balls and put them in the fridge for about 45 minutes.

Nutrition Per Serving:

- Calories: 525.27
- Carbs: 73.56 g
- Protein: 12.8 g
- Fat: 27.5 g
- Sugar: 38.6 g
- Sodium: 612.9 mg
- Fiber: 14.8 g

84. Guacamole

Preparation Time: 10 minutes
Cooking Time: 0 minutes
Servings: 3

Ingredients:

- 3 ripe avocados
- 2 large tomatoes
- 2 tablespoons lemon juice
- 1 dash chili sauce (optional)
- 1/2 onion, chopped
- 1 large garlic clove, minced
- Sea salt and pepper

Directions:

1. Peel the avocados and mix the meat with lemon juice, onion, garlic, tomatoes, sea salt, pepper, and chili sauce.
2. Serve with whole-grain tortillas and or only raw oven vegetables.

Nutrition Per Serving:

- Calories: 209.52
- Fat: 16.56 g
- Carbs: 17 g
- Fiber: 9.21 g
- Protein: 3.55 g

85. Dark Chocolate with Pomegranate Seeds

Preparation Time: 10 minutes
Cooking Time: 2-3 minutes
Servings: 3

Ingredients:

- 150 g dark chocolate (at least 70% cocoa)
- 120 g pomegranate seeds (from 1 pomegranate)
- 1 teaspoon sea salt

Directions:

1. Scatter a layer of pomegranate seeds in a muffin tin (or muffin paper).
2. Melt the chocolate in the microwave.
3. Pour the chocolate into a bag, then cut a tiny hole so that it can be spread over the seeds. Add a layer of seeds and another layer of chocolate.
4. Sprinkle with a pinch of salt and chill in the refrigerator until the mixture is hard.
5. Enjoy the cold.

Nutrition Per Serving:

- Calories: 322.63
- Carbs: 33.69 g
- Protein: 3.73 g
- Fat: 19.6 g
- Sugar: 23.82 g
- Sodium: 637.13 mg
- Fiber: 5.6 g

86. Covered Bananas

Preparation Time: 10 minutes
Cooking Time: 0 minutes
Servings: 3

Ingredients:

- 3 bananas
- 1 tablespoon oat bran
- 2 tablespoons cashew or almond butter
- 1 tablespoon honey
- 1 teaspoon chia seeds
- 1 teaspoon cinnamon

Directions:

1. Mix the oat bran, seeds, and cinnamon in a shallow bowl.
2. Mix the nut butter with honey.
3. Coat the bananas with nut butter and then add to the dry mixture so that they are coated on both sides.

Nutrition Per Serving:

- Calories: 202.3
- Carbs: 38.2 g
- Protein: 3.77 g
- Fat: 6.2 g
- Sugar: 20.2 g
- Sodium: 3.44 mg
- Fiber: 4.5 g

87. Hummus with Tahini and Turmeric

Preparation Time: 10 minutes
Cooking Time: 0 minutes
Servings: 4

Ingredients:

- 2 cans chickpeas, drained
- 50 ml lemon juice
- 60 ml tahini
- 1 garlic clove, minced
- 2 tablespoons extra-virgin olive oil
- 1/2 tablespoon turmeric powder
- 1/2 teaspoon sea salt

Directions:

1. Mix the tahini and lemon juice with olive oil, garlic, turmeric, and salt for 30 seconds using a hand blender or kitchen utensil.
2. Add the chickpeas and puree, making sure that no chickpeas remain unmixed on the sides. Pound until a uniform mixture is obtained.
3. Garnish with paprika powder and enjoy with any snacks, such as vegetable sticks.

Nutrition Per Serving:

- Calories: 361
- Carbs: 35 g
- Protein: 12.65 g
- Fat: 21 g
- Sugar: 5.44 g
- Sodium: 552 mg
- Fiber: 9.48 g

88. Fiber Bars

Preparation Time: 10 minutes
Cooking Time: 15 minutes
Servings: 4

Ingredients:

- 120 g dried dates
- 120 g nuts (cashew, hazel, walnuts)

Directions:

1. Remove the date kernels and mash the fruits with a fork.
2. Chop the nuts in a blender, but they must not get the consistency of flour.
3. Mix the two together.
4. Form small "snakes" and flatten them lightly with a fork to get the shape of a bar.

Nutrition Per Serving:

- Calories: 279.3
- Carbs: 26.6 g
- Protein: 5.11 g
- Fat: 19.6 g
- Sugar: 20.7 g
- Sodium: 0.9 mg

Chapter 7

LOW RESIDUE (BREAKFAST)

89. Coconut Chia Seed Pudding

Preparation Time: 15 minutes

Cooking Time: 0 minutes

Servings: 2

Ingredients:

- 6 tablespoons Chia seeds
- 2 cups coconut milk, unsweetened
- Blueberries for topping

Directions:

1. Merge the chia seeds and milk; mix well. Refrigerate overnight.
2. Stir in the berries and serve.

Nutrition Per Serving:

- Calories: 600
- Fat: 53 g
- Carbs: 22 g
- Fiber: 12.4 g

- Protein: 5.9 g

90. Spiced Oatmeal

Preparation Time: 2 minutes

Cooking Time: 2 minutes

Servings: 2

Ingredients:

- 1/3 cup quick oats
- 1/4 teaspoon ground ginger
- 1/8 teaspoon ground cinnamon
- A dash of ground nutmeg
- A dash of ground clove
- 1 tablespoon almond butter
- 1 cup Water

Directions:

1. Combine the oats and water. Microwave for 45 seconds, then stir and cook for another 30-45 seconds.
2. Add in the spices and drizzle on the almond butter before serving.

Nutrition Per Serving:

- Calories: 101.77
- Fat: 5.3 g
- Carbs: 11.12 g
- Fiber: 2.37 g
- Protein: 3.47 g

91. Breakfast Cereal

Preparation Time: 5 minutes

Cooking Time: 5 minutes

Servings: 4

Ingredients:

- 3 cups cooked old fashioned oatmeal
- 3 cups cooked quinoa
- 4 cups bananas, peeled and chopped

Directions:

1. Combine the oatmeal and quinoa; mix well.
2. Evenly, divide into 4 bowls and top with the bananas before serving.

Nutrition Per Serving:

- Calories: 352
- Fat: 4.18 g
- Carbs: 72.6 g
- Fiber: 9 g
- Protein: 10 g

92. Sweet Potato Hash with Sausage and Spinach

Preparation Time: 5 minutes

Cooking Time: 15 minutes

Servings: 4

Ingredients:

- 4 small chopped sweet potatoes
- 2 apples, cored and chopped
- 1 garlic clove, minced

- 1 pound ground sausage
- 10 ounces chopped spinach
- Salt and pepper

Directions:

1. Brown the sausage until no pink remains. Add the remaining ingredients.
2. Cook until the spinach and apples are tender. Season to taste and serve hot.

Nutrition Per Serving:

- Calories: 413.5
- Fat: 15 g
- Carbs: 48 g
- Fiber: 9 g
- Protein: 24 g

93. Cajun Omelet

Preparation Time: 5 minutes
Cooking Time: 8 minutes
Servings: 2

Ingredients:

- 1/4 pound spicy sausage
- 1/3 cup sliced mushrooms
- 1/2 diced onion
- 4 large eggs
- 1/2 medium bell pepper, chopped
- 2 tablespoons water
- A pinch of cayenne pepper (optional)
- Sea salt and fresh pepper to taste
- 1 tbsp. Mustard

Directions:

1. Brown the sausage in a saucepan until cooked. Add the mushrooms, onion, and bell pepper. Cook for another 3-5 minutes, or until tender.
2. Meanwhile, whisk together the eggs, water, mustard, and spices—season with salt and pepper.
3. Top with your eggs over, then reduce to low heat. Cook until the top is nearly set, and then fold the omelet in half and cover.
4. Cook for another minute before serving hot.

Nutrition Per Serving:

- Calories: 326
- Fat: 21 g
- Carbs: 9.94 g
- Fiber: 2.28 g
- Protein: 24.42 g

94. Strawberry Cashew Chia Pudding

Preparation Time: 10 minutes
Cooking Time: 0 minutes
Servings: 2

Ingredients:

- 6 tablespoon chia seeds
- 2 cups cashew milk, unsweetened
- Strawberries, for topping

Directions:

1. Merge the chia seeds and milk; mix well. Refrigerate overnight.

2. Stir in the berries and serve.

Nutrition Per Serving:

- Calories: 217
- Fat: 14.6 g
- Carbs: 18 g
- Fiber: 12.9 g
- Protein: 6 g

95. Peanut Butter Banana Oatmeal

Preparation Time: 5 minutes
Cooking Time: 0 minutes
Servings: 1

Ingredients:

- 1/3 cup quick oats
- 1/4 teaspoon cinnamon (optional)
- 1/2 sliced banana
- 1 tablespoon peanut butter, unsweetened

Directions:

1. Merge all ingredients in a bowl with a lid. Refrigerate.

Nutrition Per Serving:

- Calories: 251
- Fat: 10.13 g
- Carbs: 35.43 g
- Fiber: 5 g
- Protein: 7.75 g

96. Spinach Frittata

Preparation Time: 10 minutes
Cooking Time: 30 minutes
Servings: 4

Ingredients:

- 2 teaspoons olive oil
- 1 cup red pepper, seeded and chopped
- 1 garlic clove, minced
- 3 cups spinach leaves, chopped
- 4 large eggs, beaten
- 1/2 teaspoon salt
- 1/4 cup Parmesan cheese, freshly grated

Directions:

2. Preheat the oven to 350ºF. In a non-stick oven pan, heat 1 teaspoon of olive oil over medium heat.
3. Cook red peppers and garlic until vegetables are soft (about 10 minutes). In a medium bowl, combine the eggs, spinach, and salt; set aside.
4. Add remaining 1 teaspoon of olive oil into the pan with vegetables and add in the egg mixture.
5. Set the heat and cook for 15 minutes. Sprinkle Parmesan cheese over the mixture and broil for an additional 4 minutes.

Nutrition Per Serving:

- Calories: 126.8
- Fat: 8.56 g
- Carbs: 3.59 g
- Fiber: 1.2 g

- Protein: 9 g

97. Banana and Pear Pita Pockets

Preparation Time: 10 minutes
Cooking Time: 0 minutes
Servings: 1

Ingredients:

- 1/2 small banana, peeled and sliced
- 1 round pita bread, made with refined white flour
- 1/2 small pear, peeled, seedless, cored, cooked, and sliced
- 1/4 cup low-fat Cottage cheese

Directions:

1. Combine the banana, pear, and Cottage cheese in a small bowl. Slice the pita bread to make a pocket.
2. Fill it with the mixture.
3. Serve.

Nutrition Per Serving:

- Calories: 277.19
- Fat: 1.5 g
- Carbs: 53.9 g
- Fiber: 4.33 g
- Protein: 13 g

98. Pear Pancakes

Preparation Time: 10 minutes
Cooking Time: 15 minutes
Servings: 4

Ingredients:

- 2 eggs
- 1 cup pear, peeled mashed
- 1 teaspoon cinnamon
- 2 teaspoons sugar
- 1 ½ cup refined white flour
- 1/2 cup flour, whole-wheat
- 2 teaspoons baking powder
- 2 teaspoons vanilla
- Non-stick cooking spray

Directions:

1. In a large bowl, beat the eggs until fluffy. Add baking powder, cinnamon, vanilla, sugar, flours, and pear, then continue to stir just until smooth.
2. Sprinkle with non-stick cooking spray. Pour a sizable amount of the batter that you want your pancake to be into the hot pan.
3. Cook the pancakes until puffy and dry around the edges. Turn and cook another side until golden.
4. Serve pancakes with additional pear if desired.

Nutrition Per Serving:

- Calories: 301.54
- Fat: 4.55 g
- Carbs: 56.41 g

- Fiber: 3.6 g
- Protein: 9.36 g

99. Ripe Plantain Bran Muffins

Preparation Time: 10 minutes
Cooking Time: 20 minutes
Servings: 12

Ingredients:

- 1 ½ cup refined cereal
- 2/3 cup low-fat milk
- 4 large eggs, lightly beaten
- 1/4 cup canola oil
- 2 medium ripe plantains, mashed
- 1/2 cup brown sugar
- 1 cup refined white flour
- 2 teaspoons baking powder
- 1/2 teaspoon salt

Directions:

1. Preheat the oven to 400ºF. In a bowl, mix the bran cereal and milk; set aside.
2. Add eggs and oil; stir in brown sugar and mashed ripe plantain. In another bowl, combine salt, flour, and baking powder.
3. Dissolve the dry ingredients into the ripe plantain mixture, stir until combined.
4. Pour the batter evenly into paper-lined muffin tins; bake for 18 minutes or until golden brown and firm. Allow cooling before serving.

Nutrition Per Serving:

- Calories: 202.4
- Fat: 7.7 g

- Carbs: 31.13 g
- Fiber: 2.5 g
- Protein: 5.5 g

100. Easy Breakfast Bran Muffins

Preparation Time: 10 minutes
Cooking Time: 20 minutes
Servings: 10

Ingredients:

- 2 cups refined cereal
- 1 cup boiling water
- 1/2 cup brown sugar
- 1/2 cup butter
- 2 eggs
- 1/2 quart buttermilk
- 2 ½ cups refined white flour
- 2 ½ teaspoons baking soda
- 1/2 teaspoon salt

Directions:

1. Preheat the oven to 400ºF. Soak 1 cup of cereal in 1 cup of boiling water and set aside.
2. In a mixer, merge the brown sugar and butter until it is fully mixed. Add each egg separately and beat until fluffy. Then, stir in the buttermilk and the soaked cereal mixture.
3. In another bowl, combine salt, flour, and baking soda. Add the flour mixture into the batter and ensure not to over mix.
4. Add in the remaining cup of cereal. Set the batter evenly into 10 greased or paper-

lined muffin tins. Bake for 15-20 minutes. Allow cooling before serving.

Nutrition Per Serving:

- Calories: 319.9
- Fat: 13.7 g
- Carbs: 44.31 g
- Fiber: 3 g
- Protein: 9 g

101. Apple Oatmeal

Preparation Time: 10 minutes
Cooking Time: 1-2 minutes
Servings: 1

Ingredients:

- 1/2 cup instant oatmeal
- 3/4 cup milk or water
- 1/2 cup apples, peeled and cooked pureed
- 1 teaspoon brown sugar

Directions:

1. In a microwave-safe bowl, mix oats, milk or water, and apples—Cook in a microwave on high.
2. Stir and cook for another 30 seconds. Sprinkle it with brown sugar and add a splash of milk.

Nutrition Per Serving:

- Calories: 295
- Fat: 8.46 g
- Carbs: 47 g
- Fiber: 5 g

- Protein: 13 g

102. Breakfast Burrito Wrap

Preparation Time: 15 minutes
Cooking Time: 15 minutes
Servings: 1

Ingredients:

- 1 tablespoon extra-virgin olive oil
- 2 slices turkey bacon
- 1/4 cup green bell peppers, seeded and chopped
- 2 eggs, beaten
- 2 tablespoons milk
- 1/4 teaspoon salt
- 2 tablespoons low-fat Monterey Jack cheese, grated
- 1 white tortilla

Directions:

1. In a small non-stick pan, warm olive oil on medium heat and cook the turkey for about 2 minutes until slightly crispy.
2. Attach bell peppers and continue to cook until warmed through. In a small bowl, beat the eggs with milk and salt.
3. Gently stir in your eggs until almost cooked. Turn the heat down, then add the cheese.
4. Cover and continue cooking until the cheese have completely melted. Place the mixture on the tortilla and roll it into a burrito.

Nutrition Per Serving:

- Calories: 536.51
- Fat: 34.13 g
- Carbs: 33 g
- Fiber: 4.6 g
- Protein: 25.46 g

103. Zucchini Omelet

Preparation Time: 15 minutes

Cooking Time: 15 minutes

Servings: 4

Ingredients:

- 2 tablespoons extra-virgin olive oil
- 1 medium zucchini, seeded and cubed
- 1/2 medium tomato, seeded and chopped
- 4 large eggs
- 1/4 cup milk
- 1 teaspoon salt
- 4 whole-wheat English muffins

Directions:

1. In a large non-stick frying pan, warm olive oil over moderate heat. Add the zucchini and tomato.
2. Cook vegetables for 5-10 minutes or until they are soft.
3. In a separate bowl, merge the eggs, milk, and salt.
4. Attach the egg mixture to the pan and stir to cook through. Set with white English muffins.

Nutrition Per Serving:

- Calories: 269.5
- Fat: 13.7 g
- Carbs: 25.9 g
- Fiber: 4.4 g
- Protein: 12.46 g

104. Overnight Peach Oatmeal

Preparation Time: 10 minutes

Cooking Time: 0 minutes

Servings: 2

Ingredients:

- 1/2 cup old fashioned oats
- 2/3 cup skim milk
- 1/2 cup plain Greek yogurt
- 1 tablespoon chia seeds
- 1/2 teaspoon Vanilla
- 1/2 cup peach, peeled and diced
- 1 medium banana, peeled and chopped

Directions:

1. Combine the oats, milk, yogurt, chia seeds, and vanilla in a bowl with a lid.
2. Refrigerate for 12 hours.
3. Top with the fruits before serving.

Nutrition Per Serving:

- Calories: 273.3
- Fat: 6.52 g
- Carbs: 42.7 g
- Fiber: 6.7 g
- Protein: 12.68 g

105. Mediterranean Salmon and Potato Salad

Preparation Time: 15 minutes
Cooking Time: 18 minutes
Servings: 4

Ingredients:

- 1 pound red potatoes, peeled and cut into wedges
- 1/2 cup plus 2 tablespoons more extra-virgin olive oil
- 2 tablespoons balsamic vinegar
- 1 tablespoon fresh rosemary, minced
- 2 cups peas, cooked and drained
- 4 (4 ounces each) salmon fillets
- 2 tablespoons lemon juice
- 1/4 teaspoon salt
- 2 cups English cucumber, sliced and seedless

Directions:

1. In a saucepan, set water to a boil and cook potatoes until tender, about 10 minutes.
2. Drain and set potatoes back into the pan. To make the dressing, put together 1/2 cup of olive oil, vinegar, and rosemary in a bowl.
3. Combine potatoes and peas with the dressing. Set aside. In a separate medium pan, warm the remaining 2 tablespoons of olive oil over medium heat.
4. Attach salmon fillets and set with lemon juice and salt.
5. Cook on both sides or until the fish flakes easily. To serve, place cucumber slices on a serving plate top with potato salad and fish fillets.

Nutrition Per Serving:

- Calories: 666
- Fat: 49 g
- Carbs: 28.9 g
- Fiber: 6 g
- Protein: 29.05 g

106. Celery Soup

Preparation Time: 8 minutes
Cooking Time: 10 minutes
Servings: 2

Ingredients:

- 1 tablespoon olive oil
- 3 garlic cloves, minced
- 2 pounds fresh celery, chopped into 1-inch pieces
- 6 cups vegetable stock
- 1 teaspoon salt

Directions:

1. Reserve celery tops for later use. Warmth up the oil over medium heat in a soup pot.
2. Cook the garlic until softened, about 3-5 minutes. Add celery stalks, salt, and vegetable stock, then bring to a boil.
3. Cover, reduce the heat to low and simmer until the celery softens. Let the soup cool for a bit, then puree with a hand blender.
4. Add and cook the celery tops on medium heat for 5 minutes.

Nutrition Per Serving:

- Calories: 159.8
- Fat: 8.23 g
- Carbs: 18.24 g
- Fiber: 5.5 g
- Protein: 4.35 g

107. Pea Tuna Salad

Preparation Time: 15 minutes
Cooking Time: 0 minutes
Servings: 4

Ingredients:

- 3 pounds cooked peas
- 1/2 cup low-fat mayonnaise
- 1/3 cup tarragon vinegar
- 1 teaspoon honey Dijon mustard
- 2 small shallots, thinly sliced
- 2 (6 ounces) canned tuna fish.
- 2 small sprigs of fresh tarragon, finely chopped

Directions:

1. In a large bowl, merge mayonnaise, vinegar, and mustard. Add tuna fish, shallots, and peas; toss to coat with dressing.
2. Secure and refrigerate for 1 hour before serving. Set with fresh tarragon and serve.

Nutrition Per Serving:

- Calories: 427.39
- Fat: 4.74 g
- Carbs: 57 g
- Fiber: 19.65 g
- Protein: 38.95 g

108. Vegetable Soup

Preparation Time: 15 minutes
Cooking Time: 1 hour 20 minutes
Servings: 2

Ingredients:

- 2 tablespoons extra-virgin olive oil
- 4 garlic cloves, finely chopped
- 2 celery stalks, finely sliced
- 2 carrots, finely sliced
- 6 cups water or chicken broth
- 1/4 teaspoon thyme
- 1/4 teaspoon rosemary
- 1 bay leaf
- 1 can (14 ounces) peas
- 1/2 teaspoon salt

Directions:

1. Warmth up the oil over medium heat in a soup pot. Add garlic, celery, and carrots and continue to cook for 5 minutes, stirring occasionally.
2. Add water or chicken broth, thyme, rosemary, and bay leaf. Cook until it comes to a boil.
3. Set the heat and simmer gently for about 45-60 minutes. Add peas and season with salt.
4. Let soup cool slightly, remove the bay leaf and puree with a hand blender until creamy.
5. Serve in warmed soup bowls.

Nutrition Per Serving:

- Calories: 277.76
- Fat: 15.45 g
- Carbs: 29.56 g
- Fiber: 8.9 g
- Protein: 7.16 g

109. Carrot and Turkey Soup

Preparation Time: 15 minutes
Cooking Time: 40 minutes
Servings: 4

Ingredients:

- 1/2 pound lean ground turkey
- 1/2 bag frozen carrot
- 1/4 cup green peas
- 1 can (32 ounces) chicken broth
- 2 medium tomatoes, seeded and roughly chopped
- 1 teaspoon garlic powder
- 1 teaspoon paprika
- 1 teaspoon oregano
- 1 bay leaf

Directions:

1. Over medium heat, set the ground turkey in a soup pot. Add peas, frozen carrot, paprika, tomatoes, garlic powder, bay leaf, oregano, and broth.
2. Set the pot to a boil, lower heat, cover, and simmer for 30 minutes.

Nutrition Per Serving:

- Calories: 436

- Fat: 12 g
- Carbs: 20 g
- Fiber: 6 g
- Protein: 59 g

110. Creamy Pumpkin Soup

Preparation Time: 15 minutes
Cooking Time: 1 hour 10 minutes
Servings: 4

Ingredients:

- 1 pumpkin, cut lengthwise, seeds removed, and peeled
- 1 sweet potato, cut lengthwise and peeled
- 2 tablespoons olive oil
- 4 garlic cloves, unpeeled
- 4 cups vegetable stock
- 1/4 cup light cream
- Salt
- 1 tbsp. chopped Shallots

Directions:

1. Preheat the oven to 375°F. Cut all the sides of the pumpkin, shallots, and sweet potato with oil.
2. Transfer your vegetables with the garlic to a roasting pan. Set to roast for about 40 minutes or until tender.
3. Let the vegetables cool for a time and scoop out the flesh of the sweet potato and pumpkin.
4. In a soup pot, place the flesh of roasted vegetables, shallots, and peeled garlic. Add the broth and set to a boil.

5. Set the heat, and let it simmer, covered for 30 minutes, stirring occasionally. Let the soup cool.
6. Set the soup with a hand blender until smooth. Add the cream.
7. Season to taste and simmer until warmed through, about 5 minutes. Serve in warm soup bowls.

Nutrition Per Serving:

- Calories: 186.88
- Fat: 10.34 g
- Carbs: 22.68 g
- Fiber: 2.22 g
- Protein: 3.44 g

111. Chicken Pea Soup

Preparation Time: 15 minutes
Cooking Time: 55 minutes
Servings: 4

Ingredients:

- 1 pound chicken breast, skinless, boneless, and cubed
- 2 tablespoons olive oil
- 3 garlic cloves, minced
- 3 carrots, grated
- 1 teaspoon salt
- 1 bay leaf
- 8 cups chicken broth
- 1 teaspoon poultry seasoning
- 1/2 cup dried split peas, well washed and drained
- 1 cup green peas

Directions:

1. Warmth up the olive oil over medium heat in a soup pot. Add the chicken and cook for 5 minutes, until lightly browned.
2. Attach the garlic, bay leaf, carrots, salt, and seasoning. Cook until vegetables soften, stirring occasionally.
3. Pour the broth and split peas into the pot; bring to a boil. Set the heat, cover, and simmer on low heat for 30-45 minutes.
4. Stir the green peas in the soup and heat for 5 minutes, stirring to combine all ingredients.

Nutrition Per Serving:

- Calories: 325.18
- Fat: 10.8 g
- Carbs: 28 g
- Fiber: 9.56 g
- Protein: 29.48 g

112. Coconut Pancakes

Preparation Time: 10 minutes
Cooking Time: 10 minutes
Servings: 2

Ingredients:

- 1/2 cup coconut milk, plus additional as needed
- 1/2 tablespoon maple syrup
- 1/4 cup coconut flour
- 1/2 teaspoon salt
- 2 eggs
- 1/2 tablespoon coconut oil or almond butter, plus extra for greasing the pan

- 1/2 teaspoon vanilla extract
- 1/2 teaspoon baking soda

Directions:

1. Using an electric mixer, combine the coconut milk, maple syrup, eggs, coconut oil, and vanilla in a medium mixing cup.
2. Combine the baking soda, coconut flour, and salt in a shallow mixing bowl.
3. Set the dry ingredients with the wet ingredients in a mixing bowl and beat until smooth and lump-free.
4. If the batter is too dense, add more liquid to thin it down to a typical pancake batter consistency.
5. Using coconut oil, lightly grease a big skillet or pan—Preheat the oven to medium-high.
6. Cook until golden brown on the rim for another 2 minutes.
7. Continue cooking the leftover batter while stacking the pancake on a tray.

Nutrition Per Serving:

- Calories: 307.4
- Fat: 23.87 g
- Carbs: 15 g
- Sugar: 7.2 g
- Fiber: 7.3g
- Protein: 8.9 g
- Sodium: 664.16 mg

113. Bright Red Juice

Preparation Time: 10 minutes
Cooking Time: 0 minutes
Servings: 3

Ingredients:

- 6 tomatoes
- 2 carrots, peeled
- 1 celery stalk
- ¼ cup filtered water
- Pinch of salt and ground black pepper
- 2-3 ice cubes

Directions:

1. Put all the ingredients in a blender and pulse until well combined.
2. Through a cheesecloth-lined strainer, strain the juice and transfer into 3 glasses.
3. Serve immediately.

Nutrition Per Serving:

- Calories: 58.7
- Carbohydrates: 12.9g
- Protein: 2.5g
- Fat: 0.5g
- Sugar: 7.9g
- Sodium: 95mg
- Fiber: 4g

114. Enticing Fresh Juice

Preparation Time: 10 minutes
Cooking Time: 0 minutes
Servings: 2

Ingredients:

- 3 cup fresh spinach
- 3 cup fresh arugula
- 1 large carrot, peeled and chopped roughly
- 2 celery stalks
- 1 lemon
- 1 (1-inch) piece fresh ginger

Directions:

1. Add all ingredients into a juicer and extract the juice according to the manufacturer's method.
2. Through a cheesecloth-lined strainer, strain the juice and transfer into 2 glasses.
3. Serve immediately.

Nutrition Per Serving:

- Calories: 44
- Carbohydrates: 9g
- Protein: 2.8g
- Fat: 0.5g
- Sugar: 3.35g
- Sodium: 98mg
- Fiber: 3.5g

115. Super-Food Scramble

Preparation Time: 10 minutes
Cooking Time: 7 minutes
Servings: 3

Ingredients:

- 2 cup fresh spinach, chopped finely
- 1 tbsp. olive oil
- Salt and freshly ground black pepper, to taste
- ½ cup cooked salmon, chopped finely
- 4 eggs, beaten

Directions:

1. Heat the oil over high heat in a skillet and cook the spinach with black pepper for about 2 minutes.
2. Stir in the salmon and reduce the heat to medium.
3. Add the eggs and cook for about 3-4 minutes, stirring frequently.
4. Serve immediately.

Nutrition Per Serving:

- Calories: 200.7
- Carbohydrates: 1.3g
- Protein: 15.3g
- Fat: 14.7g
- Sugar: 0.3g
- Sodium: 375 mg
- Fiber: 0.52g

116. Family Favorite Scramble

Preparation Time: 10 minutes
Cooking Time: 5 minutes
Servings: 2

Ingredients:

- 4 eggs
- ¼ tsp. red pepper flakes, crushed
- Salt and freshly ground black pepper, to taste
- ¼ cup fresh basil, chopped
- ½ cup tomatoes, peeled, seeded, and chopped
- 1 tbsp. olive oil

Directions:

1. Add eggs, red pepper flakes, salt, and black pepper in a large bowl and beat well.
2. Add the basil and tomatoes and stir to combine.
3. In a large non-stick skillet, heat the oil over medium-high heat.
4. Add the egg mixture and cook for about 3-5 minutes, stirring continuously.
5. Serve immediately.

Nutrition Per Serving:

- Calories: 195
- Carbohydrates: 2.6g
- Protein: 11.6g
- Fat: 15.9g
- Sugar: 1.5g
- Sodium: 515mg
- Fiber: 0.7g

117. Tasty Veggie Omelet

Preparation Time: 15 minutes
Cooking Time: 25 minutes
Servings: 4

Ingredients:

- 6 large eggs
- Sea salt and freshly ground black pepper, to taste
- ½ cup low-fat milk
- 1/3 cup fresh mushrooms, cut into slices
- 1/3 cup red bell pepper, seeded and chopped
- 1 tbsp. chives, minced

Directions:

1. Preheat the oven to 350 degrees F. Lightly, grease a pie dish.
2. Add the eggs, salt, black pepper, and coconut oil to a bowl and beat until well combined.
3. In another bowl, mix the onion, bell pepper, and mushrooms.
4. Transfer the egg mixture into the prepared pie dish evenly.
5. Top with the vegetable mixture evenly and sprinkle with chives evenly.
6. Bake for about 20-25 minutes.
7. Remove from the oven and set aside for about 5 minutes.
8. With a knife, cut into equal-sized wedges and serve.

Nutrition Per Serving:

- Calories: 125

- Carbohydrates: 3.1g
- Protein: 10.8g
- Fat: 7.8g
- Sugar: 2.8g
- Sodium: 288.4 mg
- Fiber: 0.4g

118. Garden Veggies Quiche

Preparation Time: 15 minutes
Cooking Time: 20 minutes
Servings: 4

Ingredients:

- 6 eggs
- ½ cup low-fat milk
- salt and freshly ground black pepper, to taste
- 2 cup fresh baby spinach, chopped
- ½ cup green bell pepper, seeded and chopped
- 1 scallion, chopped
- ¼ cup fresh parsley, chopped
- 1 tbsp. fresh chives, minced

Directions:

1. Preheat the oven to 400 degrees F. Lightly grease a pie dish.
2. Add eggs, almond milk, salt, and black pepper to a bowl and beat until well combined. Set aside.
3. In another bowl, add the vegetables and herbs and mix well.
4. In the bottom of the prepared pie dish, place the veggie mixture evenly and top with the egg mixture.

5. Bake for 20 minutes or until a wooden skewer inserted in the center comes out clean.
6. Remove the pie dish from the oven and set it aside for about 5 minutes before slicing.
7. Cut into desired-sized wedges and serve warm.

Nutrition Per Serving:

- Calories: 120.6
- Carbohydrates: 4.3g
- Protein: 10.1g
- Fat: 7g
- Sugar: 2.4g
- Sodium: 314mg
- Fiber: 0.98g

119. Stunning Breakfast Frittata

Preparation Time: 15 minutes
Cooking Time: 12 minutes
Servings: 6

Ingredients:

- 8 eggs, beaten well
- 8 tbsp. low-fat milk
- Salt and freshly ground black pepper, to taste
- 2 oz. feta cheese, crumbled
- ½ cup low-fat mozzarella cheese, grated
- ¼ cup scallion, sliced
- 2 tsp. olive oil
- 1 large avocado, peeled, pitted, and sliced lengthwise

Directions:

1. Preheat the broiler of the oven.
2. Arrange the oven rack about 4-5-inch from the heating element.
3. Add the eggs, almond milk, salt, and black pepper to a bowl and beat until well combined.
4. In a heavy oven-proof frying skillet, heat the oil over medium-low heat.
5. Add the eggs and cook for about 2 minutes.
6. Add the mozzarella and scallion and cook for about 5 minutes.
7. Arrange the avocado slices over the egg mixture and sprinkle with the feta cheese.
8. With a lid, cover the skillet and cook for about 3 minutes.
9. Remove the lid and transfer the skillet into the oven.
10. Broil for about 2 minutes.
11. Remove from the oven and serve hot.

Nutrition Per Serving:

- Calories: 195
- Carbohydrates: 4.32g
- Protein: 12.5g
- Fat: 14.6g
- Sugar: 1.4g
- Sodium: 386.86 mg
- Fiber: 1.55g

120. Fluffy Pumpkin Pancakes

Preparation Time: 10 minutes
Cooking Time: 40 minutes
Servings: 10

Ingredients:

- 2 eggs
- 1 cup buckwheat flour
- 1 tbsp. baking powder
- 1 tsp. Pumpkin pie spice
- ½ tsp. salt
- 1 cup pumpkin puree
- ¾ cup plus 2 tbsp. low-fat milk
- 3 tbsp. pure maple syrup
- 2 tbsp. olive oil
- 1 tsp. vanilla extract

Directions:

1. In a blender, add all the ingredients and pulse until well combined.
2. Transfer the mixture into a bowl and set aside for about 10 minutes.
3. Heat a greased non-stick skillet over medium heat.
4. Place about ¼ cup of the mixture and spread in an even circle.
5. Cook for about 2 minutes per side.
6. Repeat with the remaining mixture.
7. Serve warm.

Nutrition Per Serving:

- Calories: 113
- Carbohydrates: 15.9g
- Protein: 3.45g
- Fat: 4.4g

- Sugar: 5.68g
- Sodium: 285.41mg
- Fiber: 2g

121. Super-Tasty Chicken Muffins

Preparation Time: 15 minutes
Cooking Time: 45 minutes
Servings: 8

Ingredients:

- 8 eggs
- Salt and freshly ground black pepper, as required
- 2 tbsp. filtered water
- 7 oz. cooked chicken, chopped finely
- 1½ cup fresh spinach, chopped
- 1 cup green bell pepper, seeded and chopped finely
- 2 tbsp. fresh parsley, chopped finely

Directions:

1. Preheat the oven to 350 degrees F. Grease 8 CUP of a muffin tin.
2. Add eggs, salt, black pepper, and water in a bowl and beat until well combined.
3. Add the chicken, spinach, bell pepper, and parsley and stir to combine.
4. Transfer the mixture into the prepared muffin CUP evenly.
5. Bake for about 18-20 minutes or until golden brown.
6. Remove the muffin tin from the oven and place it onto a wire rack to cool for about 10 minutes.
7. Delicately invert the muffins onto a platter and serve warm.

Nutrition Per Serving:

- Calories: 103.3
- Carbohydrates: 1.5g
- Protein: 8.9g
- Fat: 6.69g
- Sugar: 0.6g
- Sodium: 177mg
- Fiber: 0.5g

122. Classic Zucchini Bread

Preparation Time: 45 minutes
Cooking Time: 15 minutes
Servings: 24

Ingredients:

- 3 cup all-purpose flour
- 2 tsp. baking soda
- 1 tsp. ground cinnamon
- 1 tsp. ground nutmeg
- 2 cup Splenda
- 1 cup olive oil
- 3 eggs, beaten
- 2 tsp. vanilla extract
- 2 cup zucchini, peeled, seeded, and grated

Directions:

1. Preheat the oven to 325 degrees F. Arrange a rack in the center of the oven. Grease 2 loaf pans.
2. In a medium bowl, mix together the flour, baking soda, and spices.

3. In another large bowl, add the Splenda and oil and beat until well combined.
4. Add the eggs and vanilla extract and beat until well combined.
5. Add the flour mixture and mix until just combined.
6. Gently, fold in the zucchini.
7. Place the mixture into the bread loaf pans evenly.
8. Bake for about 45-50 minutes or until a toothpick inserted in the center of the bread comes out clean.
9. Remove the bread pans from the oven and place them onto a wire rack to cool for about 15 minutes.
10. Carefully invert the slices of bread onto the wire rack to cool completely before slicing.
11. With a sharp knife, cut each bread loaf into desired-sized slices and serve.

Nutrition Per Serving:

- Calories: 208.85
- Carbohydrates: 27.89g
- Protein: 2.44g
- Fat: 10.2g
- Sugar: 13.8g
- Sodium: 9.46mg
- Fiber: 0.6g

Chapter 8

LOW RESIDUE (LUNCH)

123. New Year's Luncheon Meal

Preparation Time: 10 minutes
Cooking Time: 0 minutes
Servings: 2

Ingredients:

- 1 large avocado, halved and pitted
- 1 (5-oz.) can water-packed tuna, drained and flaked
- 3 tbsp. fat-free yogurt

- 2 tbsp. fresh lemon juice
- 1 tsp. fresh parsley, chopped finely
- Salt and freshly ground black pepper, to taste

Directions:

1. Carefully remove about 2-3 tbsp of flesh from each avocado half.
2. Arrange the avocado halves onto a platter and drizzle each with 1 tsp of lemon juice.

3. Chop the avocado flesh and transfer into a bowl.
4. In the bowl of avocado flesh, add tuna, yogurt, parsley, remaining lemon juice, salt, and black pepper, and stir to combine.
5. Divide the tuna mixture into both avocado halves evenly.
6. Serve immediately.

Nutrition Per Serving:

- Calories: 207.62
- Carbohydrates: 7.5g
- Protein: 20.16g
- Fat: 11.38g
- Sugar: 0.8g
- Sodium: 669.98mg
- Fiber: 4.41g

124. Entertaining Wraps

Preparation Time: 15 minutes
Cooking Time: 10 minutes
Servings: 5

Ingredients:
For Chicken:

- 2 tbsp. olive oil
- 1 tsp. fresh ginger, minced
- 1¼ lb. ground chicken
- Salt and freshly ground black pepper, to taste

For Wraps:

- 10 romaine lettuce leaves
- 1½ cup carrot, peeled and julienned

- 2 tbsp. fresh parsley, chopped finely
- 2 tbsp. fresh lime juice

Directions:

1. In a skillet, heat the oil over medium heat and sauté the ginger for about 1 minute.
2. Add the ground chicken, salt, and black pepper and cook for about 7-9 minutes, breaking the meat into smaller pieces with a wooden spoon.
3. Remove from the heat and set aside to cool.
4. Arrange the lettuce leaves onto serving plates.
5. Place the cooked chicken over each lettuce leaf and top with carrot and cilantro.
6. Drizzle with lime juice and serve immediately.

Nutrition Per Serving:

- Calories: 240
- Carbohydrates: 6.22g
- Protein: 20.91g
- Fat: 15.17g
- Sugar: 2.54g
- Sodium: 254.15 mg
- Fiber: 2.34g

125. Outdoor Chicken Kabobs

Preparation Time: 15 minutes
Cooking Time: 7 minutes
Servings: 4

Ingredients:

- ¼ cup low-fat Parmesan cheese, grated
- 3 tbsp. olive oil
- 1 cup fresh basil leaves, chopped
- Salt and freshly ground black pepper, to taste
- 1¼ lb. boneless, skinless chicken breast, cut into 1-inch cubes

Directions:

1. Add the cheese, oil, basil, garlic, salt, and black pepper in a food processor, and pulse until smooth.
2. Put the basil mixture into a large bowl.
3. Add the chicken cubes and mix well.
4. Cover the bowl with a lid and refrigerate to marinate for at least 4-5 hours.
5. Preheat the grill to medium-high heat. Abundantly, grease the grill grate.
6. Thread the chicken cubes onto pre-soaked wooden skewers.
7. Place the skewers on the grill and cook for about 3-4 minutes.
8. Flip and cook for about 2-3 minutes more.
9. Remove from the grill and place onto a platter for about 5 minutes before serving.
10. Serve hot.

Nutrition Per Serving:

- Calories: 282.79
- Carbohydrates: 0.4g
- Protein: 33.36g
- Fat: 15.7g
- Sugar: 0g
- Sodium: 353.72mg
- Fiber: 0.1g

126. Flavorful Shrimp Kabobs

Preparation Time: 15 minutes
Cooking Time: 8 minutes
Servings: 4

Ingredients:

- ¼ cup olive oil
- 2 tbsp. fresh lime juice
- 1 tsp. Honey
- ½ tsp. Paprika
- ¼ tsp. ground cumin
- Salt and freshly ground black pepper, to taste
- 1 lb. medium raw shrimp, peeled and deveined

Directions:

1. In a large bowl, add all the ingredients except for shrimp and mix well.
2. Add the shrimp and coat with the herb mixture generously.
3. Refrigerate to marinate for at least 30 minutes.
4. Preheat the grill to medium-high heat. Grease the grill grate.

5. Thread the shrimp onto pre-soaked wooden skewers.

6. Place the skewers on the grill and cook for about 2-4 minutes per side.

7. Remove from the grill and place onto a platter for about 5 minutes before serving.

Nutrition Per Serving:

- Calories: 211
- Carbohydrates: 2.56g
- Protein: 16g
- Fat: 15.2g
- Sugar: 1.7g
- Sodium: 829.78mg
- Fiber: 0.7g

127. Pan-Seared Scallops

Preparation Time: 15 minutes
Cooking Time: 7 minutes
Servings: 4

Ingredients:

- 1¼ lb. fresh sea scallops, side muscles removed
- Salt and freshly ground black pepper, to taste
- 2 tbsp. olive oil
- 1 tbsp. fresh parsley, minced

Directions:

1. Sprinkle the scallops with salt and black pepper.

2. Heat the oil over medium-high heat in a large skillet and cook the scallops for about 2-3 minutes per side.

3. Stir in the parsley and remove from the heat.

4. Serve hot.

Nutrition Per Serving:

- Calories: 161.7
- Carbohydrates: 4.73g
- Protein: 17.15g
- Fat: 7.8g
- Sugar: 0g
- Sodium: 750.16mg
- Fiber: 0g

128. Mediterranean Shrimp Salad

Preparation Time: 15 minutes
Cooking Time: 3 minutes
Servings: 5

Ingredients:

- 1 lb. shrimp, peeled and deveined
- 1 lemon, quartered
- 2 tbsp. olive oil
- 2 tsp. fresh lemon juice
- Salt and freshly ground black pepper, to taste
- 3 tomatoes, peeled, seeded, and sliced
- ¼ cup olives pitted
- ¼ cup fresh cilantro, chopped finely

Directions:

1. In a pan of lightly salted water, add the quartered lemon and bring to a boil.

2. Add the shrimp and cook for about 2-3 minutes or until pink and opaque.

3. Transfer the shrimp into a large bowl of ice water with a slotted spoon to stop the cooking process.
4. Drain the shrimp completely, and then pat dry with paper towels.
5. Add the oil, lemon juice, salt, and black pepper in a small bowl, and beat until well combined.
6. Divide the shrimp, tomato, olives, and cilantro onto serving plates.
7. Drizzle with oil mixture and serve.

Nutrition Per Serving:

- Calories: 136.39
- Carbohydrates: 3.96g
- Protein: 13.49g
- Fat: 7.63g
- Sugar: 2.1g
- Sodium: 771.73mg
- Fiber: 1.7g

129. Health Conscious People's Salad

Preparation Time: 15 minutes
Cooking Time: 0 minutes
Servings: 2

Ingredients:

- ¼ cup low-fat mozzarella cheese, cubed
- ¼ cup tomato, peeled, seeded, and chopped
- 1 tbsp. fresh dill, chopped
- 1 tsp. fresh lemon juice
- Salt, to taste
- 6 oz. cooked salmon, chopped

Directions:

1. In a medium bowl, add all the ingredients and stir to combine.
2. Serve immediately.

Nutrition Per Serving:

- Calories: 186
- Carbohydrates: 1.17 g
- Protein: 20g
- Fat: 11.3g
- Sugar: 0.7g
- Sodium: 452.2 mg
- Fiber: 0.28g

130. Bacon-Wrapped Asparagus

Preparation Time: 25 minutes
Cooking Time: 30 minutes
Servings: 6

Ingredients:

- 10 bacon slices cut in half
- 1 pound fresh asparagus, trimmed
- 1 tablespoon extra-virgin olive oil
- 1 tablespoon balsamic vinegar
- Freshly ground black pepper, to taste
- 1 lemon, sliced

Directions:

1. Heat the oven to 400ºF. Line a big baking dish with foil paper.
2. Wrap 1 bacon slice around each asparagus piece.
3. Arrange asparagus in the prepared baking dish.

4. Set with oil and vinegar. Sprinkle it with black pepper.

5. Bake for approximately 15 minutes. Change the inside and bake for 10-15 minutes more.

6. Serve immediately with lemon slices.

Nutrition Per Serving:

- Calories: 222.51
- Fat: 18.67 g
- Carbs: 3.44 g
- Fiber: 1.47 g
- Protein: 10.68 g

131. Zucchini Pasta with Shrimp

Preparation Time: 15 minutes
Cooking Time: 21 minutes
Servings: 4

Ingredients:

- 2 tablespoons ghee or coconut oil
- 1 tablespoon extra-virgin olive oil
- 3 garlic cloves, minced
- 1 pound shrimp, peeled and deveined
- 4 large zucchini, spiralized with blade C
- Salt and freshly ground black pepper
- 4-6 fresh basil leaves, chopped

Directions:

1. In a big skillet, heat the ghee and essential olive oil on medium heat.

2. Add garlic and sauté for approximately 1 minute.

3. Set the shrimp and cook for approximately 2-3 minutes.

4. Add the zucchini, tossing occasionally, and cook for approximately 2-3 minutes.

5. Stir in salt and black pepper and take off from the heat.

6. Serve while using the garnishing of basil leaves.

Nutrition Per Serving:

- Calories: 219.4
- Fat: 11.93 g
- Carbs: 10.59 g
- Fiber: 3.7 g
- Protein: 19.8 g
- Sodium: 854.07 mg

132. Sweet Potato Buns Sandwich

Preparation Time: 25 minutes
Cooking Time: 25 minutes
Servings: 1

Ingredients:

For Sweet Potato Buns:

- 1 ½ tablespoon extra-virgin olive oil, divided
- 1 large sweet potato, peeled and spiralized with blade C
- 2 teaspoons garlic powder
- Salt and freshly ground black pepper
- 1 large organic egg
- 1 organic egg white

For the Sandwich:

- 1 (1/2 ounce) salmon piece
- Salt and freshly ground black pepper
- 1 teaspoon fresh lime juice

- 1 tomato, sliced
- 1 onion, sliced
- 1/2 avocado, peeled, pitted, and chopped
- 2 teaspoons fresh cilantro, chopped
- 1 large bit fresh kale
- 1 bacon piece

Directions:

For the buns:

1. In a sizable skillet, heat 1/2 tablespoon of oil on medium heat.
2. Add the sweet potato and sprinkle with garlic powder, salt, and black pepper.
3. Cook for 5-7 minutes. Transfer the sweet potato mixture to a bowl.
4. Add the egg and egg white; mix well. Now, transfer a combination into 2 (6 ounces) ramekins, midway full.
5. Cover the ramekins with wax paper. Now, place them over noodles to press firmly down. Refrigerate for about 15-20 minutes.

For the Sandwich:

1. Preheat the grill to medium heat. Grease it.
2. In another bowl, add salmon, salt, black pepper, and lime juice. Toss to coat well.
3. In a substantial skillet, heat the remaining oil on medium-low heat.
4. Carefully transfer the sweet potato patties to the skillet.
5. Cook for 3-4 minutes. Change the medial side and cook for 2-3 minutes more.
6. Place the salmon, onion, and tomato slices over the grill.

7. Grill the tomato slice for 1 minute. Grate the onion slice for approximately 2 minutes.
8. Cook the salmon for around 4-5 minutes or till the desired doneness.
9. In a bowl, add the avocado and cilantro; mash well.
10. Place the onion slice, salmon, tomato, bacon, and kale on a plate over the bun.
11. Spread the avocado mash around the bottom side of another bun. Place the bun, avocado mash side downwards over the kale.
12. Secure having a toothpick and serve.

Nutrition Per Serving:

- Calories: 894.42
- Carbs: 92.5 g
- Protein: 33 g
- Fat: 48 g
- Sugar: 23.4 g
- Fiber: 22.8 g
- Sodium: 1301 mg

133. Shrimp, Sausage and Veggie Skillet

Preparation Time: 15 minutes
Cooking Time: 13 minutes
Servings: 3

Ingredients:

- 3 tablespoons organic olive oil, divided
- 1 pound shrimp, peeled and deveined
- 1/2 medium yellow onion, chopped

- 3/4 cup green peppers, seeded and chopped
- 3/4 cup green peppers, seeded and chopped
- 1 zucchini, chopped
- 6 ounces cooked sausage, chopped
- 2 garlic cloves, minced
- 1/4 cup chicken broth
- A pinch of red pepper flakes, crushed
- Salt and freshly ground black pepper

Directions:

1. In a sizable skillet, heat 1 tablespoon of oil on medium-high heat.
2. Attach the shrimp and cook for around 3-4 minutes. Transfer it to a bowl.
3. In the same skillet, heat the remaining oil on medium heat.
4. Add the onion and sweet peppers. Sauté for about 4-5 minutes.
5. Stir in the zucchini and sausage—cook for approximately 2 minutes.
6. Add the garlic and cooled shrimp—cook for approximately 1 minute.
7. Pour the broth and mix to combine well. Stir in red pepper flakes, salt, and black pepper—cook for approximately 1 minute.
8. Serve hot.

Nutrition Per Serving:

- Calories: 430
- Fat: 30.9 g
- Carbs: 7.65 g
- Fiber: 2.6 g
- Protein: 29.59 g

134. Sea Scallops with Spinach and Bacon

Preparation Time: 25 minutes
Cooking Time: 25 minutes
Servings: 4

Ingredients:

- 3 bacon slices
- 1 ½ pound jumbo sea scallops
- Salt and freshly ground black pepper
- 1 cup onion, chopped
- 6 garlic cloves, minced
- 12 ounces fresh baby spinach

Directions:

1. Heat a sizable non-stick skillet on medium-high heat.
2. Add the bacon and cook for approximately 8-10 minutes.
3. Transfer the bacon into a bowl, reserving 1 tablespoon of bacon fat within the skillet.
4. Chop the bacon and keep it aside.
5. Attach the scallops and sprinkle with salt and black pepper.
6. Immediately, boost the heat to high heat.
7. Cook for about 5 minutes, turning once after 2 ½ minutes.
8. Transfer the scallops into another bowl. Cover having foil paper to ensure that they're warm.
9. In the same skillet, add the onion and garlic, minimizing the temperature to medium-high.
10. Sauté them for around 3 minutes.

11. Add the spinach and cook for approximately 2-3 minutes—season with salt and black pepper. Remove from the heat.

12. Divide the spinach among serving plates. Top with scallops and bacon evenly. Serve immediately.

Nutrition Per Serving:

- Calories: 241.91
- Fat: 8.52 g
- Carbs: 13.5 g
- Fiber: 2.6 g
- Protein: 27.8 g

135. Liver with Onion and Parsley One

Preparation Time: 10 minutes
Cooking Time: 26 minutes
Servings: 4

Ingredients:

- 3 tablespoons coconut oil, divided
- 2 large onions, sliced
- Salt to taste
- 1 pound grass-fed beef liver, cut into 1/2-inch thick slices
- Freshly ground black pepper, to taste
- 1/2 cup fresh parsley
- 2 tablespoons freshly squeezed lemon juice

Directions:

1. In a sizable skillet, heat 1 tablespoon of oil on high heat.

2. Attach the onions plus some salt and sauté for about 5 minutes.

3. Set the heat to medium. Sauté for 10-15 minutes more.

4. Place the onion right into a plate.

5. In the same skillet, heat another 1 tablespoon of oil on medium-high heat.

6. Add the liver and sprinkle with salt and black pepper.

7. Cook for approximately 1-2 minutes or till browned.

8. Flip alongside it and cook for approximately 1-2 minutes till browned. Set the liver right into a plate.

9. In the skillet, heat the remaining oil on medium heat.

10. Attach the cooked onion, parsley, and lemon juice; stir well. Cook for about 2-3 minutes.

11. Set the onion mixture over the liver and serve immediately.

Nutrition Per Serving:

- Calories: 274
- Fat: 14 g
- Carbs: 11.8 g
- Fiber: 1.4 g
- Protein: 24 g

136. Egg and Avocado Wraps

Preparation Time: 10 minutes
Cooking Time: 26 minutes
Servings: 5

Ingredients:

- 1 ripe avocado, peeled, pitted, and chopped
- 1 tablespoon freshly squeezed lemon juice
- 1 tablespoon fresh parsley, chopped
- 2 tablespoons celery stalk, chopped
- 4 organic hard-boiled eggs, peeled and finely chopped
- Salt and freshly ground black pepper
- 4-5 endive bulbs
- 2 cooked bacon slices, chopped

Directions:

1. In a bowl, add the avocado and freshly squeezed lemon juice and mash until smooth and creamy.
2. Add celery, parsley, eggs, salt, and black pepper. Blend to mix well.
3. Split the endive leaves. Divide the avocado mixture over endive leaves evenly.
4. Top with bacon and serve immediately.

Nutrition Per Serving:

- Calories: 183.6
- Fat: 11.12 g
- Carbs: 12.78 g
- Fiber: 11 g
- Protein: 10.9 g

137. Creamy Sweet Potato Pasta with Pancetta

Preparation Time: 10 minutes
Cooking Time: 28 minutes
Servings: 4

Ingredients:

For the Creamy Sauce:

- 4-5 cups cauliflower florets
- 1 small shallot, minced
- 1 large garlic herb, chopped
- A pinch of red pepper flakes, crushed
- 1 cup chicken broth
- 1 tablespoon Nutrition Per Serving yeast
- Salt to taste

For the Pancetta:

- 8 pancetta slices, cubed

For the Sweet Potato Pasta:

- 1 tablespoon extra-virgin olive oil
- 3 medium sweet potatoes, peeled and spiralized with blade C
- 3 cups leeks
- Salt and freshly ground black pepper
- 1 tablespoon fresh parsley, chopped

Directions:

1. In a pan of salted boiling water, attach cauliflower florets and cook for around 7-8 minutes. Drain well.
2. In the meanwhile, heat a large non-stick skillet on medium heat.
3. Add pancetta slices and cook for approximately 5-7 minutes.

4. Transfer the pancetta into a bowl.

5. In the same skillet, add shallot, garlic, and red pepper flakes. Sauté for around 2 minutes.

6. Transfer the shallot mixture into a higher speed blender.

7. Add the cauliflower and the remaining sauce ingredients. Pulse till smooth and creamy.

8. In the identical skillet, heat extra-virgin olive oil on medium heat.

9. Add sweet potatoes and leeks. Cook, occasionally tossing for approximately 8-10 minutes.

10. Stir in the sauce and cook for about 1 minute.

11. Serve this creamy pasta with all the topping of the pancetta and parsley.

Nutrition Per Serving:

- Calories: 295.64
- Carbs: 8.55 g
- Protein: 10.1 g
- Fat: 8.5 g
- Sugar: 12.55 g
- Sodium: 1030 mg
- Fiber: 8.95 g

138. Greek Inspired Cucumber Salad

Preparation Time: 10 minutes

Cooking Time: 0 minutes

Servings: 4

Ingredients:

- 4 medium cucumbers, peeled, seeded, and chopped
- ½ cup low-fat Greek yogurt
- 1½ tbsp. fresh dill, chopped
- 1 tbsp. fresh lemon juice
- Salt and freshly ground black pepper, as required

Directions:

1. In a large bowl, add all the ingredients and mix well.

2. Serve immediately.

Nutrition Per Serving:

- Calories: 54.1
- Carbohydrates: 8.63g
- Protein: 4.56g
- Fat: 0.86g
- Sugar: 4.4g
- Sodium: 209mg
- Fiber: 1.03g

139. Light Veggie Salad

Preparation Time: 10 minutes
Cooking Time: 0 minutes
Servings: 5

Ingredients:

- 2 cup cucumbers, peeled, seeded, and chopped
- 2 cup red tomatoes, peeled, seeded, and chopped
- 2 tbsp. extra-virgin olive oil
- 2 tbsp. fresh lime juice
- Salt, to taste

Directions:

1. In a large serving bowl, add all the ingredients and toss to coat well.
2. Serve immediately.

Nutrition Per Serving:

- Calories: 72.38
- Carbohydrates: 5.1g
- Protein: 0.9g
- Fat: 5.9g
- Sugar: 2.8g
- Sodium: 159mg
- Fiber: 1.14g

140. Eastern European Soup

Preparation Time: 10 minutes
Cooking Time: 5 minutes
Servings: 3

Ingredients:

- 2 cup fat-free yogurt
- 4 tsp. fresh lemon juice
- 2 cup beets, trimmed, peeled, and chopped
- 2 tbsp. fresh dill
- Salt, as required
- 1 tbsp. fresh chives, minced

Directions:

1. In a high-speed blender, add all ingredients except for chives and pulse until smooth.
2. Transfer the soup into a pan over medium heat and cook for about 3-5 minutes or until heated.
3. Serve immediately with the garnishing of chives.

Nutrition Per Serving:

- Calories: 122.9
- Carbohydrates: 14.68g
- Protein: 16.09g
- Fat: 0.2g
- Sugar: 6.3g
- Sodium: 401.63 mg
- Fiber: 2.63g

141. Citrus Glazed Carrots

Preparation Time: 15 minutes
Cooking Time: 15 minutes
Servings: 6

Ingredients:

- 1½ lb. carrots, peeled and sliced into ½-inch pieces diagonally
- ½ cup water
- 2 tbsp. olive oil
- Salt, to taste
- 3 tbsp. fresh orange juice

Directions:

1. In a large skillet, add the carrots, water, boil, and salt over medium heat and bring to a boil.
2. Reduce heat to low and simmer; covered for about 6 minutes.
3. Add the orange juice and stir to combine.
4. Increase the heat to high and cook, uncovered for about 5-8 minutes, tossing frequently.
5. Serve immediately.

Nutrition Per Serving:

- Calories: 86.8
- Carbohydrates: 10.4g
- Protein: 0.9g
- Fat: 5.01g
- Sugar: 5.4g
- Sodium: 199mg
- Fiber: 2.8g

142. Braised Asparagus

Preparation Time: 10 minutes
Cooking Time: 8 minutes
Servings: 2

Ingredients:

- ½ cup chicken bone broth
- 1 tbsp. olive oil
- 1 (½-inch) lemon peel
- 1 cup asparagus, trimmed

Directions:

1. In a small pan, add the broth, oil, and lemon peel over medium heat and bring to a boil.
2. Add the asparagus and cook, covered for about 3-4 minutes.
3. Discard the lemon peel and serve.

Nutrition Per Serving:

- Calories: 94.8
- Carbohydrates: 3.9g
- Protein: 3.7g
- Fat: 7.8g
- Sugar: 1.7g
- Sodium: 22.7mg
- Fiber: 2.2g

143. Spring Flavored Pasta

Preparation Time: 10 minutes
Cooking Time: 10 minutes
Servings: 4

Ingredients:

- 2 tbsp. olive oil
- 1 lb. asparagus, trimmed and cut into 1½-inch pieces
- Salt and freshly ground black pepper, to taste
- ½ lb. cooked hot pasta, drained

Directions:

1. In a large cast-iron skillet, heat the oil over medium heat and cook the asparagus, salt, and black pepper for about 8-10 minutes, stirring occasionally.
2. Place the hot pasta and toss to coat well.
3. Serve immediately.

Nutrition Per Serving:

- Calories: 171.19
- Carbohydrates: 21.18g
- Protein: 5.31g
- Fat: 7.77g
- Sugar: 2.02g
- Sodium: 196mg
- Fiber: 2.9g

144. Versatile Mac 'n Cheese

Preparation Time: 15 minutes
Cooking Time: 12 minutes
Servings: 3

Ingredients:

- 2 cup elbow macaroni
- 1½ s butternut squash, peeled and cubed
- 1 cup low-fat Swiss cheese, shredded
- 1/3 cup low-fat milk
- 1 tbsp. olive oil
- Salt and freshly ground black pepper, to taste

Directions:

1. In a large pan of the salted boiling water, cook the macaroni for about 8-10 minutes.
2. Drain the macaroni and transfer it into a bowl.
3. Meanwhile, cook the squash cubes for about 6 minutes or until soft in a pan of boiling water.
4. Drain the squash cubes entirely and return to the same pan.
5. With a masher, mash the squash and place over low heat.
6. Add the cheese and milk and cook for about 2-3 minutes, stirring continuously.
7. Add the macaroni, oil, salt, and black pepper and stir to combine.
8. Remove from the heat and serve hot.

Nutrition Per Serving:

- Calories: 322.12

- Carbohydrates: 44.6g
- Protein: 17.35g
- Fat: 7.76g
- Sugar: 3.2g
- Sodium: 336.25mg
- Fiber: 1.91g

145. Gluten-Free Curry

Preparation Time: 15 minutes
Cooking Time: 20 minutes
Servings: 6

Ingredients:

- 2 cup tomatoes, peeled, seeded, and chopped
- 1½ cup water
- 2 tbsp. olive oil
- 1 tsp. fresh ginger, chopped
- ¼ tsp. ground turmeric
- 2 cup fresh shiitake mushrooms, sliced
- 5 cup fresh button mushrooms, sliced
- ¼ cup fat-free yogurt, whipped
- Salt and freshly ground black pepper, to taste

Directions:

1. In a food processor, add the tomatoes and ¼ cup of water and pulse until smooth paste forms.
2. Heat the oil over medium heat in a pan and sauté the ginger and turmeric for about 1 minute.
3. Add the tomato paste and cook for about 5 minutes.

4. Stir in the mushrooms, yogurt, and remaining water and bring to a boil.
5. Cook for about 10-12 minutes, stirring occasionally.
6. Season with salt and black pepper and remove from the heat.
7. Serve hot.

Nutrition Per Serving:

- Calories per serving: 121.13
- Carbohydrates: 14.72g
- Protein: 6g
- Fat: 5.91g
- Sugar: 6.3g
- Sodium: 147mg
- Fiber: 5.53g

146. Roasted Beet Pasta with Kale and Pesto

Preparation Time: 10 minutes

Cooking Time: 15 minutes

Servings: 3

Ingredients:

For the Pesto:

- 3 cups fresh basil leaves
- 1 large garlic clove, minced
- 1/4 cup organic olive oil
- 1/4 cup pine nuts
- Salt and freshly ground black pepper

For the Beet Pasta:

- 2 medium beets, trimmed, peeled, and spiralized with blade C

- Olive oil cooking spray, as required
- Salt and freshly ground black pepper

For the Kale:

- 2 cups fresh baby kale

Directions:

1. Heat the oven to 425°F. Lightly grease a large baking sheet.
2. In a mixer, add all pesto ingredients and pulse till smooth. Keep aside.
3. Place the beet pasta in the prepared baking sheet.
4. Drizzle with cooking spray and sprinkle with salt and black pepper. Gently, toss to coat well.
5. Roast for around 5-10 minutes or till the desired doneness.
6. Transfer the pasta to a sizable bowl.
7. Add the kale and pesto. Gently, toss to coat well.

Nutrition Per Serving:

- Calories: 288.9
- Fat: 28.82 g
- Carbs: 7.43 g
- Fiber: 2.98 g
- Protein: 3.1 g
- Sodium: 295.26 mg

147. Veggies and Apple with Orange Sauce

Preparation Time: 30 minutes
Cooking Time: 16 minutes
Servings: 4

Ingredients:

For the Sauce:

- 1 (1 inch) fresh ginger, minced
- 2 garlic cloves, minced
- 1 tablespoon fresh orange zest, grated finely
- 1/2 cup fresh orange juice
- 2 tablespoons white wine vinegar
- 2 tablespoons coconut aminos
- 1 tablespoon red boat fish sauce

For the Veggies and Apple:

- 1 tablespoon extra-virgin olive oil
- 1 cup carrot, peeled and julienned
- 1 cup celery, chopped
- 1 cup onion, chopped
- 2 apples, cored and sliced

Directions:

1. In a sizable bowl, mix all sauce ingredients. Keep aside.
2. In a big skillet, set the oil on medium-high heat.
3. Add the carrot and stir fry for about 4-5 minutes.
4. Attach celery and onion. Stir fry for approximately 4-5 minutes.
5. Pour the sauce and stir to combine. Cook for approximately 2-3 minutes.

6. Stir in apple slices and cook for about 2-3 minutes more.

7. Serve hot.

Nutrition Per Serving:

- Calories: 157.07
- Fat: 4 g
- Carbs: 29.31 g
- Fiber: 3.64 g
- Protein: 2.07 g

148. Cauliflower Rice with Prawns and Veggies

Preparation Time: 15 minutes
Cooking Time: 21 minutes
Servings: 4

Ingredients:

- 2 tablespoons coconut oil, divided
- 14 prawns, peeled and deveined
- 2 organic eggs, beaten
- 1 brown onion, chopped
- 1 garlic clove, minced
- 1 small fresh red chili, chopped
- 1/2 pound grass-fed ground chicken
- 1 cauliflower head, cut into florets, processed like rice consistency
- 1/4 red cabbage, chopped
- 1/2 cup green peas, shelled
- 1 small head of broccoli
- 1 large carrot, peeled and finely chopped
- 1 small red bell pepper
- 2 Bok choy, sliced thinly
- 3 tablespoons coconut aminos

- Salt and freshly ground black pepper

Directions:

1. In a substantial skillet, heat 1/2 tablespoon of oil on medium-high heat.
2. Add the prawns and cook for approximately 3-4 minutes. Transfer to a large bowl.
3. In the same skillet, heat 1/2 tablespoon of oil on medium heat.
4. Add the beaten eggs, and with the back of a spoon, spread the eggs—Cook for around 2 minutes.
5. Remove the eggs from the skillet and cut them into strips.
6. In the identical skillet, heat the remaining oil on high heat. Add the onion, garlic, and red chili. Sauté for about 4-5 minutes.
7. Add the chicken and cook for about 4-5 minutes.
8. Add the cauliflower rice and remaining veggies except for the Bok choy and coconut aminos and cook for 2-3 minutes.
9. Add the Bok choy, coconut aminos, cooked eggs, prawns, salt, and black pepper. Cook for 2 minutes more.

Nutrition Per Serving:

- Calories: 303.4
- Carbs: 24.8 g
- Protein: 21.32 g
- Fat: 14.41 g
- Sugar: 12.42 g
- Sodium: 857.6 mg

149. Lentils with Tomatoes and Turmeric

Preparation Time: 15 minutes
Cooking Time: 10 minutes
Servings: 2

Ingredients:

- 1/2 onion, finely chopped
- 1/2 teaspoon garlic powder
- 1/2 (14 ounces) drained canned chopped tomatoes
- 1/8 teaspoon ground black pepper
- 1 tablespoon extra-virgin olive oil, plus extra for garnishing
- 1/2 tablespoon ground turmeric
- 1/2 (14 ounces) drained canned lentils
- 1/4 teaspoon sea salt

Directions:

1. Heat the olive oil in a pot over medium-high heat until it starts shimmering.
2. Cook, stirring regularly, for around 5 minutes until the onion and turmeric are tender.
3. Add the garlic powder, salt, tomatoes, lentils, and pepper.
4. Cook, stirring regularly, for 5 minutes

Nutrition Per Serving:

- Calories: 157.32
- Fat: 8.19 g
- Carbs: 14.32 g
- Sugar: 1.13 g
- Fiber: 6.16 g
- Protein: 5.48 g
- Sodium: 376 mg

150. Fried Rice with Kale

Preparation Time: 10 minutes
Cooking Time: 12 minutes
Servings: 2

Ingredients:

- 4 ounces tofu chopped
- 1 cup kale, stemmed and chopped
- 2 tablespoons stir-fry sauce
- 1 tablespoon extra-virgin olive oil
- 3 sliced scallions
- 1 ½ cup cooked brown rice

Directions:

1. Heat the olive oil in a big skillet or pan over medium-high heat until it starts shimmering.
2. Add the scallions, tofu, and kale. Cook until the vegetables are tender.
3. Combine the stir-fry sauce and brown rice in a mixing bowl. Cook, stirring regularly until thoroughly heated.

Nutrition Per Serving:

- Calories: 308.26
- Fat: 11.32 g
- Carbs: 41.91 g
- Sugar: 5.4 g
- Fiber: 4.38 g
- Protein: 9.56 g
- Sodium: 351.1 mg

151. Tofu and Red Pepper Stir-Fry

Preparation Time: 10 minutes
Cooking Time: 12 minutes
Servings: 2

Ingredients:

- 1 chopped red bell peppers
- 1 tablespoon extra-virgin olive oil
- 1/2 chopped onion
- 1/4 cup ginger teriyaki sauce
- 4 ounces chopped tofu

Directions:

1. Heat the olive oil in a skillet or pan over medium-high heat until it starts shimmering.
2. Add the onion, red bell peppers, and tofu. Cook, stirring regularly.
3. Apply the teriyaki sauce to the skillet or pan after whisking it together. Cook, occasionally stirring, for 3-4 minutes, or until it thickens.

Nutrition Per Serving:

- Calories: 160.59
- Fat: 10 g
- Carbs: 11.89 g
- Sugar: 8.51 g
- Fiber: 1.65 g
- Protein: 7.47 g
- Sodium: 1386.92 mg

152. Sweet Potato and Bell Pepper Hash with a Fried Egg

Preparation Time: 10 minutes
Cooking Time: 25 minutes
Servings: 2

Ingredients:

- 1/2 chopped onion
- 2 cups peeled and cubed potatoes
- 2 tablespoons extra-virgin olive oil
- 1/2 chopped red bell pepper
- 1/2 teaspoon sea salt
- 2 eggs
- A pinch of freshly ground black pepper

Directions:

1. Heat olive oil in a big non-stick pan over medium-high heat until it starts shimmering.
2. Add the red bell pepper, onion, and sweet potato. Season with salt and a pinch of black pepper. Cook, stirring regularly until the potatoes are soft and browned.
3. Serve the potatoes in 4 bowls.
4. Return the skillet or pan to heat, turn the heat down to medium-low, and swirl to secure the bottom of the pan with the remaining olive oil.
5. Scatter some salt over the eggs and carefully smash them into the tray. Cook until the whites are set, around 3-4 minutes.
6. Flip the eggs gently and remove them from the heat. Allow to rest for 1 minute in the hot skillet or pan. 1 egg should be placed on top of each serving of hash.

Nutrition Per Serving:

- Calories: 320.44
- Fat: 19 g
- Carbs: 30.31 g
- Sugar: 3.45 g
- Fiber: 4.09 g
- Protein: 9.11 g
- Sodium: 546.92 mg

153. Quinoa Florentine

Preparation Time: 5 minutes
Cooking Time: 25 minutes
Servings: 2

Ingredients:

- 1/2 chopped onion
- 2 minced garlic cloves
- 2 cups no-salt-added vegetable broth
- A pinch of freshly ground black pepper
- 1 tablespoon extra-virgin olive oil
- 1 ½ cup fresh baby spinach
- 1 cup quinoa, rinsed well
- 1/4 teaspoon sea salt

Directions:

1. Heat the olive oil over medium-high heat until it starts shimmering.
2. Add the spinach and onion. Cook, stirring regularly, for 3 minutes.
3. Cook, stirring continuously, for 30 seconds after adding the garlic.
4. Combine the vegetable broth, salt, quinoa, and pepper in a mixing bowl. Set to a simmer, then reduce to low heat. Cook, covered, for 15-20 minutes, or until the

liquid has been absorbed. Using a fork, fluff the mixture.

Nutrition Per Serving:

- Calories: 414.49
- Fat: 12.41 g
- Carbs: 63.46 g
- Sugar: 5.96 g
- Fiber: 6.94 g
- Protein: 13.2 g
- Sodium: 274.67 mg

154. Tomato Asparagus Frittata

Preparation Time: 5 minutes
Cooking Time: 20 minutes
Servings: 2

Ingredients:

- 5 trimmed asparagus spears
- 3 eggs
- 1 tablespoon extra-virgin olive oil
- 5 cherry tomatoes
- 1/2 tablespoon chopped fresh thyme
- A pinch of freshly ground black pepper
- 1/4 teaspoon sea salt

Directions:

1. Preheat the broiler to the highest setting.
2. Heat the olive oil in a big ovenproof skillet or pan over medium-high heat until it starts shimmering.
3. Toss in the asparagus. Cook, stirring regularly, for 5 minutes.

4. Add in the tomatoes. Cook for 3 minutes, stirring once in a while.
5. Whisk together the thyme, salt, eggs, and pepper in a medium mixing cup. Carefully spill over the tomatoes and asparagus, turning them about in the pan to ensure equally distributed.
6. Turn the heat down to medium. Cook for 3 minutes, or until the eggs are hardened around the outside
7. Place the pan under the broiler and cook for 3-5 minutes, or until puffed and brown. To eat, cut into wedges.

Nutrition Per Serving:

- Calories: 172.24
- Fat: 13.54 g
- Carbs: 3.57 g
- Sugar: 1.96 g
- Fiber: 1.29 g
- Protein: 9.41 g
- Sodium: 333.3 mg

155. Tofu Sloppy Joes

Preparation Time: 5 minutes
Cooking Time: 15 minutes
Servings: 2

Ingredients:

- 1/2 chopped onion
- 1 (14 ounces) canned crushed tomatoes
- 1/2 tablespoon chili powder
- 1 tablespoon extra-virgin olive oil
- 5 ounces chopped tofu
- 2 tablespoons apple cider vinegar

- 1/2 teaspoon garlic powder
- a pinch of freshly ground black pepper
- 1/4 teaspoon sea salt

Directions:

1. Heat the olive oil in a big pot over medium-high heat until it starts shimmering.
2. Combine the tofu and onion in a mixing bowl. Cook, stirring regularly until the onion is tender.
3. Add the tomatoes, apple cider vinegar, salt, garlic powder, chili powder, and pepper in a large mixing bowl. Simmer for 10 minutes, stirring regularly, to enable the flavors to meld.

Nutrition Per Serving:

- Calories: 201.77
- Fat: 11.39 g
- Carbs: 19.84 g
- Sugar: 10.43 g
- Fiber: 5.2 g
- Protein: 9.66 g
- Sodium: 671.08 mg

156. Broccoli and Egg "Muffins"

Preparation Time: 5 minutes
Cooking Time: 10 minutes
Servings: 2

Ingredients:

- 1 tablespoon extra-virgin olive oil
- 1/2 cup chopped broccoli florets
- 1/2 teaspoon garlic powder

- 2 tablespoons freshly ground black pepper
- Non-stick cooking spray
- 1/2 chopped onion
- 4 beaten eggs
- 1/4 teaspoon sea salt

Directions:

1. Preheat the oven to 350ºF.
2. Using non-stick cooking oil, coat a muffin pan.
3. Heat the olive oil in a big non-stick skillet or pan over medium-high heat until it starts shimmering.
4. Add the broccoli and onion. Let it be for 3 minutes in the oven. Divide the vegetables equally among the four muffin cups.
5. Add the eggs, salt, garlic powder, and pepper. They can be poured over the vegetables in the muffin tins.
6. Bake for 15-17 minutes, or until the eggs are cooked through.

Nutrition Per Serving:

- Calories: 256.91
- Fat: 18.71 g
- Carbs: 10.78 g
- Sugar: 1.74 g
- Fiber: 3.07 g
- Protein: 12.83 g
- Sodium: 372.82 mg

157. Shrimp Scampi

Preparation Time: 10 minutes
Cooking Time: 15 minutes
Servings: 2

Ingredients:

- 1/2 finely chopped onion
- 1 pound shrimp, peeled and tails removed
- 1 lemon juice
- 2 tablespoons extra-virgin olive oil
- 1/2 chopped red bell pepper
- 3 minced garlic cloves
- 1 lemon zest
- A pinch of freshly ground black pepper
- 1/4 teaspoon sea salt

Directions:

1. Heat the olive oil in a big non-stick pan over medium-high heat until it starts shimmering.
2. Add the red bell pepper and onion. Cook, stirring regularly, for around 6 minutes, or until tender.
3. Cook for around 5 minutes, or until the shrimp are yellow.
4. Add the garlic. Cook for 30 seconds while continuously stirring.
5. Stir in the zest and lemon juice and the pepper and salt—Cook for 3 minutes on low heat.

Nutrition Per Serving:

- Calories: 291.39
- Fat: 16.48 g
- Carbs: 9.12 g

- Sugar: 2.79 g
- Fiber: 1.43 g
- Protein: 25.88 g
- Sodium: 853.5 mg

158. Shrimp with Cinnamon Sauce

Preparation Time: 5 minutes

Cooking Time: 10 minutes

Servings: 2

Ingredients:

- 1 pound shrimp, peeled
- 1/2 cup no-salt-added chicken broth
- 1/2 teaspoon onion powder
- 1/8 teaspoon ground black pepper
- 1 tablespoon extra-virgin olive oil
- 1 tablespoon Dijon Mustard
- 1/2 teaspoon ground cinnamon
- 1/4 teaspoon sea salt

Directions:

1. Heat the olive oil in a big non-stick skillet or pan over medium-high heat until it starts shimmering.
2. Toss in the shrimp. Cook, stirring regularly, for around 4 minutes, or until it is opaque.
3. Whisk together the chicken broth, mustard, onion powder, salt, cinnamon, and pepper in a shallow cup. Pour this into the skillet or pan and fry, stirring regularly, for another 3 minutes.

Nutrition Per Serving:

- Calories: 240.5

- Fat: 10.2g
- Carbs: 1.69 g
- Sugar: 0.36 g
- Fiber: 1.74 g
- Protein: 33.71 g
- Sodium: 1558.41 mg

159. Manhattan-Style Salmon Chowder

Preparation Time: 10 minutes

Cooking Time: 10 minutes

Servings: 2

Ingredients:

- 1/2 chopped red bell pepper
- 1 (28 ounces) can of crushed tomatoes
- 1 cup sweet potatoes, diced (1/2 inch)
- 2 tablespoons extra-virgin olive oil
- 1/2 pound skinless salmon, pin bones removed, chopped into ½-inch pieces
- 3 cups no-salt-added chicken broth
- 1/2 teaspoon onion powder
- 1/8 teaspoon ground black pepper
- 1/4 teaspoon sea salt

Directions:

1. Heat the olive oil in a pot over medium-high heat until it starts shimmering.
2. Add the salmon and red bell pepper. Cook, stirring until the fish is opaque and the bell pepper is tender.
3. Combine the chicken broth, tomatoes, onion powder, sweet potatoes, pepper, and salt in a large mixing bowl.
4. Lower the heat to medium-low and bring to a simmer. Cook, stirring regularly, for

around 10 minutes, or until the sweet
potatoes are tender.

Nutrition Per Serving:

- Calories: 486.09
- Fat: 20.9 g
- Carbs: 44.3 g
- Sugar: 21.3 g
- Fiber: 10.17 g
- Protein: 36.41 g
- Sodium: 1580 mg

Chapter 9

LOW RESIDUE (DINNER)

160. Italian Style Stuffed Zucchini Boats

Preparation Time: 10 minutes
Cooking Time: 25 minutes
Servings: 2

Ingredients:

- 6 large zucchini
- 1/2 tablespoon olive oil
- Kosher salt
- Freshly ground black pepper
- 1/4 teaspoon garlic powder
- 1 small yellow onion, diced
- 2 garlic cloves, minced
- 1 pound ground turkey
- 1 (28 ounces) can crush tomatoes
- 4 ounces Mozzarella cheese, shredded
- 1 ounce Parmesan cheese, freshly grated
- Flat-leaf parsley for garnishing
- Cooking spray

Directions:

1. Turn your oven on and allow to preheat up to 425°F and lightly grease a 9x13-inch baking dish with cooking spray.
2. Divide the zucchini in half lengthwise and then scoop out the seeds. Brush with olive oil and season with salt, pepper, and garlic powder.
3. Roast in the prepared dish for 20 minutes or until it begins to soften.
4. Meanwhile, sauté the onions and garlic in 1/2 tablespoon of olive oil in a large skillet over medium-high heat.
5. Cook for 3-4 minutes, then add the ground turkey and brown. Attach the tomatoes and bring them to a boil.
6. Reduce the heat to medium, and then let simmer until the zucchini is done. Stir in 1/2 teaspoon salt and pepper to taste.
7. Set to bake for about 5 minutes or at least until the Mozzarella cheese you added has melted about 3-5 minutes.
8. Serve hot, garnished with Parmesan cheese and parsley.

Nutrition Per Serving:

- Calories: 1073.51
- Fat: 67.13 g
- Carbs: 66.52 g
- Fiber: 17.6 g
- Protein: 64.25 g

161. Chicken Cutlets

Preparation Time: 10 minutes
Cooking Time: 15 minutes
Servings: 4

Ingredients:

- 4 teaspoons red wine vinegar
- 2 teaspoons minced garlic cloves
- 2 teaspoons dried sage leaves
- 1 pound chicken breast cutlets
- Salt and pepper, to taste
- 1/4 cup refined white flour
- 2 teaspoons olive oil

Directions:

1. Set a good amount of plastic wrap on the kitchen counter; sprinkle with half the combined sage, garlic, and vinegar.
2. Put the chicken breast on the plastic wrap; sprinkle with the rest of the vinegar mixture. Season lightly with pepper and salt.
3. Secure the chicken with the second sheet of plastic wrap. Use a kitchen mallet to pound the breast until it is flattened. Let stand for 5 minutes.
4. Set the chicken on both sides with flour. In a skillet, heat the oil over medium heat.
5. Add half of the chicken breast and cook for 1 ½ minutes or until it is browned on the bottom.
6. Turn on the other side and let it cook for 3 minutes.
7. Remove the chicken breast and place it on an oven-proof serving plate so that you can keep warm.

8. Reduce the liquid by half. Pour the mixture over the chicken breast; serve immediately.

Nutrition Per Serving:

- Calories: 189.18
- Fat: 5.5 g
- Carbs: 6.63 g
- Fiber: 0.23 g
- Protein: 26.48 g

162. Slow Cooker Salsa Turkey

Preparation Time: 8 minutes
Cooking Time: 7 hours
Servings: 4

Ingredients:

- 2 pounds turkey breasts, boneless and skinless
- 1 cup salsa
- 1 cup small tomatoes, diced, canned choose low-sodium
- 2 tablespoons taco seasoning
- 1/2 cup celery, finely diced
- 1/2 cup carrots, shredded
- 3 tablespoons low-fat sour cream

Directions:

1. Add the turkey to your slow cooker. Season it with taco seasoning, then top with salsa and vegetables.
2. Add in 1/2 cup of water. Set to cook on low for 7 hours (internal temperature should be 165°F when done).

3. Shred the turkey with 2 forks, add in sour cream, and stir. Enjoy.

Nutrition Per Serving:

- Calories: 387.8
- Fat: 17.25 g
- Carbs: 10.45 g
- Fiber: 2.3 g
- Protein: 48 g

163. Sriracha Lime Chicken and Apple Salad

Preparation Time: 10 minutes
Cooking Time: 15 minutes
Servings: 4

Ingredients:

Sriracha Lime Chicken:

- 2 organic chicken breasts
- 3 tablespoons sriracha
- 1 lime, juiced
- 1/4 teaspoon fine sea salt
- 1/4 teaspoon freshly ground pepper

Fruit Salad:

- 4 apples, peeled, cored, and diced
- 1 cup organic grape tomatoes
- 1/3 cup red onion, finely chopped

Lime Vinaigrette:

- 1/3 cup light olive oil
- 1/4 cup apple cider vinegar
- 2 limes, juiced
- A dash of fine sea salt

Directions:

1. Use salt and pepper to season the chicken on both sides. Spread on the sriracha and lime and let sit for 20 minutes.
2. Cook the chicken per side over medium heat or until done. Grill the apple with the chicken.
3. Meanwhile, whisk together the dressing and season to taste.
4. Arrange the salad, topping it with red onion and tomatoes.
5. Serve as a side to the chicken and apple.

Nutrition Per Serving:

- Calories: 467.6
- Fat: 29.16 g
- Carbs: 27.8 g
- Fiber: 3.23 g
- Protein: 25 g

164. Pan-Seared Scallops with Lemon-Ginger Vinaigrette

Preparation Time: 10 minutes
Cooking Time: 10 minutes
Servings: 2

Ingredients:

- 1 pound sea scallops
- 1 tablespoon extra-virgin olive oil
- 1/4 teaspoon sea salt
- 2 tablespoons lemon-ginger vinaigrette
- A pinch of freshly ground black pepper

Directions:

1. Heat the olive oil in a non-stick skillet or pan over medium-high heat until it starts shimmering.
2. Add the scallops to the skillet or pan after seasoning them with pepper and salt. Cook for 3 minutes per side or until the fish is only opaque.
3. Serve with a dollop of vinaigrette on top.

Nutrition Per Serving:

- Calories: 312
- Fat: 18
- Carbs: 7.8 g
- Sugar: 0.4 g
- Fiber: 0 g
- Protein: 29 g
- Sodium: 508 mg

165. Roasted Salmon and Asparagus

Preparation Time: 5 minutes
Cooking Time: 15 minutes
Servings: 2

Ingredients:

- 1 tablespoon extra-virgin olive oil
- 1 pound salmon, cut into two fillets
- 1/2 lemon zest and slices
- 1/2 pound asparagus spears, trimmed
- 1 teaspoon sea salt, divided
- 1/8 teaspoon freshly cracked black pepper

Directions:

1. Preheat the oven to 425ºF.

2. Stir the asparagus with half of salt and olive oil. At the base of a roasting tray, spread in a continuous sheet.

3. Season the salmon with salt and pepper. Place the asparagus on top of the skin-side down.

4. Lemon zest should be sprinkled over the asparagus, salmon, and lemon slices. Set them over the top.

5. Roast for around 15 minutes until the flesh of the fish is opaque in the preheated oven.

Nutrition Per Serving:

- Calories: 507
- Fat: 33.87 g
- Carbs: 4.43 g
- Sugar: 1.92 g
- Fiber: 2.19 g
- Protein: 48 g
- Sodium: 1057 mg

166. Orange and Maple-Glazed Salmon

Preparation Time: 15 minutes
Cooking Time: 15 minutes
Servings: 2

Ingredients:

- 1 orange zest
- 1 tablespoon low-sodium soy sauce
- 2 (4-6 ounces) salmon fillets, pin bones removed
- 1 orange juice
- 2 tablespoons pure maple syrup
- 1 teaspoon garlic powder

Directions:

1. Preheat the oven to 400ºF.

2. Set the orange juice and zest, soy sauce, maple syrup, and garlic powder in a little shallow bowl.

3. Place the salmon parts in the dish flesh-side down. Allow resting 10 minutes for marinating.

4. Put the salmon on a rimmed baking dish, skin-side up, and bake for 15 minutes, or until the flesh is opaque.

Nutrition Per Serving:

- Calories: 297
- Fat: 13.4
- Carbs: 20.87 g
- Sugar: 15.8 g
- Fiber: 0.72 g
- Protein: 24 g
- Sodium: 275.03 mg

167. Cod with Ginger and Black Beans

Preparation Time: 10 minutes
Cooking Time: 15 minutes
Servings: 2

Ingredients:

- 2 (6 ounces) cod fillets
- 1/2 teaspoon sea salt, divided
- 3 minced garlic cloves
- 2 tablespoons chopped fresh cilantro leaves
- 1 tablespoon extra-virgin olive oil
- 1/2 tablespoon grated fresh ginger

- 2 tablespoons freshly ground black pepper
- 1/2 (14 ounces) can black beans, drained

Directions:

1. Heat the olive oil in a big non-stick skillet or pan over medium-high heat until it starts shimmering.
2. Half of the salt, ginger, and pepper are used to season the fish. Cook for around 4 minutes per side in the hot oil until the fish is opaque. Detach the cod from the pan and place it on a plate with aluminum foil tented over it.
3. Add the garlic to the skillet or pan and return it to the heat. Cook for 30 seconds while continuously stirring.
4. Mix the black beans and the remaining salt. Cook, stirring regularly, for 5 minutes.
5. Add the cilantro and serve the black beans on top of the cod.

Nutrition Per Serving:

- Calories: 289.5
- Fat: 8.98 g
- Carbs: 15.9 g
- Sugar: 0.27 g
- Fiber: 6.45 g
- Protein: 36.2 g
- Sodium: 838.09 mg

168. Halibut Curry

Preparation Time: 10 minutes
Cooking Time: 10 minutes
Servings: 2

Ingredients:

- 1 teaspoon ground turmeric
- 1 pound halibut, skin, and bones removed, cut into 1-inch pieces
- 1/2 (14 ounces) canned coconut milk
- 1/8 teaspoon ground black pepper
- 1 tablespoon extra-virgin olive oil
- 1 teaspoon curry powder
- 2 cups no-salt-added chicken broth
- 1/4 teaspoon sea salt

Directions:

1. Heat the olive oil in a non-stick skillet or pan over medium-high heat until it starts shimmering.
2. Add the curry powder and turmeric to a bowl. To bloom the spices, cook for 2 minutes, stirring continuously.
3. Stir in halibut, coconut milk, chicken broth, pepper, and salt. Lower the heat to medium-low and bring to a simmer. Cook, stirring regularly, for 6-7 minutes, or until the fish is opaque.

Nutrition Per Serving:

- Calories: 373
- Fat: 31 g
- Carbs: 5 g
- Sugar: 0.08 g
- Fiber: 1 g

- Protein: 21.61 g
- Sodium: 432.63 mg

- Fiber: 5.16 g
- Protein: 39 g
Sodium: 1041.6 mg

169. Chicken Cacciatore

Preparation Time: 10 minutes
Cooking Time: 20 minutes
Servings: 2

Ingredients:

- 1 pound skinless chicken, cut into bite-size pieces
- 1/4 cup black olives, chopped
- 1/2 teaspoon onion powder
- A pinch of freshly ground black pepper
- 1 tablespoon extra-virgin olive oil
- 1 (28 ounces) can crushed tomatoes, drained
- 1/2 teaspoon garlic powder
- 1/4 teaspoon sea salt

Directions:

1. Heat the olive oil in a non-stick skillet or pan over medium-high heat until it starts shimmering.
2. Cook until the chicken is browned.
3. Add the tomatoes, garlic powder, olives, salt, onion powder, and pepper, then stir to combine. Cook, stirring regularly, for 10 minutes.

Nutrition Per Serving:

- Calories: 343
- Fat: 14.22 g
- Carbs: 20.26 g
- Sugar: 11.6 g

170. Chicken and Bell Pepper Sauté

Preparation Time: 5 minutes
Cooking Time: 15 minutes
Servings: 2

Ingredients:

- 1 chopped bell pepper
- 1 pound skinless chicken breasts, cut into bite-size pieces
- 1 ½ tablespoon extra-virgin olive oil
- 1/2 chopped onion
- 3 minced garlic cloves
- 1/8 teaspoon ground black pepper
- 1/4 teaspoon sea salt

Directions:

1. Heat the olive oil in a non-stick skillet or pan over medium-high heat until it starts shimmering.
2. Add the onion, red bell pepper, and chicken. Cook, stirring regularly, for 10 minutes.
3. Stir in the salt, garlic, and pepper in a mixing bowl. Cook for 30 seconds while continuously stirring.

Nutrition Per Serving:

- Calories: 316
- Fat: 15 g
- Carbs: 6.81 g
- Sugar: 3.13 g

- Fiber: 1.57 g
- Protein: 37 g
- Sodium: 313 mg

171. Pure Comfort Soup

Preparation Time: 10 minutes
Cooking Time: 20 minutes
Servings: 4

Ingredients:

- 6 cup chicken bone broth
- 1/3 cup orzo
- 6 large egg yolks
- 1½ cup cooked chicken, shredded
- ¼ cup fresh lemon juice
- Salt and freshly ground black pepper, to taste

Directions:

1. In a large pan, add the broth over medium-high heat and bring to a boil.
2. Add the pasta and cook for about 8-9 minutes.
3. Slowly, add in 1 cup of the hot broth, beating continuously.
4. Add the egg mixture to the pan, stirring continuously.
5. Reduce the heat to medium and cook for about 5-7 minutes, stirring frequently.
6. Stir in the cooked chicken, salt, and black pepper and cook for about 1-2 minutes.
7. Remove from the heat and serve hot.

Nutrition Per Serving:

- Calories per serving: 318

- Carbohydrates: 11.87g
- Protein: 27.47g
- Fat: 17.69g
- Sugar: 1.7g
- Sodium: 364mg
- Fiber: 0.7g

172. Good-for-You Stew

Preparation Time: 15 minutes
Cooking Time: 18 minutes
Servings: 8

Ingredients:

- 2½ cup fresh tomatoes, peeled, seeded, and chopped
- 4 cup fish bone broth
- 1 lb. salmon fillets, cubed
- 1 lb. shrimp, peeled and deveined
- 2 tbsp. fresh lime juice
- Salt and freshly ground black pepper, to taste
- 3 tbsp. fresh parsley, chopped

Directions:

1. In a large soup pan, add the tomatoes and broth and bring to a boil.
2. Reduce the heat to medium and simmer for about 5 minutes.
3. Add the salmon and simmer for about 3-4 minutes.
4. Stir in the shrimp and cook for about 4-5 minutes.
5. Stir in lemon juice, salt, and black pepper, and remove from heat.
6. Serve hot with the garnishing of parsley.

Nutrition Per Serving:

- Calories: 173
- Carbohydrates: 3.2g
- Protein: 27.1g
- Fat: 5.5g
- Sugar: 1.5g
- Sodium: 368mg
- Fiber: 0.7g

173. Zero-Fiber Chicken Dish

Preparation Time: 16 minutes
Cooking Time: 10 minutes
Servings: 6

Ingredients:

- 4 (6-oz.) boneless, skinless chicken breast halves
- Salt and freshly ground black pepper, to taste
- 2 tbsp. olive oil

Directions:

1. Season each chicken breast half with salt and black pepper evenly.
2. Place chicken breast halves over a rack set in a rimmed baking sheet.
3. Refrigerate for at least 30 minutes.
4. Remove from the refrigerator and pat dry with paper towels.
5. In a skillet, heat the oil over medium-low heat.
6. Place the chicken breast halves, smooth-side down, and cook for about 9-10 minutes, without moving.

7. Flip the chicken breasts and cook for about 6 minutes or until fully cooked.
8. Remove from the heat and let the chicken stand in the pan for about 3 minutes.
9. Now, place the chicken breasts onto a cutting board.
10. Cut each chicken breast into slices and serve.

Nutrition Per Serving:

- Calories: 178.19
- Carbohydrates: 0.1g
- Protein: 26g
- Fat: 7.7g
- Sugar: 0g
- Sodium: 180mg
- Fiber: 0.04g

174. Amazing Chicken Platter

Preparation Time: 15 minutes
Cooking Time: 18 minutes
Servings: 6

Ingredients:

- 2 tbsp. olive oil, divided
- 4 (4-oz.) boneless, skinless chicken breasts, cut into small pieces
- Salt and freshly ground black pepper, to taste
- 1 tsp. fresh ginger, grated
- 4 cup fresh mushrooms, sliced
- 1 cup chicken bone broth

Directions:

1. Heat 1 tbsp of oil in a large skillet over medium-high heat and stir fry the chicken pieces, salt, and black pepper for about 4-5 minutes or until golden brown.
2. With a slotted spoon, transfer the chicken pieces onto a plate.
3. Heat the remaining oil over medium heat in the same skillet and sauté the onion, ginger for about 1 minute.
4. Add the mushrooms and cook for about 6-7 minutes, stirring frequently.
5. Add the cooked chicken and coconut milk and stir fry for about 3-4 minutes
6. Add in the salt and black pepper and remove from the heat.
7. Serve hot.

Nutrition Per Serving:

- Calories: 200
- Carbohydrates: 1.6g
- Protein: 24.8g
- Fat: 10.4g
- Sugar: 0.8g
- Sodium: 111mg
- Fiber: 0.5g

175. Colorful Chicken Dinner

Preparation Time: 15 minutes
Cooking Time: 20 minutes
Servings: 6

Ingredients:

- 3 tbsp. olive oil, divided
- 1 large yellow bell pepper, seeded and sliced
- 1 large red bell pepper, seeded and sliced
- 1 large green bell pepper, seeded and sliced
- 1 lb. boneless, skinless chicken breasts, sliced thinly
- 1 tsp. dried oregano, crushed
- ¼ tsp. garlic powder
- ¼ tsp. ground cumin
- Salt and freshly ground black pepper, to taste
- ¼ cup chicken bone broth

Directions:

1. Heat 1 tbsp of oil over medium-high heat in a skillet and cook the bell peppers for about 4-5 minutes.
2. With a slotted spoon, transfer the peppers mixture onto a plate.
3. In the same skillet, heat the remaining over medium-high heat and cook the chicken for about 8 minutes, stirring frequently.
4. Stir in the thyme, spices, salt, black pepper, and broth, and bring to a boil.
5. Add the peppers mixture and stir to combine.
6. Reduce the heat to medium and cook for about 3-5 minutes or until all the liquid is absorbed, stirring occasionally.
7. Serve immediately.

Nutrition Per Serving:

- Calories: 175
- Carbohydrates: 4.8g
- Protein: 19g
- Fat: 9.39g

- Sugar: 1.5g
- Sodium: 170mg
- Fiber: 1.2g

176. Easiest Tuna Salad

Preparation Time: 15 minutes
Cooking Time: 0 minutes
Servings: 4

Ingredients:

For Dressing:

- 2 tbsp. fresh dill, minced
- 2 tbsp. olive oil
- 1 tbsp. fresh lime juice
- Salt and freshly ground black pepper, to taste

For Salad:

- 2 (6-oz.) cans water-packed tuna, drained and flaked
- 6 hard-boiled eggs, peeled and sliced
- 1 cup tomato, peeled, seeded, and chopped
- 1 large cucumber, peeled, seeded, and sliced

Directions:

1. For the dressing: In a bowl, add all the ingredients and beat until well combined.
2. For the salad: in another large serving bowl, add all the ingredients and mix well.
3. Divide the tuna mixture onto serving plates.
4. Drizzle with dressing and serve.

Nutrition Per Serving:

- Calories: 277
- Carbohydrates: 5.9g
- Protein: 31.2g
- Fat: 14.5g
- Sugar: 3g
- Sodium: 612mg
- Fiber: 0.96g

177. Lemony Salmon

Preparation Time: 10 minutes
Cooking Time: 14 minutes
Servings: 4

Ingredients:

- 1 tbsp. fresh lemon zest, grated
- 2 tbsp. extra-virgin olive oil
- 2 tbsp. fresh lemon juice
- Salt and freshly ground black pepper, to taste
- 4 (6-oz.) boneless, skinless salmon fillets

Directions:

1. Preheat the grill to medium-high heat. Grease the grill grate.
2. In a medium bowl, place all ingredients except for salmon fillets and mix well.
3. Add the salmon fillets and coat with garlic mixture generously.
4. Place the salmon fillets on the grill and cook for about 6-7 minutes per side.
5. Serve hot.

Nutrition Per Serving:

- Calories: 383.48
- Carbohydrates: 0.9g
- Protein: 34.5g
- Fat: 27g
- Sugar: 0.25g
- Sodium: 275 mg
- Fiber: 0.24g

178. Herbed Salmon

Preparation Time: 10 minutes
Cooking Time: 8 minutes
Servings: 4

Ingredients:

- 1 tsp. dried oregano, crushed
- 1 tsp. dried basil, crushed
- Salt and freshly ground black pepper, to taste
- ¼ cup olive oil
- 2 tbsp. fresh lemon juice
- 4 (4-oz.) salmon fillets

Directions:

1. In a large bowl, add all ingredients except for salmon and mix well.
2. Add the salmon and coat with marinade generously.
3. Cover the bowl and refrigerate to marinate for at least 1 hour.
4. Preheat the grill to medium-high heat. Grease the grill grate.
5. Place the salmon on the grill and cook for about 4 minutes per side.
6. Serve hot.

Nutrition Per Serving:

- Calories: 341.43
- Carbohydrates: 1.04g
- Protein: 23g
- Fat: 27.6g
- Sugar: 0.2g
- Sodium: 248mg
- Fiber: 0.3g

179. Delicious Combo Dinner

Preparation Time: 15 minutes
Cooking Time: 15 minutes
Servings: 5

Ingredients:

- 2 tbsp. olive oil
- 1 lb. prawns, peeled and deveined
- 1 lb. asparagus, trimmed
- Salt and freshly ground black pepper, to taste
- 1 tsp. fresh ginger, minced

2 tbsp. fresh lemon juice

Directions:

1. In a skillet, heat 1 tbsp of oil over medium-high heat and cook the prawns with salt and black pepper for about 3-4 minutes.
2. With a slotted spoon, transfer the prawns into a bowl. Set aside.
3. Heat the remaining oil over medium-high heat in the same skillet and cook the asparagus, ginger, salt, and black pepper for about 6-8 minutes, stirring frequently.

4. Stir in the prawns and cook for about 1 minute.
5. Stir in the lemon juice and remove from the heat.
6. Serve hot.

Nutrition Per Serving:

- Calories: 127.8
- Carbohydrates: 3.52g
- Protein: 14.35g
- Fat: 6.5g
- Sugar: 1.6g
- Sodium: 664mg
- Fiber: 2.05g

180. Chicken Salad Sandwiches

Preparation Time: 15 minutes
Cooking Time: 0 minutes
Servings: 2

Ingredients:

- 2 tablespoons anti-inflammatory mayonnaise
- 1 tablespoon chopped fresh tarragon leaves
- 1 cup chicken, chopped, cooked, and skinless (from 1 rotisserie chicken)
- 1/2 minced red bell pepper
- 1 teaspoon Dijon mustard
- 4 slices whole-wheat bread
- 1/4 teaspoon sea salt

Directions:

1. Combine the chicken, red bell pepper, mayonnaise, mustard, tarragon, and salt in a medium mixing bowl.
2. Spread on 2 pieces of bread and top it with the remaining bread.

Nutrition Per Serving:

- Calories: 380
- Fat: 22 g
- Carbs: 25.6 g
- Sugar: 3.5 g
- Fiber: 3.9 g
- Protein: 19 g
- Sodium: 609 mg

181. Rosemary Chicken

Preparation Time: 15 minutes
Cooking Time: 20 minutes
Servings: 2

Ingredients:

- 1 tablespoon extra-virgin olive oil
- 1 pound chicken breast tenders
- 1 tablespoon chopped fresh rosemary leaves
- 1/8 teaspoon ground black pepper
- 1/4 teaspoon sea salt

Directions:

1. Preheat the oven to 425°F.
2. Set the chicken tenders on a baking sheet with a rim. Sprinkle it with salt, rosemary, and pepper after brushing them with olive oil.

3. For 15-20 minutes, keep in the oven, just before the juices run clear.

Nutrition Per Serving:

- Calories: 336
- Fat: 13.13 g
- Carbs: 0.31 g
- Sugar: 0 g
- Fiber: 0.1 g
- Protein: 51 g
- Sodium: 339 mg

182. Gingered Turkey Meatballs

Preparation Time: 10 minutes
Cooking Time: 10 minutes
Servings: 2

Ingredients:

- 1/2 cup shredded cabbage
- 1/2 tablespoon grated fresh ginger
- 1/2 teaspoon onion powder
- 1 pound ground turkey
- 2 tablespoons chopped fresh cilantro leaves
- 1/2 teaspoon garlic powder
- 1/4 teaspoon sea salt
- 1 tablespoon olive oil
- A pinch of freshly ground black pepper

Directions:

1. Combine the cabbage, turkey, cilantro, ginger, onion powder, garlic powder, pepper, and salt in a big mixing bowl. Mix well. Make 10 (3/4 inch) meatballs out of the turkey mixture.

2. Heat the oil in a big non-stick skillet or pan over medium-high heat until it starts shimmering.

3. Cook for about 10 minutes, rotating the meatballs while they brown and you are done.

Nutrition Per Serving:

- Calories: 559.57
- Fat: 47.68 g
- Carbs: 4.5 g
- Sugar: 0.7 g
- Fiber: 0.74 g
- Protein: 28.8 g
- Sodium: 402.9 mg

183. Turkey and Kale Sauté

Preparation Time: 15 minutes
Cooking Time: 35 minutes
Servings: 2

Ingredients:

- 1 pound ground turkey breast
- 1/2 chopped onion
- 1/2 teaspoon sea salt
- 3 minced garlic cloves
- 1 tablespoon extra-virgin olive oil
- 1 cup stemmed and chopped kale
- 1 tablespoon fresh thyme leaves
- A pinch of freshly ground black pepper

Directions:

1. Heat the olive oil in a big non-stick skillet or pan over medium-high heat until it starts shimmering.

2. Add the turkey, onion, kale, thyme, pepper, and salt. Cook, crumbling the turkey with a spoon until it browns, for about 5 minutes.

3. Garlic can be included now. Cook for 30 minutes while continuously stirring.

Nutrition Per Serving:

- Calories: 342
- Fat: 9.58 g
- Carbs: 7 g
- Sugar: 1.8 g
- Fiber: 1.6 g
- Protein: 58.7 g
- Sodium: 600 mg

184. Turkey with Bell Peppers and Rosemary

Preparation Time: 15 minutes
Cooking Time: 10 minutes
Servings: 2

Ingredients:

- 1 chopped red bell peppers
- 1 pound boneless, skinless turkey breasts, cut into bite-size pieces
- 1/4 teaspoon sea salt
- 2 minced garlic cloves
- 2 tablespoons extra-virgin olive oil
- 1/2 chopped onion
- 1 tablespoon chopped fresh rosemary leaves
- A pinch of freshly ground black pepper

Directions:

1. Heat the olive oil in a non-stick skillet or pan over medium-high heat until it starts shimmering.

2. Add the onion, red bell peppers, rosemary turkey, salt, and pepper. Cook until the turkey is cooked and the veggies are soft.

3. Garlic can be included now—Cook for an additional 30 seconds.

Nutrition Per Serving:

- Calories: 413
- Fat: 17 g
- Carbs: 6.8 g
- Sugar: 3.3 g
- Fiber: 1.6 g
- Protein: 54 g
- Sodium: 496 mg

185. Mustard and Rosemary Pork Tenderloin

Preparation Time: 15 minutes
Cooking Time: 15 minutes
Servings: 2

Ingredients:

- 2 tablespoons Dijon mustard
- 2 tablespoons fresh rosemary leaves
- 1/4 teaspoon sea salt
- 1/2 (1 ½ pound) pork tenderloin
- 1/4 cup fresh parsley leaves
- 3 garlic cloves
- 1 ½ tablespoon extra-virgin olive oil
- 1/8 teaspoon ground black pepper

Directions:

1. Preheat the oven to 400°F.
2. Combine the mustard, parsley, garlic, olive oil, rosemary, pepper, and salt in a blender or food processor.
3. Pulse 20 times in 1-second intervals before a paste emerges.
4. Rub the tenderloin with the paste and place it on a rimmed baking sheet.
5. Bake the pork for around 15 minutes or until an instant-read meat thermometer reads 165°F.
6. Allow resting for 5 minutes before slicing and serving.

Nutrition Per Serving:

- Calories: 540.45
- Fat: 24.7 g
- Carbs: 3.24 g
- Sugar: 0.2 g
- Fiber: 0.94 g
- Protein: 72 g
- Sodium: 456.6 mg

186. Thin-Cut Pork Chops with Mustardy Kale

Preparation Time: 10 minutes
Cooking Time: 25 minutes
Servings: 2

Ingredients:

- 1 teaspoon sea salt, divided
- 2 tablespoons Dijon mustard, divided
- 1/2 finely chopped red onion
- 1 tablespoon apple cider vinegar
- 2 thin-cut pork chops
- 1/8 teaspoon ground black pepper, divided
- 1 ½ tablespoon extra-virgin olive oil
- 2 cups stemmed and chopped kale

Directions:

1. Preheat the oven to 425°F.
2. Half of salt and pepper are used to season the pork chops. Place them on a rimmed baking sheet and spread 1 tablespoon of mustard over them. Bake for 15 minutes until an instant-read meat thermometer detects a temperature of 165°F.
3. When the pork cooks, heat the olive oil in a big non-stick skillet or pan over medium-high heat until it starts shimmering.
4. Add the red onion and kale. Cook, stirring regularly, for around 7 minutes, or until the veggies soften.
5. Whisk the remaining tablespoon of mustard, the remaining half salt, the cider vinegar, and the remaining pepper in a wide mixing bowl. Toss with the kale. Cook for 2 minutes, stirring occasionally.

Nutrition Per Serving:

- Calories: 415
- Fat: 27 g
- Carbs: 7.6 g
- Sugar: 2.3 g
- Fiber: 2.8 g
- Protein: 35 g
- Sodium: 1091 mg

187. Beef Tenderloin with Savory Blueberry Sauce

Preparation Time: 10 minutes
Cooking Time: 15 minutes
Servings: 2

Ingredients:

- 1 teaspoon sea salt, divided
- 2 tablespoons extra-virgin olive oil
- 1/4 cup tawny port
- 1 ½ tablespoon very cold butter, cut into pieces
- 2 beef tenderloin fillets, about 3⁄4 inch thick
- 1/8 teaspoon ground black pepper, divided
- 1 finely minced shallot
1 cup fresh blueberries

Directions:

1. Half salt and pepper are to be used to season the beef.
2. Heat the olive oil in a big skillet or pan over medium-high heat until it starts shimmering.
3. Add the seasoned steaks to the pan. Cook per side until an instant-read meat thermometer detects an internal temperature of 130°F. Set aside on a plate of aluminum foil tented over it.
4. Get the skillet or pan back up to heat. Add the port, shallot, blueberries, and the remaining salt and pepper to the pan. Scrape some browned pieces off the bottom of the skillet or pan with a wooden spoon. Set the heat to medium-low and bring to a simmer. Cook, stirring from time to time, gently crush the blueberries for around 4 minutes or until the liquid has reduced by half.
5. Set in the butter 1 slice at a time. Toss the meat back into the skillet or pan. Mix it once with the sauce to coat it. The rest of the sauce can be spooned over the meat before serving.

Nutrition Per Serving:

- Calories: 330
- Fat: 24.3 g
- Carbs: 20.9 g
- Sugar: 8.36 g
- Fiber: 2.2 g
- Protein: 2.5 g
- Sodium: 954 mg

188. Ground Beef Chili with Tomatoes

Preparation Time: 10 minutes
Cooking Time: 15 minutes
Servings: 2

Ingredients:

- 1/2 chopped onion
- 1 (14 ounces) canned kidney beans, drained
- 1/2 pound extra-lean ground beef
- 1 (28 ounces) can chopped tomatoes, undrained
- 1/2 tablespoon chili powder
- 1/4 teaspoon sea salt
- 1/2 teaspoon garlic powder

Directions:

1. Cook the beef and onion in a big pot over medium-high heat for around 5 minutes.
2. Add the kidney beans, tomatoes, garlic powder, chili powder, salt, and stir to combine. Bring to a boil, then reduce to low heat.
3. Cook for 10 minutes, stirring occasionally.

Nutrition Per Serving:

- Calories: 355.7
- Fat: 8.77 g
- Carbs: 36.17 g
- Sugar: 3.64 g
- Fiber: 6.8 g
- Protein: 35.17 g
- Sodium: 1.2 g

189. Fish Taco Salad with Strawberry Avocado Salsa

Preparation Time: 20 minutes
Cooking Time: 15 minutes
Servings: 2

Ingredients:

For the salsa:

- 2 hulled and diced strawberries
- 1/2 diced small shallot
- 2 tablespoons finely chopped fresh cilantro
- 2 tablespoons freshly squeezed lime juice
- 1/8 teaspoon cayenne pepper
- 1/2 diced avocado
- 2 tablespoons canned black beans, well rinsed and drained
- 1 thinly sliced green onions
- 1/2 teaspoon finely chopped peeled ginger
- 1/4 teaspoon sea salt

For the fish salad:

- 1 teaspoon agave nectar
- 2 cups arugula
- 1 tablespoon extra-virgin olive or avocado oil
- 1/2 tablespoon freshly squeezed lime juice
- 1 pound light fish (halibut, cod, or red snapper), cut into 2 fillets
- 1/4 teaspoon ground black pepper
- 1/2 teaspoon sea salt

Directions:

For the salsa:

1. Preheat the grill, whether it's gas or charcoal.
2. Add the avocado, beans, strawberries, shallot, cilantro, green onions, salt, ginger, lime juice, and cayenne pepper in a medium mixing cup. Put aside after mixing until all the components are well combined.

For the fish salad:

1. Whisk the agave, oil, and lime juice in a small bowl. Set the arugula with the vinaigrette in a big mixing bowl.
2. Season the fish fillets with pepper and salt. Grill the fish for 7-9 minutes over

direct high heat, flipping once during cooking. The fish should be translucent and quickly flake.

3. Place 1 cup of arugula salad on each plate to eat. Cover each salad with a fillet and a heaping spoonful of salsa.

Nutrition Per Serving:

- Calories: 251
- Fat: 11.9 g
- Carbs: 10.16 g
- Sugar: 3.8 g
- Fiber: 3.38 g
- Protein: 24.3 g
Sodium: 813 mg

190. Beef and Bell Pepper Stir-Fry

Preparation Time: 5 minutes
Cooking Time: 10 minutes
Servings: 2

Ingredients:

- 3 scallions, white and green parts, chopped
- 1 tablespoon grated fresh ginger
- 2 minced garlic cloves
- 1/2 pound extra-lean ground beef
- 1 chopped red bell peppers
- 1/4 teaspoon sea salt

Directions:

1. Cook the beef for around 5 minutes in a big non-stick skillet or pan until it browns.

2. Add the scallions, ginger, red bell peppers, and salt. Cook, occasionally stirring, for around 4 minutes or until the bell peppers are tender.

3. Garlic can be included now. Cook for 30 seconds while continuously stirring. Switch off the flame, and you are done.

Nutrition Per Serving:

- Calories: 181
- Fat: 5.8 g
- Carbs: 6 g
- Sugar: 2.6 g
- Fiber: 1.7 g
- Protein: 25.4 g
- Sodium: 318 mg

191. Veggie Pizza with Cauliflower-Yam Crust

Preparation Time: 5 minutes
Cooking Time: 1hour 10 minutes
Servings: 2

Ingredients:

- 1/2 medium peeled and chopped garnet yam
- 1 teaspoon sea salt, divided
- 1/2 tablespoon coconut oil, plus more for greasing pizza stone
- 1/4 cup sliced cremini mushrooms
- 1/4 medium head cauliflower, cut into small florets
- 1/2 tablespoon dried Italian herbs
- 1/2 cup flour brown rice
- 1/2 sliced small red onion

- 1/2 zucchini or yellow summer squash
- 2 tablespoons vegan pesto
- 1/2 cup spinach

Directions:

1. Heat the oven to 400°F or preheat the pizza stone if you have one.

2. Set a big pot with 1 inch of water, place a steamer basket. Put yam and cauliflower in a steamer basket and steam for 15 minutes until both are quickly pricked with a fork. If you overcook the vegetables, they can get too soggy.

3. Place the vegetables in a food blender or processor and pulse until smooth. Blend in the Italian herbs and half a teaspoon of salt until smooth. Set the mixture in a big mixing bowl. Gradually whisk in the flour until it is well mixed.

4. Use coconut oil to grease the pizza stone or a pizza plate. In the middle of the pizza stone, pile the cauliflower mixture. Spread the pizza dough uniformly roundly or circularly (much like frosting) with a spatula until the crust is around 1/8 inches thick.

5. Bake for around 45 minutes. To get the top crispy, switch on the broiler and cook it for 2 minutes.

6. In a medium skillet or pan, melt the coconut oil over medium heat—Cook for 2 minutes after adding the onion. Add the squash, mushrooms, and the remaining ingredients to a large mixing bowl. Sauté for 3-4 minutes with a quarter teaspoon of salt. Detach the spinach from the heat as soon as it starts to wilt.

7. Evenly, plate the pesto around the pizza crust. Over the pesto, spread the sautéed vegetables. It's time to slice the pizza and eat it.

Nutrition Per Serving:

- Calories: 343
- Fat: 7 g
- Carbs: 63 g
- Sugar: 3.7 g
- Fiber: 7.2 g
- Protein: 7.4 g
- Sodium: 1.1 g

192. Toasted Pecan Quinoa Burgers

Preparation Time: 5 minutes
Cooking Time: 30 minutes
Servings: 2

Ingredients:

- 2 cups vegetable broth, divided
- 1 teaspoon sea salt
- 2 tablespoons sesame seeds
- 1/2 teaspoon dried oregano
- 1/4 cup canned black beans,
- 2 tablespoons pecans
- 1/2 cup quinoa, rinsed and drained
- 1/4 cup sunflower seeds
- 1/2 teaspoon ground cumin
- 1/2 shredded carrot
- Freshly ground black pepper
- 1/2 thinly sliced avocado
- 1/2 teaspoon coconut or sunflower oil

Directions:

1. Preheat the oven to 375°F.
2. Roast the pecans for 5-7 minutes on a baking sheet.
3. In a big saucepan, bring 1 cup of broth, quinoa, and salt to a boil over medium-high heat. Set the heat to a minimum, cover, and cook for 20 minutes, stirring occasionally.
4. Grind the pecans, cumin, sesame seeds, sunflower seeds, and oregano to a medium-coarse texture in a food processor.
5. Combine a half cup of quinoa, carrots, nut mixture, and beans in a big mixing bowl. Slowly pour the remaining cup of broth, constantly stirring, before the paste becomes tacky—season with pepper and salt as per taste.
6. Set the mixture into 2 (1/2-inch thick) patties and cook; refrigerate them right away.
7. In a big skillet or pan over medium-high heat, melt the coconut oil—Cook for around 2 minutes on either side. Carry on for the remaining patties in the same manner. Avocado slices can be placed on top of the burgers.

Nutrition Per Serving:

Calories: 454.89

Fat: 27 g

Carbs: 42 g

Sugar: 2.8 g

Fiber: 10 g

Protein: 14.7 g

Sodium: 1.7 g

193. Sizzling Salmon and Quinoa

Preparation Time: 10 minutes

Cooking Time: 30 minutes

Servings: 2

Ingredients:

- 1/2 teaspoon extra-virgin olive oil
- 1/2 cup quinoa, rinsed and drained
- 1/4 pound sliced chanterelle mushrooms
- 1/2 cup frozen small peas
- 1 tablespoon chopped fresh basil
- 1 head garlic
- 1 ½ cup mushroom broth, divided
- 1 tablespoon coconut oil
- 1/2 cup shredded brussels sprouts
- 1 tablespoon Nutrition Per Serving yeast
- 1/2 tablespoon dried oregano
- Sea salt and freshly ground black pepper
- 1/4 pound salmon, skin, and bones removed, cut into 1-inch cubes

Directions:

1. Preheat the oven to 350°F.
2. Detach the top of the garlic head to reveal the cloves. Cover the head in foil and drizzle with olive oil. Set in the oven for 50 minutes to roast.
3. Meanwhile, in a big saucepan, mix 1 cup of broth and the quinoa. Set to a boil over high heat, then reduce to low heat, cover, and simmer without stirring for 20 minutes. To make this dish, measure 1/4 cup of quinoa, reserving any leftovers for another use.

4. Heat the coconut oil in a big skillet or pan over medium heat. Sauté for 5 minutes or before the mushrooms release liquid and become tender.

5. Cook for 3 minutes with the brussels sprouts, adding up to 1/4 cup of broth if required to keep the mushrooms and sprouts from sticking to the skillet or pan.

6. Sauté for 5 minutes, stirring regularly, with the peas, basil, Nutrition Per Serving yeast, and oregano.

7. Toss the salmon in the pan to mix. Squeeze the garlic cloves gently into it. Cook, secured, for 4-5 minutes, stirring periodically.

8. Stir in the remaining 1/4 cup of broth and 1/4 cup of quinoa in the skillet or pan until all is well mixed—season with pepper and salt to taste.

9. Serve.

Nutrition Per Serving:

- Calories: 433
- Fat: 18 g
- Carbs: 46 g
- Sugar: 4 g
- Fiber: 8.8 g
- Protein: 22.8 g
- Sodium: 921 mg

Chapter 10

LOW RESIDUE (SNACKS)

194. Papaya-Mango Smoothie

Preparation Time: 5 minutes

Cooking Time: 0 minutes

Servings: 2

Ingredients:

- 1 cup mango, diced
- 1 cup papaya chunks
- 1 cup almond or lactose-free milk
- 1 tablespoon honey or maple syrup

Directions:

1. Blend all ingredients in a blender and then pulse until smooth.
2. Pour into a large glass. Enjoy!

Nutrition Per Serving:

- Calories: 162
- Fat: 1.86 g
- Carbs: 37.44 g
- Sugar: 33 g
- Fiber: 3 g
- Protein: 1.6 g

- Sodium: 90 mg

195. Cantaloupe Smoothie

Preparation Time: 5 minutes
Cooking Time: 0 minutes
Servings: 2

Ingredients:

- 1 cup cantaloupe, diced
- 1/2 cup vanilla yogurt or lactose-free yogurt
- 1/2 cup of orange juice
- 1 tablespoon honey or maple syrup
- 2 ice cubes

Directions:

1. Merge all ingredients in a blender and then pulse until smooth.
2. Pour into a large glass. Enjoy!

Nutrition Per Serving:

- Calories: 149
- Fat: 2.2 g
- Carbs: 30 g
- Sugar: 28 g
- Fiber: 0.87 g
- Protein: 4.1 g
- Sodium: 54 mg

196. Cantaloupe-Mix Smoothie

Preparation Time: 5-10 minutes
Cooking Time: 0 minutes
Servings: 2

Ingredients:

- 1 cup cantaloupe, diced
- 1/2 cup mango, diced
- 1/2 cup almond milk or lactose-free cow milk
- 1/2 cup of orange juice
- 2 tablespoons lemon
- 1 tablespoon honey or maple syrup
- 2 ice cubes

Directions:

1. Merge all ingredients in a blender until smooth.
2. Pour into a large glass. Enjoy!

Nutrition Per Serving:

- Calories: 142
- Fat: 1.15 g
- Carbs: 33.5 g
- Sugar: 30.33 g
- Fiber: 2.17 g
- Protein: 1.91 g
- Sodium: 55 mg

197. Applesauce-Avocado Smoothie

Preparation Time: 5-10 minutes
Cooking Time: 0 minutes
Servings: 1

Ingredients:

- 1 cup unsweetened almond or lactose-free milk
- 1/2 avocado
- 1/2 cup applesauce
- 1/4 teaspoon ground cinnamon
- 1/2 cup ice
- 1/2 teaspoon stevia or 1 tablespoon honey for sweetness (optional)

Directions:

1. Blend all ingredients in a blender. Pulse the mix until smooth.
2. Pour into a large glass. Enjoy!

Nutrition Per Serving:

- Calories: 213
- Fat: 11.2 g
- Carbs: 30 g
- Sugar: 18 g
- Fiber: 5.5 g
- Protein: 2.88 g
- Sodium: 194 mg

198. Pina Colada Smoothie

Preparation Time: 5-10 minutes
Cooking Time: 0 minutes
Servings: 1

Ingredients:

- 1 cup papaya chunks
- 1/2 cup unsweetened almond milk or lactose-free milk
- 1 banana
- 1/2 teaspoon vanilla extract, to taste
- 1 tablespoon honey, maple syrup, or 1 teaspoon stevia (optional)

Directions:

1. Blend all ingredients in a blender and then pulse until smooth and creamy.
2. Pour into a large glass. Enjoy!

Nutrition Per Serving:

- Calories: 358
- Fat: 2.23 g
- Carbs: 87g
- Sugar: 67g
- Fiber: 5.5g
- Protein: 2.8g
- Sodium: 112mg

199. Diced Fruits

Preparation Time: 10 minutes
Cooking Time: 40 minutes
Servings: 6

Ingredients:

- 4 peaches, skin removed and thinly sliced
- 1 pound apple, pitted and skin removed
- 1 teaspoon cinnamon powder
- 1 cup honey or maple syrup
- 1 teaspoon vanilla extract

Directions:

1. In a large pot, cook the fruits in boiling water over medium heat until softened.
2. In a large bowl, mix well all ingredients (except the fruits).
3. Pour the syrup over fruits and let the compote thicken.
4. Pour the compote into a jar. Serve hot or cold. Enjoy!

Nutrition Per Serving:

- Calories: 234
- Fat: 0.2 g
- Carbs: 62 g
- Fiber: 2.3 g
- Protein: 1.06 g

200. Avocado Dip

Preparation Time: 10 minutes
Cooking Time: 0 minutes
Servings: 4

Ingredients:

- 6 avocados, peeled
- 1/2 tablespoon extra-virgin olive oil
- 1/4 cup chopped fresh cilantro
- 2 tablespoons fresh lime juice
- 1 teaspoon fresh lemon juice
- 1/2 teaspoon salt

Directions:

1. In a large bowl, set avocados with a fork.
2. Add extra-virgin olive oil and the other ingredients.
3. Enjoy!

Nutrition Per Serving:

- Calories: 285
- Carbs: 14.96 g
- Protein: 3.39 g
- Fat: 26 g
- Sugar: 1 g
- Sodium: 303 mg

201. Homemade Hummus

Preparation Time: 10 minutes
Cooking Time: 60 minutes
Servings: 4

Ingredients:

- 1/4 pound dried chickpeas (soaked in water for a night)

- 11/2 tablespoon tahini
- 1 tablespoon lemon juice
- 2 tablespoons extra-virgin olive oil, divided
- 1/4 teaspoon cumin powder
- 1/2 teaspoon salt
- 1 tablespoon water
- 1 teaspoon baking soda (optional)
- 1 teaspoon paprika powder (optional)

Directions:

1. Before cooking, you will need to soak the chickpeas overnight in water and optionally add baking soda to the water.
2. Cook your chickpeas in a large pot with water over medium heat for about 1 hour. Check if they are cooked well by crushing one of them with a fork in your hand.
3. When chickpeas are cooked, drain and put them in a blender.
4. Add 1 tablespoon of extra-virgin olive oil, lemon juice, tahini, cumin powder, and salt to the blender. Blend until your hummus gets a soft, creamy texture equally.
5. Drizzle with one tablespoon of extra-virgin olive oil or paprika powder (optional).
6. Serve immediately or fridge it.

Nutrition Per Serving:

- Calories: 328
- Fat: 22 g
- Carbs: 24 g
- Sugar: 3 g
- Fiber: 4.9 g

- Protein: 11 g
- Sodium: 301.17 mg

202. Almond Butter Sandwich

Preparation Time: 10 minutes
Cooking Time: 5 minutes
Servings: 1

Ingredients:

- 2 slices white bread or gluten-free white bread
- 1 tablespoon organic smooth almond butter

Directions:

1. Set 1 piece of bread with almond butter.
2. Toast and enjoy!

Nutrition Per Serving:

- Calories: 238
- Fat: 9.9 g
- Carbs: 29 g
- Fiber: 7 g
- Protein: 9.6 g

203. Gluten-Free Muffins

Preparation Time: 15 minutes
Cooking Time: 30 minutes
Servings: 10-15

Ingredients:

- 2 tablespoons extra-virgin olive oil
- 2 ½ cups almond flour, blanched

- 3 large organic free-range eggs
- 1/4 cup organic maple syrup
- 2 teaspoons vanilla extract
- 1/4 cup banana, mashed
- 1 teaspoon lemon juice
- 3/4 teaspoon baking soda
- 1/4 teaspoon cinnamon powder
- 1/2 teaspoon salt

Nutrition Per Serving:

- Calories: 143
- Fat: 10.9 g
- Carbs: 7.8 g
- Sugar: 4 g
- Fiber: 2 g
- Protein: 4.7 g
- Sodium: 92 mg

Directions:

1. Preheat your oven to 375°F.
2. In a bowl, set almond flour, cinnamon, baking soda, and salt. Mix well.
3. Add extra-virgin olive oil, vanilla extract, eggs, ripe banana, maple syrup, and lemon juice in another bowl. Whisk well.
4. Mix both bowls and stir with a wooden spoon until the flour is mixed well with the other ingredients.
5. Prepare 10 muffin cups. Pour them to the top and then bake for 15 minutes.
6. To avoid browning quickly, loosely cover muffins with aluminum foil. Cook for another 15 minutes.
7. Put a toothpick in a muffin to check if it cooks well or not. If cooked well, the toothpick should not stick to the muffin.
8. Remove from the oven. Let the muffins cool for 15 more minutes. Enjoy!

Chapter 11

HIGH-FIBER (BREAKFAST)

204. Baked Oatmeal

Preparation Time: 10 minutes
Cooking Time: 30 minutes
Servings: 6

Ingredients:

- 1/2 cup (125 g) applesauce
- 3/4 cup (170 g) brown sugar
- 2 eggs
- 1 cup (235 ml) skim milk
- 3 cups (240 g) quick-cooking oats
- 2 teaspoons baking powder
- 1/2 teaspoon cinnamon
- 1 cup (80 g) chopped walnuts

Directions:

1. Combine the applesauce, sugar, eggs, and milk; mix well.
2. Merge remaining ingredients and then combine with the first mixture.

3. Bake in a 9 x 13-inch (23 x 33 cm) pan coated with non-stick vegetable oil spray for 30 minutes at 350ºF (180ºC, gas mark 4). Serve with hot milk.

Nutrition Per Serving:

- Calories: 397
- Fat: 12 g
- Carbs: 62 g
- Sugar: 33 g
- Fiber: 5 g
- Protein: 10.6 g

205. Homestyle Pancake Mix

Preparation Time: 10 minutes
Cooking Time: 30 minutes
Servings: 16

Ingredients:

- 6 cups whole-wheat pastry flour
- 1 ½ cups (210 g) cornmeal
- 1/2 cup (100 g) sugar
- 11/2 cups (102 g) non-fat dry milk
- 2 tablespoons (28 g) baking powder

Directions:

1. Merge all ingredients and store them in a tightly covered jar. To cook, attach 1 cup of water to 1 cup of the mix; use less water if you want a thicker pancake. Stir until lumps disappear.

2. Coat a non-stick skillet or griddle with non-stick vegetable oil spray and preheat until drops of cold water bounce and sputter.

3. Drop the batter to the desired size and cook until bubbles form and edges begin to dry. Turn only once.

Nutrition Per Serving:

- Calories: 264
- Carbs: 53.67 g
- Protein: 9.16 g
- Fat: 0.9 g
- Sugar: 11.4 g
- Sodium: 222 mg

206. Multigrain Pancakes

Preparation Time: 10 minutes
Cooking Time: 30 minutes
Servings: 6

Ingredients:

- 1 ½ cup whole-wheat pastry flour
- 1/4 cup (35 g) cornmeal
- 1/4 cup (20 g) rolled oats
- 2 tablespoons oat bran
- 2 tablespoons wheat germ
- 2 tablespoons (18 g) toasted wheat cereal, such as Wheatena
- 1 teaspoon baking soda
- 1/2 teaspoon baking powder
- 1 teaspoon vanilla extract
- 11/2 cups (355 ml) skim milk
- 2 egg whites

Directions:

1. Mix all dry ingredients. Add milk to make the batter. The thicker batter makes

thicker pancakes. Put aside to rest for half an hour. Beat the egg whites until stiff peaks form.

2. Gently fold into the batter after it has rested. Spoon onto the moderate griddle and cook until bubbles break. Turn and cook until done. Bake more slowly than with regular pancakes because of the heavy batter.

Nutrition Per Serving:

- Calories: 256.95
- Fat: 1.9 g
- Carbs: 44.8 g
- Sugar: 12 g
- Fiber: 5.4 g
- Protein: 15 g
- Sodium: 159 mg

207. Cinnamon–Oat Bran Pancakes

Preparation Time: 10 minutes
Cooking Time: 30 minutes
Servings: 6

Ingredients:

- 3/4 cup (75 g) oat bran
- 3/4 cup whole-wheat pastry flour
- 1 tablespoon sugar
- 1/2 teaspoon baking powder
- 1/2 teaspoon cinnamon
- 1/4 teaspoon baking soda
- 1 ¼ cup (295 ml) buttermilk
- 1 tablespoon (15 ml) canola oil
- 1/2 cup (55 g) finely chopped pecans

Directions:

1. In a mixing bowl, mix all dry ingredients. Set aside.
2. In another mixing bowl, combine the buttermilk and oil. Add to dry ingredients, stirring until just combined. Stir in the pecans.
3. Cook on the hot grill. Set 1/4 cup of the batter for each pancake.

Nutrition Per Serving:

- Calories: 209.78
- Fat: 11.6 g
- Carbs: 25.4 g
- Sugar: 5.6 g
- Fiber: 4.9 g
- Protein: 6.6 g
- Sodium: 94.8 mg

208. Whole-Wheat Buttermilk Pancakes

Preparation Time: 10 minutes
Cooking Time: 30 minutes
Servings: 6

Ingredients:

- 1 cup whole-wheat flour
- 1/2 teaspoon baking soda
- 1/4 teaspoon cinnamon
- 1 ¼ cup (295 ml) buttermilk
- 2 eggs
- 3 tablespoons (45 ml) canola oil

Directions:

1. Blend all dry ingredients. Merge the wet ingredients except for oil.
2. Mix both mixtures. It will be slightly lumpy—heat oil in a cast-iron skillet.
3. Pour 1/4 of the butter into the pan. When the pancake bubbles, turn and cook for 1-2 minutes more.

Nutrition Per Serving:

- Calories: 183
- Fat: 10.31 g
- Carbs: 18.5 g
- Sugar: 2.7 g
- Fiber: 2.8 g
- Protein: 5.5 g
- Sodium: 75.3 mg

209. Cornmeal Pancakes

Preparation Time: 10 minutes
Cooking Time: 30 minutes
Servings: 6

Ingredients:

- 1 cup (235 ml) boiling water
- 3/4 cup (105 g) cornmeal
- 1 ¼ cup (295 ml) buttermilk
- 2 eggs
- 1 cup whole-wheat pastry flour
- 1 tablespoon baking powder
- 1/4 teaspoon baking soda
- 1/4 cup (60 ml) canola oil

Directions:

1. Pour water over the cornmeal, stir until thick. Add the buttermilk; beat in the eggs: mix flour, baking powder, and baking soda.
2. Add to the cornmeal mixture. Stir in canola oil—Bake on a hot grill.

Nutrition Per Serving:

- Calories: 272.3
- Fat: 12.8 g
- Carbs: 31.8 g
- Sugar: 3.4 g
- Fiber: 3.35 g
- Protein: 7.39 g
- Sodium: 320 mg

210. Oven-Baked Pancake

Preparation Time: 10 minutes
Cooking Time: 30 minutes
Servings: 6

Ingredients:

- 3 eggs
- 1/2 cup whole-wheat pastry flour
- 1/2 cup (120 ml) skim milk
- 1/4 cup (55 g) unsalted butter, divided
- 2 tablespoons (26 g) sugar
- 2 tablespoons (18 g) slivered almonds, toasted
- 2 tablespoons (30 ml) lemon juice

Directions:

1. Set the eggs with an electric mixer at medium speed until well blended. Gradually add flour, beating until smooth. Add milk and 2 tablespoons (28 g) melted butter; beat until the batter is smooth.

2. Pour the batter into a 10-inch (25 cm) skillet coated with non-stick vegetable oil spray. Bake at 400ºF for 15 minutes until the pancake is puffed and golden brown.

3. Sprinkle it with sugar and toasted almonds. Combine the remaining butter and lemon juice; heat until butter melts. Serve over the hot pancake.

Nutrition Per Serving:

- Calories: 176.57
- Fat: 11.27 g
- Carbs: 13.8 g
- Sugar: 5.98 g
- Fiber: 1.27 g
- Protein: 5.55 g

211. Baked Pancake

Preparation Time: 10 minutes
Cooking Time: 30 minutes
Servings: 4

Ingredients:

- 1 ½ cup whole-wheat pastry flour
- 1 ½ cup (355 ml) skim milk
- 4 eggs, slightly beaten
- 1/4 cup (55 g) unsalted butter
- 1 cup (170 g) sliced strawberries

Directions:

1. Gradually, add flour and milk to the eggs. Melt the butter in a 9 x 13-inch (23 x 33 cm) pan.

2. Pour the batter over melted butter—Bake at 400ºF for about 30 minutes.

Serve with fresh sliced strawberries.

Nutrition Per Serving:

- Calories: 373.05
- Fat: 16.4 g
- Carbs: 40.81 g
- Sugar: 8 g
- Fiber: 6.8 g
- Protein: 15.16 g
- Sodium: 105 mg

212. Wheat Waffles

Preparation Time: 10 minutes
Cooking Time: 30 minutes
Servings: 8

Ingredients:

- 2 cups whole-wheat pastry flour
- 4 teaspoons (18 g) baking powder
- 2 tablespoons (40 g) honey
- 1 ¾ cup (410 ml) skim milk
- 4 tablespoons (60 ml) canola oil
- 2 eggs

Directions:

1. Mix all dry ingredients. Stir in the remaining ingredients. For lighter waffles,

separate the eggs. Beat the egg whites and carefully fold in.

2. Set into a waffle iron coated with non-stick vegetable oil spray.

Nutrition Per Serving:

- Calories: 221.87
- Fat: 8.52 g
- Carbs: 29.36 g
- Sugar: 7.7 g
- Fiber: 4 g
- Protein: 7.29 g
- Sodium: 279 mg

213. Oatmeal Waffles

Preparation Time: 10 minutes

Cooking Time: 30 minutes

Servings: 5

Ingredients:

- 1 ½ cup whole-wheat pastry flour
- 1 cup (80 g) quick-cooking oats
- 1 tablespoon baking powder
- 1 teaspoon cinnamon
- 2 tablespoons (30 g) brown sugar
- 3 tablespoons (42 g) unsalted butter
- 1 ½ cup (355 ml) skim milk
- 2 eggs, slightly beaten

Directions:

1. In a bowl, merge all dry ingredients and set aside. Melt the butter, add milk and eggs. Mix well and then add to the flour mixture. Stir until well blended.

2. Set into a waffle iron coated with non-stick vegetable oil spray.

Nutrition Per Serving:

- Calories: 330.38
- Fat: 10.3 g
- Carbs: 47.91 g
- Sugar: 10 g
- Fiber: 6.6 g
- Protein: 12 g

214. Bran Applesauce Muffins

Preparation Time: 10 minutes

Cooking Time: 30 minutes

Servings: 12

Ingredients:

- 3/4 cup (30 g) bran flakes cereal, crushed
- 1/2 cup (100 g) sugar
- 1 teaspoon baking soda
- 1 teaspoon cinnamon
- 1/2 teaspoon nutmeg
- 1 cup (245 g) applesauce
- 1/2 cup (120 ml) canola oil
- 1 teaspoon vanilla extract
- 2 eggs
- 1/2 cup (75 g) raisins
- 1 tablespoon sugar
- 1/2 teaspoon cinnamon

Directions:

1. Heat the oven to 400ºF. Set 12 muffin cups with baking paper or sprinkle with non-stick vegetable oil spray.

2. Combine all ingredients in a bowl except the sugar and cinnamon; mix well. Set the batter into the prepared muffin cups, filling 2/3 full. In a bowl, combine the sugar and cinnamon; sprinkle over the top of each muffin. Bake at 400ºF for 20 minutes or until a toothpick inserted in the center comes out clean. Immediately remove from the pan. Serve warm.

Nutrition Per Serving:

- Calories: 170.5
- Fat: 9.9 g
- Carbs: 20.44 g
- Sugar: 16.6 g
- Fiber: 1.14 g
- Protein: 1.41 g
- Sodium: 25.41 mg

215. Oat Bran Muffins

Preparation Time: 10 minutes
Cooking Time: 15-17 minutes
Servings: 12

Ingredients:

- 2 ¼ cup (225 g) oat bran
- 1 tablespoon baking powder
- 1/4 cup (35 g) raisins
- 1/4 cup (28 g) chopped pecans
- 2 eggs
- 2 tablespoons (28 ml) olive oil
- 1/4 cup (85 g) honey
- 1 ¼ cup (295 ml) water

Directions:

1. Heat the oven to 425ºF. Put all dry ingredients, raisins, and pecans in a mixing bowl.
2. Beat the eggs, olive oil, honey, and water lightly.
3. Attach this mixture to the dry ingredients and stir until moistened. Line muffin pans with paper liners or spray with non-stick vegetable oil spray and fill about half full. Bake for 15-17 minutes.

Nutrition Per Serving:

- Calories: 124.5
- Fat: 6.08 g
- Carbs: 21 g
- Sugar: 7.9 g
- Fiber: 3.2 g
- Protein: 4.4 g
- Sodium: 134 mg

216. Orange Bran Muffins

Preparation Time: 10 minutes
Cooking Time: 25 minutes
Servings: 12

Ingredients:

- 2 ½ cups (300 g) whole-wheat pastry flour
- 1 tablespoon baking soda
- 3 cups (177 g) raisin bran cereal
- 1/2 cup (100 g) sugar
- 1 teaspoon cinnamon
- 1 ½ tablespoon orange peel
- 2 cups (460 g) plain fat-free yogurt

- 2 eggs, beaten
- 1/2 cup (120 ml) cooking oil

- 1 teaspoon black pepper
- 1 cup (235 ml) water

Directions:

1. In a bowl, merge flour and baking soda. Add the cereal, sugar, cinnamon, and orange peel, mixing well.
2. Briefly, but thoroughly mix in the yogurt, beaten eggs, and cooking oil. Set into muffin tins lined with paper liners or sprayed with non-stick vegetable oil spray.
3. Bake for 20 minutes in a 375ºF (190ºC, gas mark 5) oven.

Nutrition Per Serving:

- Calories: 284
- Fat: 11 g
- Carbs: 41.6 g
- Sugar: 16 g
- Fiber: 5.5 g
- Protein: 7.5 g

217. Pasta Fritters

Preparation Time: 10 minutes
Cooking Time: 30 minutes
Servings: 6

Ingredients:

- 2 cups (280 g) leftover spaghetti
- 1/4 cup (25 g) chopped scallions
- 1/2 cup (56 g) shredded zucchini
- 78 ml canola oil
- 1 egg
- 1 cup whole-wheat pastry flour

Directions:

1. About 35 minutes before serving, coarsely chop the cooked spaghetti, onions, and shred zucchini; set aside. In a 12-inch (30 cm) skillet, heat canola oil until very hot over high heat.
2. Meanwhile, prepare the batter. Mix the egg, flour, pepper, and water in a bowl with a wire whisk or fork.
3. Stir in the spaghetti mixture. Drop it into hot oil in the skillet by 1/4 cup into 4 mounds about 2 inches (5 cm) apart. With a spatula, flatten each to make a 3-inch (7.5 cm) pancake.
4. Set the fritters until golden brown on both sides; drain them on paper towels. Keep warm. Repeat with the remaining mixture, adding more oil to the skillet if needed.

Nutrition Per Serving:

- Calories: 365
- Fat: 13.5 g
- Carbs: 50.3 g
- Fiber: 4.4 g
- Protein: 9.89 g

218. Cinnamon Honey Scones

Preparation Time: 10 minutes
Cooking Time: 20 minutes
Servings: 5

Ingredients:

- 1 ¾ cup (220 g) whole-wheat pastry flour
- 1 ½ teaspoon baking powder
- 1/4 teaspoon cinnamon
- 6 tablespoons (85 g) unsalted butter, softened
- 1 tablespoon (20 g) honey
- 1/2 cup (120 ml) skim milk
- 1 egg

Directions:

1. Heat the oven to 450ºF. Line a baking sheet with aluminum foil.
2. In a bowl, merge the flour, baking powder, and cinnamon with a wooden spoon. Work the butter into the mixture by hand until it is yellow.

Add honey and milk, then the egg. Using a wooden spoon, stir until thoroughly mixed.

3. Scoop a spoonful of dough and drop it onto the baking sheet. Leave 1 inch (2.5 cm) between each. Bake for 15 minutes or until golden brown. Cool for 5 minutes.

Nutrition Per Serving:

- Calories: 318
- Fat: 15.4 g
- Carbs: 37.2 g
- Sugar: 5.9 g
- Fiber: 5.93 g

- Protein: 8 g
- Sodium: 171 mg

219. Oatmeal Raisin Scones

Preparation Time: 10 minutes
Cooking Time: 20-25 minutes
Servings: 10

Ingredients:

- 2 cups whole-wheat pastry flour
- 3 tablespoons (45 g) brown sugar
- 1 teaspoon baking powder
- 1/2 teaspoon baking soda
- 1/2 cup unsalted butter, chilled
- 1 ½ cup (120 g) rolled oats
- 1/2 cup (75 g) raisins
- 1 cup (235 ml) buttermilk
- 2 tablespoons cinnamon
- 2 tablespoons (26 g) sugar

Directions:

1. Heat the oven to 375ºF. Merge flour, brown sugar, baking powder, and baking soda. Divide in the butter until the mixture resembles coarse crumbs.
2. Stir in oats and raisins. Add the buttermilk and mix with a fork until the dough forms a ball. Set out on a lightly floured board and knead for 6-8 minutes. Pat the dough into 1/2-inch (1 cm) thickness. Divide 8-10 rounds or wedges and place them on an ungreased baking sheet. Sprinkle it with sugar and cinnamon.

Bake for 20-25 minutes.

Nutrition Per Serving:

- Calories: 280.9
- Fat: 10.9 g
- Carbs: 41.33 g
- Sugar: 13.55 g
- Fiber: 5 g
- Protein: 5.9 g
- Sodium: 430 mg

220. Whole Grain Scones

Preparation Time: 10 minutes
Cooking Time: 30 minutes
Servings: 5

Ingredients:

- 1 egg
- 1/2 cup (100 g) sugar
- 5 tablespoons (75 ml) canola oil
- teaspoon lemon peel
- 1/2 cup (40 g) rolled oats
- 1/4 cup (25 g) wheat bran
- 1 ½ cup whole-wheat pastry flour
- 2 tablespoons poppy seeds
- 1 tablespoon baking powder
- 1/2 teaspoon cinnamon
- 1/2 cup (120 ml) skim milk

Lemon Topping:

- 3 tablespoons (45 ml) lemon juice
- 1/4 cup (25 g) confectioners' sugar

Directions:

1. Heat the oven to 375ºF. Set the egg, sugar, and oil together in a bowl. Mix the lemon peel and all the dry ingredients in a separate bowl. Stir using a wooden spoon until all of them are dispersed evenly.
2. Slowly, add the dry ingredients into the egg, sugar, and oil. Mix to create a thick dough. Add the milk and mix well. Coat a baking sheet with non-stick vegetable oil spray
3. Bake until the crust is barely golden brown and the dough is dry. Detach from the oven and let cool for 10 minutes. Mix the lemon topping ingredients with a fork until the sugar is completely melded in—drizzle 1 tablespoon over each scone.

Nutrition Per Serving:

- Calories: 433.9
- Fat: 17 g
- Carbs: 63.8 g
- Sugar: 27 g
- Fiber: 8.6 g
- Protein: 9.25 g
- Sodium: 317 mg

221. Toasty Nut Granola

Preparation Time: 10 minutes
Cooking Time: 35 minutes
Servings: 30

Ingredients:

- 6 cups (480 g) rolled oats
- 1 cup (110 g) chopped pecans
- 3/4 cup (84 g) wheat germ

- 1/2 cup (115 g) firmly packed brown sugar
- 1/2 cup (40 g) shredded coconut
- 1/2 cup (72 g) sesame seeds
- 1/2 cup (120 ml) canola oil
- 1/2 cup (170 g) honey
- 1 ½ teaspoon vanilla extract

Directions:

1. Toast the oats in a 9 x 13-inch (23 x 33 cm) pan at 350ºF (180ºC, gas mark 4) for 10 minutes.
2. Merge the remaining ingredients in a large bowl and add the toasted oats.
3. Bake on 2 baking sheets at 350ºF (180ºC, gas mark 4) for 20-25 minutes. Stir when cool and store in the refrigerator.

Nutrition Per Serving:

- Calories: 184
- Fat: 9.9 g
- Carbs: 21.8 g
- Sugar: 8.8 g
- Fiber: 2.8 g
- Protein: 3.69 g
- Sodium: 4.18 mg

222. Breakfast Bars

Preparation Time: 10 minutes
Cooking Time: 30 minutes
Servings: 30

Ingredients:

- 1 cup (80 g) quick-cooking oats
- 1/2 cup whole-wheat flour
- 1/2 cup (58 g) crunchy wheat-barley cereal, such as Grape-Nuts
- 1/2 teaspoon cinnamon
- 1 egg
- 1/4 cup (60 g) applesauce
- 1/4 cup (85 g) honey
- 3 tablespoons (45 g) brown sugar
- 2 tablespoons (28 ml) canola oil
- 1/4 cup (36 g) sunflower seeds, unsalted
- 1/4 cup (30 g) chopped walnuts
- 7 ounces (198 g) dried fruit

Directions:

1. Heat the oven to 325ºF. Set a 9-inch (23 cm) square baking pan with aluminum foil. Spray the foil with non-stick vegetable oil.
2. In a medium bowl, stir together the flour, oats, cinnamon, and cereal. Add the applesauce, egg, brown sugar, honey, and oil. Merge well.
3. Using a wooden spoon, stir in the sunflower seeds, walnuts, and dried fruit. Spread the mixture evenly in the prepared pan.
4. Bake for 30 minutes or 'till firm and lightly browned around the edges. Let it cool. Use the foil to remove from the pan. Cut into bars and store in the refrigerator.

Nutrition Per Serving:

- Calories: 80
- Fat: 2.58g
- Carbs: 13.8g
- Sugar: 4.6 g
- Fiber: 1.56 g
- Protein: 1.51 g

223. Whole-Wheat Coffee Cake

Preparation Time: 10 minutes
Cooking Time: 30-45 minutes
Servings: 12

Ingredients:

For the cake:

- 1 ¾ cup (210 g) whole-wheat pastry flour
- 1 teaspoon baking powder
- 1 teaspoon baking soda
- 1/2 cup (112 g) unsalted butter, softened
- 1 cup (133 g) sugar
- 2 eggs
- 1 teaspoon vanilla extract
- 1 cup (230 g) sour cream

For the Bran Nut Filling:

- 1 cup (75 g) packed brown sugar
- 1/2 cup bran flakes (20 g) cereal
- 1/2 cup (60 g) chopped walnuts
- 1 teaspoon cinnamon

Directions:

For the cake:

1. Merge flour, baking powder, and baking soda; set aside.
2. Beat the butter, sugar, eggs, and vanilla until light and fluffy in a large bowl. At low speed, stir in the sour cream alternately with the flour mixture until blended.

For the Bran Nut Filling:

1. Stir all filling ingredients in a small bowl. To assemble the cake, spread 1/3 of the sour cream mixture in a 9-inch (23 cm) square pan coated with non-stick vegetable oil spray.
2. Sprinkle on about 1/2 cup of the filling. Repeat layering twice. Bake in a preheated oven at 350ºF (180C, gas mark 4) for 30-45 minutes. Cool slightly.

Nutrition Per Serving:

- Calories: 286
- Fat: 15g
- Carbs: 33.4g
- Sugar: 18g
- Fiber: 3g
- Protein: 4.7g

224. Crunchy Breakfast Topping

Preparation Time: 10 minutes
Cooking Time: 30 minutes
Servings: 12

Ingredients:

- 1/4 cup (55 g) unsalted butter
- 1 ¼ cup (140 g) wheat germ
- 1/2 cup packed brown sugar
- 1/2 cup (47 g) ground almonds
- 1 tablespoon grated orange peel
- 1/2 teaspoon cinnamon

Directions:

1. Melt the butter in a 9 x 13-inch (23 x 33 cm) baking pan into the oven for about 4 minutes.
2. Add the remaining ingredients and mix well. Bake until deep golden brown. Stir.

Cool and store in the refrigerator for up to 3 months.

Nutrition Per Serving:

- Calories: 132
- Fat: 6 g
- Carbs: 14.5 g
- Fiber: 1.9 g
- Protein: 3.81 g

225. Vegetables and Fruits Breakfast

Preparation Time: 10 minutes
Cooking Time: 55 minutes
Servings: 6

Ingredients:

- 1/4 cup (60 ml) olive oil
- 2 baking potatoes, peeled and thinly sliced
- 1 cup (160 g) thinly sliced onion
- 2 cups (226 g) thinly sliced zucchini
- 1 cup red bell pepper, cut in 1/2-inch (1 cm) cubes
- 1 cup green bell pepper, cut in 1/2-inch (1 cm) cubes
- 12 eggs
- 2 tablespoons chopped fresh parsley
- Salt and pepper

Directions:

1. Heat the oven to 450°F. Pour oil into a 12-inch (30 cm) square or round baking dish. Heat oil in the oven for 5 minutes and then remove.

2. Place potatoes and onion over the bottom of the dish and bake until potatoes are just tender, 20 minutes.

3. Arrange zucchini slices over potatoes and onion, then sprinkle peppers overall—set eggs and season with salt and pepper.

4. Add the chopped parsley to the eggs. Pour the eggs over vegetables—Bake for about 25 minutes. The top should be golden brown. Serve hot or at room temperature.

Nutrition Per Serving:

- Calories: 276
- Fat: 18 g
- Carbs: 15.6 g
- Sugar: 4.4 g
- Fiber: 3.11 g
- Protein: 13 g

226. Cinnamon Apple Omelet

Preparation Time: 10 minutes
Cooking Time: 30 minutes
Servings: 2

Ingredients:

1. 4 teaspoons unsalted butter, divided
2. 1 apple, peeled and thinly sliced
3. 1/2 teaspoon cinnamon
4. 1 tablespoon (15 g) brown sugar
5. 3 eggs
6. 1 tablespoon cream
7. 1 tablespoon sour cream

Directions:

1. Melt two teaspoons of butter in a pan. Add apple, cinnamon, and brown sugar.
2. Sauté until tender. Pour into a bowl and set aside. Clean the skillet.
3. Whip the eggs and cream until fluffy; set aside. Melt the remaining butter and pour in the egg mixture.
4. Cook as you would for an omelet. When the eggs are ready to flip, turn them. Add the sour cream to the center of the eggs and top that with the apple mixture. Fold it onto a plate.

Nutrition Per Serving:

- Calories: 262
- Fat: 17 g
- Carbs: 19 g
- Sugar: 16 g
- Fiber: 1 g
- Protein: 8.9 g
- Sodium: 101 mg

227. Vitamins Packed Green Juice

Preparation Time: 10 minutes
Cooking Time: 0 minutes
Servings: 2

Ingredients:

- 6 pears, cored and chopped
- 3 celery stalks
- 3 cup fresh kale
- 2 tbsp. fresh parsley

Directions:

1. Put all the ingredients in a blender and pulse until well combined.
2. Through a cheesecloth-lined strainer, strain the juice and transfer into 2 glasses. Serve immediately.

Nutrition Per Serving:

- Calories: 288
- Carbohydrates: 71.5g
- Protein: 5.1g
- Fat: 1.59g
- Sugar: 41.2g
- Sodium: 90 mg
- Fiber: 15.2g

228. Healthier Breakfast Juice

Preparation Time: 10 minutes
Cooking Time: 0 minutes
Servings: 2

Ingredients:

- 2 large Granny Smith apples, cored and sliced
- 4 medium carrots, peeled and chopped
- 2 medium grapefruit, peeled and seeded
- 1 cup fresh kale
- 1 tsp. fresh lemon juice

Directions:

1. Place all the ingredients in a blender and pulse until well combined.
2. Through a cheesecloth-lined strainer, strain the juice and transfer into 2 glasses.

3. Serve immediately.

Nutrition Per Serving:

- Calories: 219.3
- Carbohydrates: 52g
- Protein: 4.2g
- Fat: 1.07g
- Sugar: 34.1g
- Sodium: 89mg
- Fiber: 11.7g

229. Summer Perfect Smoothie

Preparation Time: 10 minutes
Cooking Time: 0 minutes
Servings: 2

Ingredients:

- 2 cup frozen peaches, pitted
- ½ cup rolled oats
- ¼ tsp. ground cinnamon
- 1½ cup plain yogurt
- ½ cup fresh orange Juice

Directions:

1. In a blender, add all the ingredients and pulse until smooth and creamy.
2. Transfer the smoothie into 2 serving glasses and serve immediately.

Nutrition Per Serving:

- Calories: 296.3
- Carbohydrates: 45.3g
- Protein: 11g
- Fat: 7.7g
- Sugar: 23g
- Sodium: 86mg
- Fiber: 4.8g

Chapter 12

HIGH-FIBER (LUNCH)

230. Secretly Amazing Salad

Preparation Time: 15 minutes

Cooking Time: 35 minutes

Servings: 6

Ingredients:

For Lentils:

- 4 cup water
- 2 cup dried green lentils, rinsed

- 2 large garlic cloves, halved lengthwise
- 2 tbsp. olive oil

For Dressing:

- 1 garlic clove, minced
- ¼ cup fresh lemon juice
- 2 tbsp. olive oil
- 1 tsp. maple syrup
- 1 tsp. Dijon mustard

- Salt and freshly ground black pepper, to taste

For Salad:

- 1½ (15-oz.) cans chickpeas, rinsed and drained
- 2 large avocados, peeled, pitted, and chopped
- 2 cup radishes, trimmed and sliced
- ¼ cup fresh mint leaves, chopped

Directions:

1. For lentils: in a medium pot, add all ingredients over medium-high heat and bring to a boil.
2. Reduce the heat to very low and simmer for about 25-35 minutes or until the lentils are cooked through and tender.
3. Drain the water from the lentils and discard the garlic cloves.
4. For the dressing: add all ingredients in a small bowl and beat until well combined.
5. Add lentils, chickpeas, radishes, avocados, and mint in a large serving bowl and mix.
6. Add the dressing and toss to coat well.
7. Serve immediately.

Nutrition Per Serving:

- Calories: 431
- Carbohydrates: 60.5g
- Protein: 20.2g
- Fat: 14.36g
- Sugar: 6g
- Sodium: 319mg
- Fiber: 17.8g

231. Crowd Pleasing Salad

Preparation Time: 15 minutes
Cooking Time: 0 minutes
Servings: 5

Ingredients:

- 2 cup cooked quinoa
- 2 cup canned red kidney beans, well rinsed and drained
- 5 cup fresh baby spinach
- ¼ cup tomatoes, peeled, seeded, and chopped
- ¼ cup fresh dill, chopped
- ¼ cup fresh parsley, chopped
- 3 tbsp. fresh lemon juice
- Salt and freshly ground black pepper, to taste

Directions:

1. In a large bowl, add all the ingredients and toss to coat well.

Serve immediately.

Nutrition Per Serving:

- Calories: 185.5
- Carbohydrates: 32.7g
- Protein: 9.77g
- Fat: 2.3g
- Sugar: 3.8g;
- Sodium: 343mg;
- Fiber: 6.7g

232. Great Luncheon Salad

Preparation Time: 20 minutes
Cooking Time: 5 minutes
Servings: 4

Ingredients:

For Salad:

- ½ cup homemade vegetable broth
- ½ cup couscous
- 3 cup canned red kidney beans, well rinsed and drained
- 2 large tomatoes, peeled, seeded, and chopped
- 5 cup fresh spinach, torn

For Dressing:

- 1 garlic clove, minced
- 2 tbsp. shallots, minced
- 2 tsp. lemon zest, grated finely
- ¼ cup fresh lemon juice
- 2 tbsp. extra-virgin olive oil
- Salt and freshly ground black pepper, to taste

Directions:

2. In a pan, add the broth over medium heat and bring to a boil.
3. Add the couscous and stir to combine.
4. Put the lid on the pan and immediately remove it from the heat.
5. Set aside, covered for about 5-10 minutes or until all the liquid is absorbed.
6. For the salad: in a large bowl, add the couscous and remaining ingredients and stir to combine.

7. For the dressing: in another small bowl, add all the ingredients and beat until well combined.
8. Pour the dressing over the salad and gently toss to coat well.
9. Serve immediately.

Nutrition Per Serving:

- Calories: 341
- Carbohydrates: 51.2g
- Protein: 15.7g
- Fat: 8.5g
- Sugar: 6.6g
- Sodium: 613mg
- Fiber: 10.2g

233. Flavors Powerhouse Lunch Meal

Preparation Time: 15 minutes
Cooking Time: 0 minutes
Servings: 2

Ingredients:

- 1 large avocado
- 1¼ cup cooked chickpeas
- ¼ cup celery stalks, chopped
- 1 scallion (greed part), sliced
- 1 small garlic clove, minced
- 1½ tbsp. fresh lemon juice
- ½ tsp. olive oil
- Salt and freshly ground black pepper, to taste
- 1 tbsp. fresh cilantro, chopped

Directions:

1. Cut the avocado in half and then remove the pit.
2. With a spoon, scoop out the flesh from each avocado half.
3. Then, cut half of the avocado flesh into equal-sized cubes.
4. Add avocado cubes and remaining ingredients in a large bowl except for sunflower seeds and cilantro and toss to coat well.
5. Stuff each avocado half with chickpeas mixture evenly.
6. Serve immediately with the garnishing of cilantro.

Nutrition Per Serving:

- Calories: 324.6
- Carbohydrates: 41.8g
- Protein: 12.6g
- Fat: 13.7g
- Sugar: 7g
- Sodium: 413 mg
- Fiber: 13.8g

234. Mexican Enchiladas

Preparation Time: 15 minutes
Cooking Time: 20 minutes
Servings: 8

Ingredients:

- 1 (14-oz.) can red beans, drained, rinsed, and mashed
- 2 cup cheddar cheese, grated
- 2 cup tomato sauce

- ½ cup onion, chopped
- ¼ cup black olives, pitted and sliced
- 2 tsp. garlic salt
- 8 whole-wheat tortillas

Directions:

1. Preheat the oven to 350 degrees F.
2. Add the mashed beans, cheese, 1 cup of tomato sauce, onions, olives, and garlic salt in a medium bowl and mix well.
3. Place about 1/3 cup of the bean mixture along the center of each tortilla.
4. Roll up each tortilla and place enchiladas in a large baking dish.
5. Place the remaining tomato sauce on top of the filled tortillas.
6. Bake for about 15-20 minutes.
7. Serve warm.

Nutrition Per Serving:

- Calories: 305
- Carbohydrates: 30.4g
- Protein: 13.8g
- Fat: 14.7g
- Sugar: 4.9g

Sodium: 1.1g
Fiber: 6.8g

235. Unique Banana Curry

Preparation Time: 15 minutes
Cooking Time: 15 minutes
Servings: 3

Ingredients:

- 2 tbsp. olive oil

- 2 yellow onions, chopped
- 8 garlic cloves, minced
- 2 tbsp. curry powder
- 1 tbsp. ground ginger
- 1 tbsp. ground cumin
- 1 tsp. ground turmeric
- 1 tsp. ground cinnamon
- 1 tsp. red chili powder
- Salt and freshly ground black pepper, to taste
- 2/3 cup plain yogurt
- 1 cup tomato puree
- 2 bananas, peeled and sliced
- 3 tomatoes, peeled, seeded, and chopped finely

Directions:

1. Heat the oil over medium heat and sauté onion for about 4-5 minutes in a large pan.
2. Add the garlic, curry powder, and spices, and sauté for about 1 minute.
3. Add the yogurt and tomato sauce and bring to a gentle boil.
4. Stir in the bananas and simmer for about 3 minutes.
5. Stir in the tomatoes and simmer for about 1-2 minutes.
6. Remove from the heat and serve hot.

Nutrition Per Serving:

- Calories: 310.8
- Carbohydrates: 47.03g
- Protein: 7.5g
- Fat: 13.2g
- Sugar: 19.6g

- Sodium: 321 mg
- Fiber: 9.9g

236. Vegan-Friendly Platter

Preparation Time: 10 minutes
Cooking Time: 30 minutes
Servings: 4

Ingredients:

- 1 tbsp. olive oil
- 2 small onions, chopped
- 5 garlic cloves, chopped finely
- 1 tsp. of dried oregano
- 1 tsp. Ground cumin
- ½ tsp. ground ginger
- Salt and freshly ground black pepper, to taste
- 2 cups tomatoes, peeled, seeded, and chopped
- 2 (13½-oz.) cans black beans, rinsed and drained
- ½ cup homemade vegetable broth

Directions:

1. Heat the olive oil over medium heat in a pan and cook the onion for about 5-7 minutes, stirring frequently.
2. Add the garlic, oregano, spices, salt, and black pepper and cook for about 1 minute.
3. Add the tomatoes and cook for about 1-2 minutes.
4. Add in the beans and broth and bring to a boil.
5. Reduce the heat to medium-low and simmer, covered for about 15 minutes.

6. Serve hot.

Nutrition Per Serving:

- Calories: 196
- Carbohydrates: 25.7g
- Protein: 10.11g
- Fat: 4.6g
- Sugar: 4.1g
- Sodium: 725 mg
- Fiber: 10.03g

237. Armenian Style Chickpeas

Preparation Time: 15 minutes
Cooking Time: 15 minutes
Servings: 4

Ingredients:

- 2 tbsp. olive oil
- 1 medium yellow onion, chopped
- 4 garlic cloves, minced
- 1 tsp. dried thyme, crushed
- 1 tsp. Dried oregano, crushed
- ½ tsp. paprika
- 1 cup tomato, chopped finely
- 2½ cup canned chickpeas, rinsed and drained
- 5 cup Swiss chard, chopped
- 2 tbsp. water
- 2 tbsp. fresh lemon juice
- Salt and freshly ground black pepper, to taste
- 3 tbsp. fresh basil, chopped

Directions:

1. Heat the olive oil over medium heat in a skillet and sauté the onion for about 6-8 minutes.
2. Add the garlic, herbs, and paprika, and sauté for about 1 minute.
3. Add the Swiss chard and 2 tbsp. Water and cook for about 2-3 minutes.
4. Add the tomatoes and chickpeas and cook for about 2-3 minutes.
5. Add in the lemon juice, salt, and black pepper and remove from the heat.
6. Serve hot with the garnishing of basil.

Nutrition Per Serving:

- Calories: 233
- Carbohydrates: 30g
- Protein: 8.6g
- Fat: 10.11g
- Sugar: 5.8g
- Sodium: 529 mg
- Fiber: 8.46g

238. High-Fiber Dumplings

Preparation Time: 10 minutes
Cooking Time: 10 minutes
Servings: 8

Ingredients:

- 200 g cream quark
- 60 g psyllium husks
- 10 g bamboo fibers
- 1 bowl vegetable broth
- 2 eggs

Directions:

1. Take a bowl and add the psyllium husks along with the bamboo fibers. Mix well with a spoon.

2. Put the eggs in the same bowl, add the cream curd and vegetable stock. Knead, well, it's best done by hand. Alternatively, the kneading hooks of the mixer can be used.

3. Set a large saucepan with water and bring to a boil on the stove. In the meantime, moisten your hands with water and roll the dough into 12 balls.

4. Put the balls in hot water and cook for 10 minutes, then serve. High-fiber vegetables like beans and matching sauces also taste great.

Nutrition Per Serving:

- Calories: 75
- Carbs: 0.1 g
- Protein: 13.4 g
- Fat: 1.7 g
- Sugar: 0 g
- Sodium: 253 mg

239. Pizza Made with Bamboo Fibers

Preparation Time: 10 minutes
Cooking Time: 20 minutes
Servings: 4

Ingredients:

- 2 eggs
- 60 g bamboo fibers
- 80 g sour cream
- 40 g olive oil
- 150 g grated Gouda cheese
- Salt and pepper

Directions:

1. First, preheat the oven to 180ºC and cover a baking sheet with baking paper.

2. Take a bowl and beat in the eggs. Whisk briefly with a fork, then add the remaining ingredients and knead everything well. That is best done by hand, but you can also work with the dough hook on the mixer.

3. Finally, flavor with salt and pepper to taste, then place the dough on the baking tray and roll out evenly. If necessary, flour the dough with a bit of bamboo fiber to not stick to the rolling pin.

4. Bake the tray for 10 minutes on the lower rack. The pizza base can now be topped with delicious low-carb foods, depending on your taste. Then bake for another 10 minutes on the lower rack and then enjoy hot.

Nutrition Per Serving:

- Calories: 297.6
- Fat: 26 g
- Carbs: 9 g
- Sugar: 2.05 g
- Fiber: 2 g
- Protein: 13 g
- Sodium: 539 mg

240. Lamb with Carrot and Brussels Sprouts Spaghetti

Preparation Time: 10 minutes
Cooking Time: 30 minutes
Servings: 4-8

Ingredients:

- 250 g Brussels sprouts
- 300 g carrots
- 5 tablespoons sesame oil
- 3 tablespoons soy sauce
- 1 lime juice
- A pinch of sugar
- Salt
- 600 g loosened saddle of lamb
- Pepper
- 2 tablespoons butter
- 2 tablespoons sesame seeds

Directions:

1. First, preheat the oven to 100ºc.
2. Take the Brussels sprouts, wash, and clean. Then, cut them into strips.
3. To prepare the marinade, place 3 tablespoons of sesame oil with soy sauce, sugar, salt, and lime juice in a bowl; merge well.
4. Put the vegetable spaghetti in the marinade and let it steep for a moment.
5. In the meantime, flavor the lamb with salt and pepper. Pour the remaining oil into a coated pan and heat on high.
6. Set the meat in the hot oil, sear it on all sides, then put it in the oven and let it cook gently for 10 minutes.

7. After that, melt the butter in the same pan and fry the marinated vegetables for about 3-4 minutes. Arrange on a plate with the sliced lamb and garnish with sesame seeds.

Nutrition Per Serving:

- Calories: 341.58
- Fat: 28 g
- Carbs: 6.95 g
- Sugar: 2.34 g
- Fiber: 2.36 g
- Protein: 12.59 g
- Sodium: 500 mg

241. Cabbage Wrap

Preparation Time: 10 minutes
Cooking Time: 30 minutes
Servings: 4-8

Ingredients:

- 1 head white cabbage
- Salt
- 100 ml milk
- 1 roll (from the day before)
- 350 g mixed minced meat
- 1 egg freshly ground pepper
- 2 tablespoons clarified butter
- 250 ml meat stock
- 1 tablespoon flour
- 4 tablespoons cream

Directions:

1. First, separate the large outer leaves (12-16 pieces) from the cabbage and cut out the strong leaf veins with a knife. Set a saucepan with water and bring to a boil. Salt well and add the large cabbage leaves with the rest of the cabbage. Cook everything for 5-10 minutes.

2. Heat the milk in a saucepan. Put the roll on it and soak for a few minutes.

3. Squeeze out the bun and place it in a bowl. Also, add the minced meat, egg, pepper, and salt. Mix everything well until a batter is formed.

4. Cut the cooked cabbage (not the large leaves) and add to the dough, mix again.

5. Take 3-4 cabbage leaves and stack them on top of each other. Spread some butter on top, then roll the leaves and fix with toothpicks, roulade needles, or kitchen twine.

6. Put the clarified butter in a pan and heat over medium fire until it melts. Then, place the cabbage rolls in the hot oil and fry them lightly brown.

7. Extinguish with the broth, cover the pan and simmer the cabbage rolls over low heat for 25 minutes. Take out the cabbage rolls and briefly keep them warm.

8. Now, stir in the flour in a bit of cream and add everything to the sauce. Bring to a boil briefly.

9. Arrange on plates with the cabbage rolls.

Nutrition Per Serving:

- Calories: 211.13
- Fat: 13.7 g
- Carbs: 10.7 g
- Sugar: 4.4 g
- Fiber: 2.44 g
- Protein: 11.86 g

242. Veal with Asparagus

Preparation Time: 10 minutes
Cooking Time: 30 minutes
Servings: 4-8

Ingredients:

- 800 g green asparagus
- Salt
- 3-4 tablespoons rapeseed oil
- A pinch of sugar
- Pepper
- 1/2 fresh lemon zest, grated
- Oil for frying
- 8 slices veal from the back (60 g each)
- 8 slices Parma ham
- 8 sage leaves
- 125 ml white wine
- 1 tablespoon butter

Directions:

1. First, peel the lower part of the sticks with a vegetable peeler, then remove the woody ends. Wash the asparagus thoroughly.

2. At the same time, fill a saucepan with water and bring it to a boil. Salt well, add the asparagus, and cook for 8 minutes; they must not become too soft. Drain them and rinse directly with ice water.

3. Place the asparagus on a kitchen roll to dry, then put them in a baking dish.

4. Take a small bowl and add the oil, salt, pepper, sugar 0, and lemon zest. Mix everything well and pour over the asparagus stalks. Let sit in the marinade for 25 minutes.

5. Put the oil in a pan and heat over medium fire. Detach the asparagus from the marinade and place them in the hot oil. Fry while turning.

6. Now, pepper the meat and cover it with Parma ham and a sage leaf. Secure everything with a toothpick.

7. Put the oil in a pan, heat it and place the meat in it. Fry briefly on medium heat and turn for 3 minutes.

8. Serve with the asparagus on a plate. Extinguish the now-empty pan with white wine so that the roasting residue dissolves, then stir in the butter and briefly bring to a boil.

9. Pour the sauce over the asparagus and meat. Enjoy hot.

Nutrition Per Serving:

- Calories: 265.22
- Fat: 17.6 g
- Carbs: 3.94 g
- Sugar: 1.7 g
- Fiber: 1.9 g
- Protein: 20.3 g
- Sodium: 152.9 mg

243. Salmon with Sesame Seeds and Mushrooms

Preparation Time: 10 minutes
Cooking Time: 30 minutes
Servings: 4-8

Ingredients:

- 500 g salmon fillet
- 4 tablespoons fish sauce
- 200 g mushrooms
- 400 g fresh spinach leaves
- 2 tablespoons vegetable oil
- 2 tablespoons sesame oil
- 1 tablespoon sesame seeds
- 1 teaspoon Sambal Oelek

Directions:

1. First, take the salmon, rinse under running water, dry with a little kitchen roll, and then cut to form strips. Take a bowl, pour in the fish sauce. Soak the salmon in the sauce for 10 minutes.

2. In the meantime, it is best to carefully clean the mushrooms with a brush, and cut them to make slices. Rinse and dry the spinach under the tap.

3. Now, take a wok, add the vegetable and sesame oil. Heat on high, add the mushrooms to the hot oil and fry briefly. Put the spinach in the wok and fry until it collapses.

4. Now, move the vegetables away from the center to the edge of the wok and reduce the heat.

5. Place the salmon on the resulting surface and fry gently while turning.

6. Arrange it with the vegetables on a plate, carefully refine with Sambal Oelek to taste.

Nutrition Per Serving:

- Calories: 205.2
- Fat: 15.1 g
- Carbs: 3.16 g
- Sugar: 1.1 g
- Fiber: 1.4 g
- Protein: 15.4 g
- Sodium: 787.8 mg

244. **Stuffed Trout with Mushrooms**

Preparation Time: 10 minutes
Cooking Time: 30 minutes
Servings: 4-8

Ingredients:

- 4 ready-to-cook trout
- 1 lemon juice
- Salt
- Pepper
- 1/2 bunch dill
- 500 g mushrooms
- 2 tablespoons butter
- 2 tablespoons freshly chopped parsley
- 3 tablespoons chopped almonds
- 4 tablespoons oil

Directions:

1. First, preheat the oven to 220ºc.

2. Take the lemon juice and use it to drizzle the trout inside and out. Wash the dill, shake dry and chop.

3. Salt and pepper the trout and refine each with 1 tablespoon of dill. It is best to carefully clean the mushrooms with a brush and cut them into slices.

4. Then, put them in a bowl. Also, add butter, almonds, and parsley. Stir everything well.

5. Now, distribute the filling over the trout's abdominal cavities. Fix the abdomen with wooden skewers, wrap the trout well in aluminum foil coated with oil. Let it cook in the oven for 20 minutes.

6. Finally, put the fish on a plate and enjoy the hot.

Nutrition Per Serving:

- Calories: 385.5
- Fat: 23 g
- Carbs: 3.2 g
- Sugar: 1.5 g
- Fiber: 1 g
- Protein: 40.3 g
- Sodium: 198.4 mg

245. **Salmon with Basil and Avocado**

Preparation Time: 10 minutes
Cooking Time: 30 minutes
Servings: 4-8

Ingredients:

- 1 avocado
- 1 teaspoon pickled capers

- 3 garlic cloves
- A handful of basil leaves
- 1 tablespoon fresh lemon zest
- 4 salmon fillets (approximately 200 g each)
- Coconut oil for greasing the tray

Directions:

1. Preheat the oven at 180°C and use a brush to spread coconut oil on a baking sheet.
2. Divide the avocado in half, then remove the core and skin.
3. Mash the pulp with a fork in a small bowl.
4. Put the capers in a colander and drain, chop finely.
5. Peel the garlic cloves and mash them with a press. Alternatively, chop them very finely with a sharp knife.
6. Then, wash the basil and shake it dry, pluck the leaves off and chop them too.
7. Attach everything to the avocado in the bowl, refine with lemon zest and mix well.
8. Wash the salmon, dry with a little kitchen roll, and place on the baking sheet. It is best to spread the avocado mixture over the fish with a spoon.
9. Put the tray in the oven and bake briefly for 10 minutes. Switch on the grill function and bake for another 4 minutes until the avocado takes on a light brown color.
10. Set the salmon fillets on a plate and enjoy hot.

Nutrition Per Serving:

- Calories: 226.22
- Fat: 15.4 g
- Carbs: 1.7 g
- Sugar: 0.1 g
- Fiber: 10.5 g
- Protein: 20.6 g
- Sodium: 52.8 mg

246. Leek Quiche with Olives

Preparation Time: 10 minutes
Cooking Time: 30 minutes
Servings: 4-8

Ingredients:

- 140 g almonds
- 40 g walnuts
- 25 g coconut oil
- 1 teaspoon salt
- 1 leek
- 50 g spinach
- 2 sprigs rosemary
- 40 g fresh basil
- 30 g pine nuts
- 4 tablespoons extra-virgin olive oil
- 2 tablespoons lime juice
- 1/2 garlic clove
- 50 g pitted black olives
- 1 teaspoon red pepper berries

Directions:

1. First, coarsely grind the almonds and walnuts in a food processor or blender,

then put them in a small bowl with coconut oil and 1/2 teaspoon of salt.

2. Merge thoroughly, pour the mixture into a cake springform pan. Press the dough with your fingers simultaneously and distribute it in the mold so that a border of 4 cm high is created. Put it in the freezer for 15 minutes.

3. Now, wash the leek, spinach, and herbs, then pat dry. Slice the leek and place it in a bowl.

4. Stir in the remaining salt and set aside to draw.

5. Meanwhile, put the basil, pine nuts, olive oil, and lime juice in a blender. Pulse until you have a creamy puree.

6. Alternatively, a large mixing vessel or a hand blender can also be used here.

7. Now, peel the garlic clove and chop half. Remove the needles from the rosemary and also finely chop them.

8. Cut the spinach into narrow strips and halve the olives.

9. Add everything to the leek in the bowl, and then add the basil puree. Mix well.

10. Distribute the mixture to the base of the springform pan, sprinkle the pepper berries over it. Finally, cut the quiche into pieces and enjoy.

Nutrition Per Serving:

*   Calories: 266
*   Fat: 25.6 g
*   Carbs: 6.9 g
*   Sugar: 1.2 g
*   Fiber: 3.6 g
*   Protein: 5.41 g

*   Sodium: 300.49 mg

247. Vegetarian Hamburgers

Preparation Time: 10 minutes
Cooking Time: 30 minutes
Servings: 4

Ingredients:

*   90 g protein flour
*   120 ml egg white
*   100 g carrots, grated
*   2 tablespoons coconut oil
*   100 g low-fat quark
*   2 eggs
*   6 g baking powder
*   20 g gold linseed (alternatively other nuts and grains)
*   Preferred spices (Worcester sauce, soy sauce, salt, or chili)
*   Preferred topping (tomatoes, cucumbers, radishes)

Directions:

1. First, preheat the oven to 180ºC and line 6-7 muffin tins with paper cases.

2. Take a bowl, add 50 g of flour and the egg white and carrots, and then stir well. Divide the dough into 6-7 parts and shape a meatball from each one.

3. Now, put 2 tablespoons of coconut oil in a non-stick pan and heat over medium heat until it has melted. Put the meatballs in the hot pan and fry vigorously on both sides.

4. Take a separate bowl, add the remaining flour along with the low-fat quark, eggs, baking powder, and gold linseed.

5. Mix well, then pour into the prepared muffin cups. Bake in the oven for 25 minutes, let the finished rolls cool down well. Finally, cut the rolls in half with a sharp knife, top with a meatball of your choice, and season. Then, skewer the finished burger with a toothpick and enjoy.

Nutrition Per Serving:

- Calories: 258.31
- Fat: 11.1 g
- Carbs: 28.5 g
- Fiber: 8 g
- Protein: 12.5 g

248. Pork Steaks with Avocado

Preparation Time: 10 minutes
Cooking Time: 30 minutes
Servings: 8

Ingredients:

For the salsa:

- 6 limes
- 3 tablespoons fruity olive oil
- 1 ½ dried chili pepper
- Salt and freshly ground pepper
- 2 mangoes (ripe, but still firm)
- 2 shallots
- 2 avocados
- A bunch of coriander

For the steaks:

- 4 pork neck steaks (approximately 150 g each)
- 1 teaspoon ground anise
- 1 teaspoon ground cumin
- Salt
- freshly ground pepper
- 2 tablespoons clarified butter

Directions:

For the salsa:

1. Halve the limes and squeeze them thoroughly; measure out 10 tablespoons of lime juice—place in a small bowl.

2. Add olive oil and stir well with a whisker. Crumble the chili pepper and mix it into the dressing together with salt and pepper.

3. Now, peel the mangoes with a vegetable peeler, remove the stone and dice the pulp. Finely chop the shallots with a sharp knife.

4. Take a separate bowl, add the mangoes and shallots; stir well.

5. Remove the stone and skin from the avocados, dice the meat and then fill the mango mixture. Immediately, pour the dressing over it so that the avocado doesn't tarnish. Mix gently.

6. Finally, wash the coriander thoroughly under running water and dry it carefully. Remove the tender leaves and also add to the salsa. Mix again.

For the steaks:

1. Preheat the oven to 60°c. Rinse the steaks under running water and dry them

carefully with a little kitchen roll. Sprinkle the anise, cumin, salt, and pepper over them. Place the clarified butter in a pan and heat over medium heat until melted. Set the steaks in the hot pan and fry briefly while turning for 3 minutes.

2. Put the steaks on a piece of aluminum foil and seal it tightly around the steak. Place in the oven and let rest briefly for 3 minutes.

3. Arrange on a plate with the meat juice and salsa. Enjoy immediately!

Nutrition Per Serving:

- Calories: 331.66
- Fat: 20 g
- Carbs: 18.6 g
- Sugar: 10 g
- Fiber: 4.9 g
- Protein: 21.46 g
- Sodium: 454.8 mg

249. Chicken with Asparagus Salad

Preparation Time: 10 minutes
Cooking Time: 30 minutes
Servings: 4

Ingredients:

- 800 g green asparagus
- 1/2 bunch spring onions
- 3 tablespoons white wine vinegar
- Salt
- Pepper
- 1 teaspoon mustard

- 1/2 teaspoon honey
- 8 tablespoons olive oil
- 4 chicken breast fillets (approximately 200 g each)
- 250 g sliced breakfast bacon
- 2 tablespoons clarified butter
- Basil leaves for garnishing

Directions:

1. First, preheat the oven to 180°C and place baking paper on a baking sheet.

2. Take the asparagus and peel only the bottom stick.

3. Remove the woody ends, then wash thoroughly. Halve the asparagus lengthways and cut so that oblique pieces are created. Now, wash the spring onions and cut them into large pieces.

4. Take a bowl, pour the white wine vinegar into it. Also, attach 2 tablespoons of water along with mustard, honey, salt, and pepper. Stir well.

5. Finally, slowly add 6 tablespoons of olive oil, spoon by spoon. Stir.

6. Take the meat, rinse under running water, and dry with a little kitchen roll, then season with salt and pepper on both sides.

7. Take the bacon slices and wrap the meat in them.

8. Put the clarified butter in a non-stick pan and heat over medium fire until the fat has melted. Set the chicken breasts in the hot pan, first placing them to the point where the ends of the bacon slice meet. Turn after 2 minutes and fry again briefly for 2 minutes.

9. Remove from the pan and place on the tray so the meat can cook in the oven for another 15 minutes.

10. In the meantime, set the remaining olive oil in a pan and heat over medium fire. Put the vegetables in the hot oil and fry briefly—meanwhile, salt and pepper. After 4 minutes, take the vegetables out of the pan, add them to the vinegar mixture, and mix well.

11. Finally, arrange the meat with the asparagus salad on a plate and enjoy immediately.

Nutrition Per Serving:

- Calories: 875.2
- Fat: 65g
- Carbs: 8.03g
- Sugar: 4g
- Fiber: 3.7g
- Protein: 62.7g
- Sodium: 1.2g

250. Hot Pepper and Lamb Salmon

Preparation Time: 10 minutes
Cooking Time: 20 minutes
Servings: 6

Ingredients:

For the Meat:

- 700 g lamb salmon
- 2 garlic cloves
- 1/2 bunch mint
- 2 sprigs rosemary
- 1/2 bunch oregano
- 10 peppercorns
- 4 tablespoons olive oil
- Salt
- Pepper

For the Peperonata:

- 1 small zucchini
- 2 red peppers
- 2 yellow peppers
- 1 onion
- 3 garlic cloves
- 3 tomatoes
- 1 chili pepper
- 3 tablespoon small capers
- 2 tablespoons olive oil
- Salt
- Pepper
- 2 tablespoons chopped parsley

Directions:

For the Meat:

1. First, rinse the meat under running water, dry it with a little kitchen roll, and carefully remove the tendons and fat. Peel and cut the garlic to make fine slices.

2. Wash the rosemary, oregano, and mint, pat dry carefully. Then, chop the leaves and needles (not too fine). Put the peppercorns in the mortar and press lightly. Take a bowl, add the herbs and peppercorns.

3. Attach 2 tablespoons of olive oil and stir well, then rub the meat with the mixture. Finally, wrap it in foil and refrigerate for 4 hours.

4. Preheat the oven to 70°C, placing a baking dish in it that will be used for the meat later.

5. Now, take the meat and remove the marinade with the back of a knife, then season with salt and pepper. Set the remaining oil in a pan and heat over medium fire.

6. Place the meat in the hot oil and fry briefly while turning for 2 minutes. Put it in the pan into the oven and cook for another 40 minutes.

For the Peperonata:

1. Wash the zucchini thoroughly and dice it with the skin. Halve and core the peppers, wash them too. Cut so that narrow strips are created. First, peel the onion and garlic, then process into fine cubes.

2. Score the tomatoes, pour hot water; at that time, peel them and remove the seeds. Cut the pulp into small pieces. Alternatively, canned tomatoes can also be used here. Halve and core the chili pepper, wash it well, and cut it into small pieces. Finally, rinse the capers in a sieve and let them drain.

3. Now, pour olive oil over the pan and heat over medium fire. Put the onion in the hot oil and fry briefly, then add the peppers, zucchini, garlic, and chili. Cook for 5 minutes, stirring evenly. Attach tomatoes and season with salt and pepper.

4. Let everything fry for 10 minutes, stir in the capers and cook for another 5 minutes.

Nutrition Per Serving:

- Calories: 400.3
- Fat: 28.6 g
- Carbs: 12.5 g
- Sugar: 4.5 g
- Fiber: 3.9 g
- Protein: 26.07 g
- Sodium: 296.7 mg

251. Pork Rolls À La Ratatouille

Preparation Time: 10 minutes
Cooking Time: 30 minutes
Servings: 8

Ingredients:

For the Ratatouille:

- 2 yellow peppers
- 2 red peppers
- 2 small zucchini
- 2 red onions
- 3 garlic cloves
- 250 g cherry tomatoes
- A bunch of thyme
- 3 tablespoons olive oil
- Salt
- Freshly ground pepper
- 250 ml vegetable stock
- 3 tablespoons tomato paste

For the Pork Rolls:

- 2 bunches basil
- 30 g Parmesan cheese
- 30 g pine nuts
- 5 tablespoons olive oil

- Salt
- Freshly ground pepper
- 75 g sun-dried tomatoes in oil
- 8 small pork schnitzel (approximately 75 g each)

Directions:

For the Ratatouille:

1. First, preheat the oven to 180°c
2. Halve and core the peppers, wash thoroughly, and cut so that narrow strips are formed.
3. Wash the zucchini as well, then cut into cubes with the skin on. First, peel the onion and garlic, then cut into strips. Clean the tomatoes thoroughly, cut them in half.
4. Rinse the thyme under running water and pat dry carefully, remove the leaves. Take a bowl, add the vegetables with the thyme and mix well.
5. Flavor with salt, pepper, and olive oil; mix again. Take the frying pan from the oven and distribute the vegetable mixture in it—Bake for 20 minutes.

For the Pork Rolls:

1. Now, rinse the basil with water and shake dry, pluck the leaves and chop finely. Coarsely or finely grate the Parmesan with the grater to taste.
2. Take a small pan, add the pine nuts, briefly toast them without adding any further fat, and then put them in the blender. Also, add half of the chopped basil along with the Parmesan and 3 tablespoons of olive oil. Puree everything

into a pesto, then season with salt and pepper.

3. Wash the tomatoes and cut them to make strips. Clean the pork, dry it with a little kitchen roll and then plate with a meat tenderizer or a saucepan. Sprinkle it with salt and pepper, spread some pesto on top.
4. Spread the sun-dried tomatoes and the remaining basil on top, roll into roulades, and set. Add the remaining oil to a pan and heat over medium fire; place the rolls in the hot oil and fry on all sides for 5 minutes.
5. Take a small bowl, add the vegetable stock and tomato paste. Stir.
6. Add the cherry tomatoes and the mixture to the cooked vegetables in the oven. Put the meat on it and bake for another 15 minutes. Enjoy served on a plate with the remaining pesto.

Nutrition Per Serving:

- Calories: 332.8
- Fat: 23
- Carbs: 12.5 g
- Sugar: 4.2 g
- Fiber: 3.6 g
- Protein: 20 g

252. Pepper Fillet with Leek

Preparation Time: 10 minutes
Cooking Time: 30 minutes
Servings: 8

Ingredients:

For the Vegetables:

- 50 g sun-dried tomatoes
- 100 g pine nuts
- 4 large leeks
- 2 tablespoon raisins
- 2 cups Peppercorns
- 2 tablespoons olive oil
- Salt
- Freshly ground pepper

For the Meat:

- 2 tablespoons black pepper
- 4 tablespoons sesame seeds
- 1 teaspoon salt
- 4 sprigs rosemary
- 4 beef fillet steaks (approximately 180 g each)
- 4 tablespoons sunflower oil

Directions:

1. Place the tomatoes in a heat-resistant bowl and pour boiling water over them. Let stand for 10 minutes, then take out the tomatoes and chop with a sharp knife.
2. Now, put the pine nuts in a small pan and briefly toast them without adding further fat, stirring well. Set aside and wash the leek thoroughly and cut so that rings are formed. Rinse the raisins under cold running water.
3. Take a non-stick pan and pour in olive oil. Heat on high and add the leek. Sauté briefly, add tomatoes and raisins over low heat and stir well—Cook for 10 minutes, season with salt and pepper. Add the pine nuts, then carefully stir in.
4. At the same time, put the peppercorns in the mortar and coarsely crush them, stirring in a small bowl with salt and sesame seeds.
5. Rinse off the rosemary and steaks, then dry them with a little paper towel. Place the steaks with the edges in the pepper mixture so that the spices stick to the edges.
6. Heat oil in a non-stick pan on a high level and sear the meat on both sides for 3 minutes. Immediately, wrap in a piece of aluminum foil, covering a sprig of rosemary with it.
7. After resting for 5 minutes, remove the steaks and arrange them on a plate with the leek vegetables. Garnish with meat juice and enjoy instantly.

Nutrition Per Serving:

- Calories: 560
- Fat: 38.5 g
- Carbs: 37 g
- Sugar: 5 g
- Fiber: 12 g
- Protein: 25 g
- Sodium: 464 mg

253. Lamb Chops with Beans

Preparation Time: 10 minutes
Cooking Time: 50 minutes
Servings: 8

Ingredients:

- 1 kg lamb chops
- 2 lemons juice
- Salt
- Pepper
- 150 ml olive oil (approximately)
- 6 garlic cloves
- 6 sprigs rosemary
- 6 sprigs thyme
- 2 onions
- 12 cocktail tomatoes
- 300 g green beans
- 2 shallots
- 70 g bacon
- 2 teaspoons butter
- Savory to taste

Directions:

1. First, rinse the lamb chops briefly under running water and carefully dry them with a little kitchen roll. Pour the lemon juice into a bowl, add 100 ml of olive oil, salt, and pepper, stir well. Take the garlic and remove the peel. Cut so that thin slices are formed; also add to the lemon marinade.

2. Now, put the marinade together with the chops in a freezer bag, squeeze out the air, and seal.

3. Set aside for at least 2 hours and let it soak in.

4. Preheat the oven to 180°c Rinse the rosemary, thyme, and pat dry. Take a baking dish and grease it with olive oil. Spread the herb sprigs in it.

5. Add the onions and cut into 4 parts, place them in the mold as well. Wash the tomatoes thoroughly and cut in half depending on the size, then add to the onions.

6. Set the meat out of the marinade and place it on top of the vegetables. Spread the soak and a little olive oil on top— Bake on the middle rack for 40 minutes.

7. In the meantime, take the beans and cut the ends, then wash. Set the water to a boil in a saucepan, season with salt, and add the beans—Cook for 8 minutes. Meanwhile, take the shallots and remove the skin, cut into small cubes. Finely dice the bacon as well.

8. Put the butter in a pan and heat over medium fire until it has melted.

9. Place the shallots and bacon in the hot oil and fry until everything takes on a brown color.

10. Add the beans with a little savory, stir well.

11. Salt and pepper, then serve with the lamb and the bed of vegetables. Enjoy hot.

Nutrition Per Serving:

- Calories: 472
- Fat: 40 g
- Carbs: 9 g
- Sugar: 3.8 g

- Fiber: 2.4 g
- Protein: 20 g
- Sodium: 234.4 mg

254. Fillet of Beef on Spring Vegetables

Preparation Time: 10 minutes
Cooking Time: 30 minutes
Servings: 8

Ingredients:

- 500 g green asparagus
- 2 bulbs kohlrabi
- 1 bunch flat-leaf parsley
- 1 bunch tarragon
- Salt
- Pepper
- 4 beef fillet steaks (approximately 150 g each)
- 4 tablespoons olive oil
- 300 ml cream

Directions:

1. Wash the asparagus, peel only the bottom stick with the vegetable peeler. Divide off the woody ends, then cut the asparagus in half. Now, peel the kohlrabi with the knife, cut so that narrow sticks are formed.
2. Rinse the herbs under running water, dry them carefully and remove the leaves. Finely chop with a sharp knife. Take a bowl, pour in 2/3 of the herbs, set aside the rest for now.
3. After that, add the vegetables to the herbs in the bowl, season with salt and pepper,

and mix well. Put the mixture in a roasting tube (must be closed on one side).
4. Take a large saucepan, pour water up to 1/3 full. Set on the stove and bring to a boil.
5. In the meantime, rinse the steaks with water and dry them carefully with a little kitchen roll.
6. Season with salt and pepper on both sides. Put the oil in a pan and heat over medium fire.
7. Set the meat in the hot oil and fry briefly on all sides for 3 minutes. Place it on the vegetables in the roasting tube.
8. Pour the oil out of the pan and add in the cream. Bring to the boil briefly so that the roasting loosens, then pour over the meat in the roasting tube.
9. Now, close the hose and add it to the boiling water. Cook gently over low heat and cover for 12 minutes.
10. Finally, arrange the meat with the bed of vegetables on a plate and garnish with the remaining herbs.

Nutrition Per Serving:

- Calories: 209
- Fat: 10 g
- Carbs: 21 g
- Sugar: 13 g
- Fiber: 8 g
- Protein: 11 g
- Sodium: 644 mg

255. Bolognese with Zucchini Noodles

Preparation Time: 10 minutes
Cooking Time: 50 minutes
Servings: 4-8

Ingredients:

- 4 zucchini (approximately 200 g each)
- Salt
- 1 onion
- 3 garlic cloves
- 2 tablespoons coconut oil
- 4 tablespoons tomato paste
- 3 tablespoons balsamic vinegar
- 600 g chunky tomatoes (canned)
- 4 sprigs rosemary
- 1 handful basil leaves
- 1/2tbsp. Dried oregano
- 1/4tsp. Dried thyme
- Freshly ground black pepper
- 600 g mixed minced meat
- 2 tablespoons olive oil

Directions:

1. First, wash the zucchini and cut them into thin, narrow slices.
2. For preparing the Bolognese, peel the onion and garlic; cut into fine cubes. Set the oil in a saucepan and heat over medium fire. Put the onion in the hot oil and fry until it becomes translucent.
3. Stir well and fry briefly before adding the tomato paste. Cook them together again, pour in the balsamic vinegar until the bottom can no longer be seen. Bring to a boil, add the tomatoes.

4. Wash the rosemary, and basil then dry them carefully. Pluck the needles and leaves, chop and add to the Bolognese. Season with the remaining herbs to taste.
5. Reduce the heat and simmer gently for 30 minutes before stirring in the minced meat. Cook for another 15 minutes, then cook over high heat for 5 minutes.
6. At the same time, attach olive oil to the zucchini noodles and mix well.
7. Put the oiled zucchini in a pan and cook only briefly over medium heat without becoming too soft.
8. Arrange the Bolognese on a plate and enjoy hot.

Nutrition Per Serving:

- Calories: 283
- Carbs: 12.9 g
- Protein: 17.01 g
- Fat: 18.8 g
- Sugar: 8.1 g
- Sodium: 300 mg

256. Chicken with Chickpeas

Preparation Time: 10 minutes
Cooking Time: 30 minutes
Servings: 4

Ingredients:

- 12 sun-dried tomatoes in oil
- 2 garlic cloves
- 2 zucchini
- 500 g chickpeas (canned, drained weight)
- 4 tablespoons olive oil

- 100 ml poultry stock
- 2 bags saffron threads
- Salt
- Freshly ground black pepper
- 1/4 teaspoon ground coriander
- 4 chicken breasts (approximately 200 g each)
- 1 tbsp. Ras-el-Hanout

Directions:

1. First, get the sun-dried tomatoes out of the oil, dry them with a little kitchen roll, and then cut them to form narrow strips.
2. Take the garlic, remove the skin and cut it into slices.
3. Wash the zucchini and cut into cubes with the skin on.
4. Rinse the chickpeas in a colander and drain well.
5. Set a saucepan, add 2 tablespoons of olive oil. Warmth on medium heat, add the tomatoes with garlic to the hot oil. Fry briefly for 1 minute.
6. Place the zucchini with chickpeas, stir well and fry briefly together before deglazing with the broth. Add saffron threads, coriander, salt, and pepper. Bring to a boil.
7. Set the heat, cover the saucepan and let the vegetables simmer for 5 minutes.
8. In the meantime, rinse the meat under running water and dry it with a little kitchen roll. Set the remaining oil in a pan and heat over medium fire.
9. For now, sprinkle the meat on both sides with salt, pepper, and Ras el Hanout, then add to the hot oil and fry for 7 minutes, turning.
10. Serve the meat with the vegetables on a large plate and enjoy hot.

Nutrition Per Serving:

- Calories: 534
- Fat: 32 g
- Carbs: 24 g
- Sugar: 2.5 g
- Fiber: 7 g
- Protein: 38.9 g
- Sodium: 921 mg

257. Ham with Chicory

Preparation Time: 10 minutes
Cooking Time: 30 minutes
Servings: 4-8

Ingredients:

- 4 sprigs chicory (approximately 200 g each)
- 150 g Emmental cheese
- 8 sage leaves
- 40 g butter
- 3 tablespoons orange juice
- Salt
- Pepper
- 8 slices of the Black Forest ham

Directions:

1. First, preheat the oven to 200°c
2. Wash and clean the chicory and cut it lengthwise in half. Remove the stalk with a knife.

3. Shred the cheese coarsely or finely with a grater to taste.

4. Rinse the sage leaves under running water and gently shake dry.

5. Put the butter in a pan and heat over medium fire. Extinguish with orange juice and so froth the butter. Add the sage.

6. Place the chicory with the cut side in the hot oil. Reduce the heat and fry for 5 minutes.

7. Remove the chicory, cover with a sage leaf and sprinkle with salt and pepper.

8. Chop the ham and put it on the baking dish. Sprinkle with cheese and drizzle with liquid orange and butter.

9. Bake in the oven for 20 minutes, then serve hot.

Nutrition Per Serving:

- Calories: 159
- Carbs: 5.7 g
- Protein: 11.5 g
- Fat: 11.18 g
- Sugar: 1.6 g
- Sodium: 440 mg

258. Fried Egg on Onions with Sage

Preparation Time: 10 minutes
Cooking Time: 30 minutes
Servings: 4-8

Ingredients:

- 275 g onions
- 1/2 bunch sage
- 3 tablespoons clarified butter
- 1 ½ tablespoon coconut flour
- Salt
- 1 teaspoon sweet paprika powder
- 8 eggs
- Freshly ground black pepper

Directions:

1. First, remove the skin from the onions, then cut into thin rings.

2. Rinse the sage under running water, pat dry, and remove the leaves.

3. Now, put 1 ½ tablespoon of clarified butter in a pan and heat over medium fire until it has melted. Put the sage leaves in the hot oil and fry until they are crispy. Place on kitchen paper to drain.

4. Meanwhile, put the remaining clarified butter in the same pan, heat it, and then place the onion rings.

5. Scatter the coconut flour on top and fry for 10 minutes, stirring at regular intervals. Sprinkle salt and paprika too.

6. Take the eggs and beat them one by one on the onions in the pan. Let the eggs sink to the bottom of the pan; if necessary, use a wooden spoon to help.

7. Now, cover the pan and fry everything for 10 minutes until the eggs are completely set.

8. Arrange the fried eggs with the onions on flat plates, season with salt and pepper. Garnish with the roasted sage.

Nutrition Per Serving:

- Calories: 179
- Fat: 13 g

- Carbs: 6 g
- Sugar: 3 g
- Fiber: 1 g
- Protein: 10 g
- Sodium: 265 mg

259. Quinoa Mushroom Risotto

Preparation Time: 10 minutes
Cooking Time: 30 minutes
Servings: 4-8

Ingredients:

- 1 garlic clove
- 30 g hazelnuts
- Salt
- 1 fresh lemon zest, grated
- 2 shallots
- 650 g small mushrooms
- 1 bunch flat-leaf parsley
- 70 g quinoa
- 2 tablespoons olive oil
- Pepper
- 100 g baby spinach
- 30 g grated Parmesan cheese
- 20 g butter
- Red pepper to taste
- 500 ml hot water

Directions:

1. First, peel the garlic clove and put it in a blender. Also, add the hazelnuts, lemon zest, and a little salt; mix until everything is finely ground. Put aside.
2. Peel the shallots, then cut them into fine cubes. It is best to carefully clean the mushrooms with a brush and chop them to form thin slices.
3. Rinse and dab the parsley under running water, remove the leaves and chop with a sharp knife.
4. Place the quinoa in a colander and wash well under the tap; drain thoroughly.
5. Pour olive oil into a non-stick pan and warm over medium heat. Put the shallots in it and fry until they turn slightly brown.
6. Add the mushrooms to the shallots and fry them together until they turn brown. Attach the quinoa, but at the same time pour in hot water. Season with salt and pepper, stir well.
7. Cook over low heat until all the water has boiled away. The quinoa should be soft.
8. Now, add the parsley, spinach, Parmesan, and butter; stir thoroughly.
9. Salt and pepper again and set with garlic and the hazelnut mixture.
10. Arrange on a plate and serve garnished with red pepper if necessary.

Nutrition Per Serving:

- Calories: 166
- Fat: 10 g
- Carbs: 17 g
- Sugar: 3.9 g
- Fiber: 3.8 g
- Protein: 8.7 g
- Sodium: 216 mg

260. Vegetarian Lentil Stew

Preparation Time: 10 minutes
Cooking Time: 30 minutes
Servings: 4

Ingredients:

- 50 g carrots
- 30 g parsnip or parsley root
- 30 g celery
- 1 leek
- 1 yellow pepper
- 250 g red lentils
- 1 ½ teaspoon ground cumin
- 3 tablespoons balsamic vinegar
- 3 tablespoons walnut oil
- 2-3 tablespoons maple syrup
- Salt and pepper
- A pinch of cayenne pepper
- 1/2 bunch flat-leaf parsley

Directions:

1. Measure 1000 ml of water and pour into a saucepan. Warm on high heat until boiling.
2. In the meantime, cut the peppers in half, remove the seeds and wash them together with the leek. Peel the carrots, parsnips, and celery.
3. Process everything into fine cubes; only use the white part of the leek.
4. Pour everything into the boiling water and bring to a boil. Then, add the lentils— Cook for 10 minutes, or until they are soft.

5. Ideally, most of the liquid has boiled away, if necessary, drain—season with cumin, balsamic vinegar, maple syrup, walnut oil, salt, and pepper. Add the cayenne pepper to taste.
6. Turn off the stove and set the vegetarian lentils stew aside briefly to steep.
7. In the meantime, rinse the parsley under the tap, pat dry, pluck the leaves off and sprinkle them into stew.
8. Arrange in deep plates and enjoy hot.

Nutrition Per Serving:

- Calories: 376
- Fat: 11 g
- Carbs: 54 g
- Sugar: 10.4 g
- Fiber: 8.2 g
- Protein: 16.4 g
- Sodium: 223 mg

261. Lemon Chicken Soup with Beans

Preparation Time: 10 minutes
Cooking Time: 50 minutes
Servings: 4

Ingredients:

- 1 onion
- 6 garlic cloves
- 600 g chicken breast
- 3 tablespoons olive oil
- 1 chicken broth
- 1 fresh lemon
- 250 g cooked white beans (canned)
- Salt

- Pepper
- 120 g Feta
- A bunch of chives

Directions:

1. First, peel the onion, then the garlic cloves. Divide the onion in half and cut it into thin slices.
2. Rinse the meat under running water and dry it with a little paper towel.
3. Put the olive oil in a large saucepan and heat over medium fire; add the onion and garlic to the hot oil.
4. Fry until everything is soft, deglaze with the chicken stock. Also, add the meat and bring it to a boil.
5. In the meantime, wash and dry the lemon, then rub and peel it with a grater; alternatively, you can also use a zester. Add the lemon zest to the broth and cook everything for 40 minutes before adding the beans. Salt and pepper, then cook again for 10 minutes.
6. Now, remove the meat and tear it into small pieces on a plate or board with 2 forks. Put the chicken back into the soup, then crumble the Feta over the soup.
7. Finally, rinse the chives with water, dry and cut them so that small rolls are created. Sprinkle it into the soup, stir well and immediately enjoy hot.

Nutrition Per Serving:

- Calories: 470
- Fat: 28 g
- Carbs: 20 g

- Sugar: 3.91 g
- Fiber: 3.9 g
- Protein: 35 g
- Sodium: 1.6 g

262. Chicken, Lettuce and Avocado Salad

Preparation Time: 5 minutes
Cooking Time: 0 minutes
Servings: 4

Ingredients:

- 2 grilled chicken breasts, diced
- 1 avocado, peeled and diced
- 5-6 green lettuce leaves, cut in stripes
- 3-4 green onions, finely chopped
- 5-6 radishes, sliced
- 7-8 grape tomatoes, halved
- 3 tbsp lemon juice
- 3 tbsp extra virgin olive oil
- 1 tsp dried mint
- salt and black pepper, to taste

Directions:

1. Combine avocados, lettuce, chicken, onions, radishes, and grape tomatoes in a deep salad bowl.
2. Season with dried mint, salt, and pepper to taste. Sprinkle with lemon juice and olive oil, toss lightly, and serve.

Nutrition Per Serving:

- Calories: 410
- Fat: 26g

- Protein: 30.41g
- Carbs: 17.5g
- Fiber: 8.2g
- Sodium: 394mg

263. Mediterranean Beef Salad

Preparation Time: 5 minutes
Cooking Time: 15 minutes
Servings: 4-5

Ingredients:

- 8 oz quality roast beef, thinly sliced
- 1 avocado, peeled and diced
- 2 tomatoes, diced
- 1 cucumber, peeled and diced
- 1 yellow pepper, sliced
- 2 carrots, shredded
- 1 cup black olives, pitted and halved
- 2-3 fresh basil leaves, torn
- 2-3 fresh oregano leaves
- 1 tbsp balsamic vinegar
- 4 tbsp extra virgin olive oil
- salt and black pepper, to taste

Directions:

1. Combine the avocado and all vegetables in a large salad bowl. Add in basil and oregano leaves.
2. Season with salt and pepper, drizzle with balsamic vinegar and olive oil and toss to combine. Top with roast beef and serve.

Nutrition Per Serving:

- Calories: 273
- Fat: 22.4g
- Protein: 10.04g
- Carbs: 9.5g
- Fiber: 3.2g
- Sodium: 911mg

Chapter 13

HIGH-FIBER (DINNER)

264. Sweet Potato Black Bean Chili for Two

Preparation Time: 10 minutes
Cooking Time: 20 minutes
Servings: 2

Ingredients:

- 2 teaspoons virgin olive oil
- 1 small onion

- 1 small sweet potato
- 2 garlic cloves
- 1 tablespoon chili powder
- 2 teaspoons ground cumin
- 1/4 teaspoon ground chipotle Chile
- 1/8 teaspoon salt, or to taste
- 1 1/3 cup water
- 1 (15 ounces) can black beans, rinsed
- 1 cup canned diced tomatoes
- 2 teaspoons lime juice
- 2 tablespoons chopped fresh cilantro

Directions:

1. Heat a big pan with oil over medium-high heat, add potato and onion, then cook, frequently stirring, until the onion becomes slightly soft, roughly 4 minutes.

2. Add salt, chipotle, cumin, chili powder, and garlic, then cook continuously for around 30 seconds until aromatic.

3. Attach the water and bring to a simmer, cover, turn the heat down to keep it gently simmering.

4. Cook until the potato becomes tender, around 10-12 minutes.

5. Add lime juice, tomatoes, and beans, then turn the heat up to high and simmer, stirring frequently.

6. Turn the heat down to keep at a simmer and cook until the mixture reduces slightly, roughly 4 minutes.

Nutrition Per Serving:

- Calories: 365
- Fat: 7 g
- Sodium: 629 mg
- Carbs: 67 g
- Sugar: 16 g
- Protein: 14 g
- Saturated Fat: 1 g
- Fiber: 18 g
- Cholesterol: 0 g

265. Tabbouleh, Hummus Pita Plate

Preparation Time: 10 minutes
Cooking Time: 0 minutes
Servings: 4

Ingredients:

- 2 cups tabbouleh
- 1 cup beet hummus
- 1 cup sugar snap peas, stem ends snapped off
- 1 cup mixed olives
- 1 cup blackberries
- 1 cup raspberries
- 4 radishes
- 2/3 cup unsalted dry-roasted pistachios
- 4 whole-wheat pita breads
- 4 vegan cookies

Directions:

1. Distribute all the ingredients among 4 serving plates.

Nutrition Per Serving:

- Calories: 537
- Fat: 31 g
- Sugar: 12 g
- Protein: 13 g
- Saturated Fat: 5 g
- Sodium: 655 g
- Fiber: 14 g
- Cholesterol: 0 g
- Carbs: 55 g

266. Tex Mex Bean Tostadas

Preparation Time: 10 minutes
Cooking Time: 10 minutes
Servings: 1

Ingredients:

- 4 tostada shells
- 1 ½ cup shredded iceberg lettuce
- 1 can pinto beans, rinsed and drained
- 1/2 cup prepared salsa
- 1/2 cup shredded reduced-fat Cheddar cheese, plus 1/4 for garnishing
- 1 cup chopped tomato (1 large)
- 1/2 teaspoon salt-free Southwest chipotle seasoning blend
- Lime wedges (optional)

Directions:

1. Start preheating the oven at 350°F.
2. Arrange tostada shells on a baking sheet.
3. Bake until warm, about 3-5 minutes.
4. In the meantime, in a large bowl, mix the seasoning blend, salsa, and beans.
5. Coarsely mash the mixture using a potato masher or fork.
6. Separate the bean mixture among tostada shells, spreading evenly.
7. Spread on top with 1/2 cup of cheese.
8. Bake until the cheese is melted, about 5 minutes. Spread on top of the tostadas with the remaining 1/4 cup of cheese (if wanted), chopped tomato, and shredded lettuce.
9. Serve with lime wedges.

Nutrition Per Serving:

- Calories: 230
- Sodium: 660 mg
- Sugar: 2 g
- Cholesterol: 10 mg
- Carbs: 33 g
- Protein: 12 g
- Fat: 6 g
- Saturated Fat: 3 g
- Fiber: 8 g

267. Tomato Artichoke Gnocchi

Preparation Time: 10 minutes
Cooking Time: 20 minutes
Servings: 4

Ingredients:

- 2 tablespoons extra-virgin olive oil
- 1 (16 ounces) package shelf-stable gnocchi
- 1 small onion, sliced
- 1 small red bell pepper
- 4 large garlic cloves
- 1 tablespoon chopped fresh oregano
- 1 (15 ounces) canned chickpeas
- 1 (14 ounces) can no-salt-added diced tomatoes
- 1 (9 ounces) box frozen artichoke hearts
- 8 pitted Kalamata olives, sliced
- 1 tablespoon red-wine vinegar
- 1/4 teaspoon ground pepper

Directions:

1. In a non-stick skillet, heat 1 tablespoon of oil over medium-high heat.
2. Put in the gnocchi; cook and often stir for about 5 minutes, until plumped and beginning to brown.
3. Place them in a bowl and cover
4. -up to keep warm.
5. Lower heat to medium. Attach in the onion and the remaining tablespoon of oil.
6. Cook for 2-3 minutes, occasionally stirring, until beginning to brown.
7. Add in bell pepper; cook for about 3 minutes, occasionally stirring, until crisp-tender.
8. Put in the oregano and garlic; cook for half a minute, stirring.
9. Set in artichokes, tomatoes, and chickpeas; cook for about 3 minutes, stirring, until hot.
10. Mix in the gnocchi, pepper, vinegar, and olives.
11. Sprinkle oregano on top, if desired.

Nutrition Per Serving:

- Calories: 427
- Fat: 11 g
- Sugar: 5 g
- Protein: 12 g
- Carbs: 64 g
- Saturated Fat: 1 g
- Sodium: 825 mg
- Fiber: 10 g
- Cholesterol: 0 g

268. Vegan Buddha Bowl

Preparation Time: 10 minutes
Cooking Time: 20 minutes
Servings: 4

Ingredients:

- 1 medium sweet potato
- 3 tablespoons extra-virgin olive oil
- 1/2 teaspoon salt
- 1/2 teaspoon ground pepper
- 2 tablespoons tahini
- 2 tablespoons water
- 1 tablespoon lemon juice
- 1 small clove garlic
- 2 cups cooked quinoa
- 1 (15 ounces) canned chickpeas, rinsed
- 1 firm-ripe avocado, diced
- 1/4 cup cilantro or parsley

Directions:

1. Set the oven temperature to 425°F to preheat.
2. In a medium bowl, mix the sweet potato with 1/4 teaspoon each of salt and pepper plus 1 tablespoon of oil.
3. Move to a rimmed baking sheet. For 15-18 minutes, roast, stir once, until tender.
4. In a small bowl, mix the leftover 2 tablespoons of oil, lemon juice, tahini, garlic, water, and the leftover 1/4 teaspoon each of salt and pepper.
5. Split the quinoa among 4 bowls to serve.
6. Garnish with equal amounts of chickpeas, sweet potato, and avocado.
7. Drizzle with the tahini sauce.

8. Top with parsley or cilantro.

Nutrition Per Serving:

- Calories: 455
- Fat: 25 g
- Sodium: 472 mg
- Sugar: 3 g
- Protein: 11 g
- Carbs: 51 g
- Saturated Fat: 3 g
- Fiber: 11 g
- Cholesterol: 0 g

269. Vegan Cauliflower Fried Rice

Preparation Time: 10 minutes
Cooking Time: 15 minutes
Servings: 4

Ingredients:

- 3 tablespoons peanut oil, divided
- 3 scallions, sliced
- 1 tablespoon grated fresh ginger
- 1 tablespoon minced garlic
- 1/2 cup diced red bell pepper
- 1 cup trimmed and halved snow peas
- 1 cup shredded carrots
- 1 cup frozen shelled edamame, thawed
- 4 cups riced cauliflower
- 1/3 cup unsalted roasted cashews
- 3 tablespoons tamari or soy sauce
- 1 teaspoon toasted sesame oil

Directions:

1. In a cooking pan or wok, heat 1 tablespoon of peanut oil over high heat.
2. Cook and stir the ginger, garlic, and scallions in the hot oil for 30-40 seconds until scallions have softened.
3. Add the snow peas, bell pepper, edamame, and carrots, then cook while stirring until just tender for 2-4 minutes.
4. Move everything to a dish or plate.
5. Set the remaining 2 tablespoons of peanut oil into the pan.
6. Stir the cauliflower in the oil for about 2 minutes until it's mostly softened.
7. Put the vegetables back in the pan; add tamari or soy sauce, cashews, and sesame oil.
8. Stir together until blended properly.

Nutrition Per Serving:

- Calories: 287
- Fat: 19 g
- Saturated Fat: 3 g
- Fiber: 6 g
- Cholesterol: 0 g
- Carbs: 18 g
- Sodium: 451 mg
- Sugar: 6 g
- Protein: 10 g

270. Oatmeal Bread to Live for

Preparation Time: 10 minutes
Cooking Time: 30 minutes
Servings: 12

Ingredients:

- 1 ¼ cup (295 ml) water
- 2 teaspoons (10 ml) canola oil
- 1 tablespoon (15 g) brown sugar
- 1 cup (80 g) quick-cooking oats
- 2 ¼ cups whole-wheat flour, divided
- 1 tablespoon vital wheat gluten
- 1 ¼ teaspoon yeast
- 1 tablespoon shelled sunflower seeds

Directions:

1. Put water, oil, and sugar in the bread machine.
2. Add the oats and let them sit for 5 minutes.
3. Pour 2 cups (240 g) of flour and the gluten.
4. Set a well in the middle of the flour for the yeast.
5. Turn on the bread machine. (Use a setting for 1 ½-pound [680 g] loaf, dark if you have it). If the dough seems too sticky, attach additional flour as required.
6. Add the sunflower seeds to the beep.

Nutrition Per Serving:

- Calories: 287
- Fat: 19 g
- Saturated Fat: 3 g
- Fiber: 6 g
- Cholesterol: 0 g
- Carbs: 18 g

271. Vermicelli Puttanesca

Preparation Time: 10 minutes
Cooking Time: 15 minutes
Servings: 6

Ingredients:

- 4 large tomatoes
- 1/4 cup chopped flat-leaf parsley
- 16 large black olives
- 3 tablespoons capers
- 4 anchovy fillets
- 2 tablespoons olive oil
- 3 large garlic cloves
- 1/2 teaspoon ground pepper
- 1 pound whole-wheat vermicelli, or spaghettini
- 1/4 cup freshly grated Pecorino Romano

Directions:

1. Combine pepper, garlic, oil, anchovies, capers, olives, parsley, and tomatoes in a large pasta serving bowl.
2. In the meantime, in a pot of boiling salted water, cook pasta for 8-10 minutes, until just tender, or follow the package directions.
3. Drain the pasta and put it into the bowl with the sauce.
4. Next, toss well to combine.
5. Then taste and adjust seasonings.
6. Dust with cheese and immediately serve.

Nutrition Per Serving:

- Calories: 379
- Saturated Fat: 2 g

- Sodium: 379 mg
- Fiber: 4.8 g
- Sugar: 6 g
- Fat: 10 g
- Cholesterol: 2.2 mg
- Carbs: 62 g
- Protein: 14 g

272. Quinoa Chickpea Salad with Roasted Bell Pepper Hummus Dressing

Preparation Time: 10 minutes

Cooking Time: 0 minutes

Servings: 1

Ingredients:

- 2 tablespoons hummus
- 1 tablespoon lemon juice
- 1 tablespoon chopped and roasted bell pepper
- 2 cups mixed salad greens
- 1/2 cup cooked quinoa
- 1/2 cup chickpeas, rinsed
- 1 tablespoon unsalted sunflower seeds
- 1 tablespoon chopped fresh parsley
- A pinch of salt
- A pinch of ground pepper

Directions:

1. In a small bowl, combine hummus, red peppers, and lemon extract. To achieve the desired consistency, add enough water to thin.
2. In a large dish, place chickpeas, greens and quinoa. Flavor with salt and pepper to taste and garnish with parsley and sunflower seeds. Serve with dressing.

Nutrition Per Serving:

- Calories: 379
- Saturated Fat: 1 g
- Sodium: 607 mg
- Fiber: 13 g
- Cholesterol: 0 g
- Sugar: 3 g
- Protein: 16 g
- Fat: 10
- Carbs: 59 g

273. Rainbow Buddha Bowl with Cashew Tahini Sauce

Preparation Time: 10 minutes

Cooking Time: 0 minutes

Servings: 2

Ingredients:

- 3/4 cup unsalted cashews
- 1/4 cup packed parsley leaves
- 1/2 cup water
- 1 tablespoon lemon juice or cider vinegar
- 1/2 cup cooked quinoa
- 1/2 cup shredded red cabbage
- 1 tablespoon extra-virgin olive oil
- 1/4 cup grated raw beet
- 1/4 teaspoon salt
- 1/4 cup chopped bell pepper
- 1/2 cup cooked lentils
- 1/4 cup grated carrot
- 1/2 teaspoon reduced-sodium tamari or soy sauce
- 1/4 cup sliced cucumber

- Toasted chopped cashews for garnishing (optional)

Directions:

1. In a blender, mix soy sauce or tamari, cashews, salt, water, oil, lemon juice or vinegar, and parsley until smooth.
2. Put in quinoa and lentils in the middle of a serving bowl; add cucumber, cabbage, carrot, pepper, and beet on top. Ladle 2 tablespoons of cashew sauce over the vegetables; reserve the extra sauce for future use. If desired, add cashews on top.

Nutrition Per Serving:

- Calories: 361
- Fat: 10 g
- Saturated Fat: 2 g
- Cholesterol: 0 g
- Sodium: 139 mg
- Fiber: 14 g
- Carbs: 54 g
- Sugar: 9 g
- Protein: 17 g

274. Rice Bean Freezer Burritos

Preparation Time: 10 minutes
Cooking Time: 0 minutes
Servings: 8

Ingredients:

- 2 (15 ounces) cans of low-sodium black or pinto beans, rinsed
- 4 teaspoons chili powder
- 1 teaspoon ground cumin
- 2 cups shredded sharp Cheddar cheese

- 1 cup chopped grape tomatoes
- 4 scallions, chopped
- 1/4 cup chopped pickled jalapeños
- 2 tablespoons chopped fresh cilantro
- 8 (8 inches) whole-wheat tortillas, at room temperature
- 2 cups cooked brown rice

Directions:

1. In a big bowl, mash the beans with cumin and chili powder until it becomes almost smooth. Stir in cilantro, jalapeños, scallions, tomatoes, and cheese, then mix to blend.
2. Put about 1/2 cup of the filling on the bottom of every tortilla, then spread, and put about 1/4 cup of rice on top. Roll it up snugly and tuck the ends as you go. Use a foil to wrap each burrito. You can freeze it for up to 3 months.
3. Note: To warm your frozen burritos, unwrap the foil and put it on a microwave-safe plate. Use a paper towel to cover it and heat for 1-2 minutes on high, until it becomes steaming hot.

Nutrition Per Serving:

- Calories: 401
- Fat: 13 g
- Saturated Fat: 6 g
- Cholesterol: 28 mg
- Sodium: 646 mg
- Fiber: 12 g
- Carbs: 53 g
- Sugar: 4 g
- Protein: 17 g

275. Roasted Veggie Hummus Pita Pockets

Preparation Time: 10 minutes
Cooking Time: 0 minutes
Servings: 1

Ingredients:

- 1 (6 ½ inches) whole-wheat pita bread
- 4 tablespoons hummus
- 1/2 cup mixed salad greens
- 1/2 cup Sheet-Pan Roasted Root Vegetables, roughly chopped (see associated recipe)
- 1 tablespoon crumbled Feta cheese

Directions:

1. Halve the pita bread. Set the inside of each half of the pita pocket with 2 tablespoons of hummus.
2. Stuff with Feta, roasted vegetables, and greens on each pita pocket.

Nutrition Per Serving:

- Calories: 292
- Sodium: 545 mg
- Cholesterol: 8.3 mg
- Carbs: 46 g
- Sugar: 2.9 g
- Protein: 11 g
- Saturated Fat: 3 g
- Fiber: 10 g
- Fat: 9 g

276. Salmon Sushi Buddha Bowl

Preparation Time: 10 minutes
Cooking Time: 0 minutes
Servings: 1

Ingredients:

- 1/2 teaspoon rice vinegar
- 1/2 teaspoon honey
- 1/2 cup cooked short-grain brown rice
- 3 ounces sliced smoked salmon
- 1/2 avocado, sliced
- 1/2 cup cucumber
- 1 teaspoon reduced-sodium tamari or soy sauce
- 1 teaspoon toasted sesame oil
- 1/4 teaspoon wasabi paste
- Sesame seeds for garnishing (optional)

Directions:

1. In a small-size bowl, mix honey and rice vinegar. Into a shallow serving bowl, put the rice.
2. Place the smoked salmon, cucumber, and avocado on top.
3. In a small-size bowl, mix sesame oil, wasabi, and soy sauce or tamari; sprinkle on top of all. If wished, put sesame seeds on top.

Nutrition Per Serving:

- Calories: 370
- Sugar: 4.5 g
- Fiber: 5.9 g
- Saturated Fat: 4 g
- Sodium: 870 mg
- Cholesterol: 20 mg
- Carbs: 34.5 g

- Protein: 20.1 g
- Fat: 17.4 g

277. Sausage Peppers Baked Ziti

Preparation Time: 10 minutes
Cooking Time: 30 minutes
Servings: 4

Ingredients:

- 8 ounces whole-wheat penne or ziti pasta
- 1 (16 ounces) bag frozen pepper and onion mix
- 6 ounces turkey sausage crumbled
- 2 (8 ounces) cans of no-salt-added tomato sauce
- 1 teaspoon garlic powder
- 1 teaspoon dried oregano
- 1/4 teaspoon salt
- 1/2 cup reduced-fat Cottage cheese
- 3/4 cup Italian blend shredded cheese

Directions:

1. Following the package instructions, cook the pasta properly in a pot of boiling water. Strain.
2. Meanwhile, place a large ovenproof skillet on medium-high heat. Put in the sausage and frozen vegetables; cook while occasionally stirring for 10-15 minutes, till most of the liquid from the vegetables has evaporated.
3. Set a rack in the upper third of the oven; preheat the broiler.
4. Combine salt, oregano, garlic powder, and tomato sauce into the skillet. Set the heat down to medium-low; mix in the pasta and Cottage cheese.
5. Cook while stirring for around 2 minutes, till heated. Place shredded cheese on top.
6. Place the skillet under the preheat broiler; brown the cheese for 1-2 minutes.

Nutrition Per Serving:

- Calories: 408
- Fat: 10 g
- Sodium: 702 mg
- Fiber: 11 g
- Cholesterol: 48 g
- Carbs: 58 g
- Sugar: 9 g
- Saturated Fat: 4 g
- Protein: 27 g

278. Sauteed Butternut Squash

Preparation Time: 10 minutes
Cooking Time: 15 minutes
Servings: 7

Ingredients:

- 1 large butternut squash (2-3 pounds), peeled, seeded, and cubed
- 1 tablespoon extra-virgin olive oil

Directions:

1. In a big saucepan, heat oil on moderate fire.

2. Put in the squash and cook for 15 minutes while often stirring, until brown slightly and soften.

Nutrition Per Serving:

- Calories: 75
- Sugar: 3 g
- Protein: 1 g
- Fat: 2 g
- Saturated Fat: 0 g
- Sodium: 5 mg
- Fiber: 3 g
- Cholesterol: 0 g
- Carbs: 15 g

279. Seared Salmon with Pesto Fettuccine

Preparation Time: 10 minutes
Cooking Time: 20 minutes
Servings: 4

Ingredients:

- 8 ounces whole-wheat Fettuccine
- 2/3 cup pesto
- 1 ¼ pound wild salmon, skinned and cut into 4 portions
- 1/4 teaspoon salt
- 1/4 teaspoon ground pepper
- 1 tablespoon extra-virgin olive oil

Directions:

1. Boil a large pot of water. Include in the Fettuccine; cook for around 9 minutes, or till just tender. Strain; transfer into a large bowl. Toss with pesto.
2. Meanwhile, season with pepper and salt on salmon. Set a large, non-stick, or cast-iron skillet on medium-high heat; heat oil. Include in the salmon; cook for 2-4 minutes per side, or till just opaque in the center, turning once. Serve the salmon accompanied with the pasta.

Nutrition Per Serving:

- Calories: 540
- Protein: 23 g
- Fat: 28 g
- Saturated Fat: 7 g
- Sodium: 274 mg
- Fiber: 6.6 g
- Cholesterol: 43.22 mg
- Carbs: 45 g
- Sugar: 1.3

280. Sesame Ginger Chicken Salad

Preparation Time: 10 minutes
Cooking Time: 0 minutes
Servings: 1

Ingredients:

- 4 cups chopped romaine lettuce
- 3 ounces shredded cooked chicken breast
- 1/2 cup fresh spinach
- 1/4 cup shredded carrot
- 1/4 cup sliced radishes
- 1 scallion, sliced

- 3 tablespoons prepared sesame-ginger dressing

Directions:

1. In a medium bowl, mix scallion, radishes, carrot, spinach, chicken, and lettuce, then put in the dressing and toss to coat well.

Nutrition Per Serving:

- Calories: 238
- Fat: 8.7 g
- Saturated Fat: 1.7 g
- Cholesterol: 39 mg
- Carbs: 23 g
- Protein: 17 g
- Sodium: 500 mg
- Fiber: 6 g
- Sugar: 15 g

281. Protein-Packed Soup

Preparation Time: 15 minutes
Cooking Time: 1 hour 10 minutes
Servings: 8

Ingredients:

- 2 tbsp. olive oil
- 1½ lb. ground turkey
- Salt and freshly ground black pepper, to taste
- 1 large carrot, peeled and chopped
- 1 large celery stalk, chopped
- 1 large onion, chopped
- 6 garlic cloves, chopped
- 1 tsp. dried rosemary

- 1 tsp. dried oregano
- 2 large potatoes, peeled and chopped
- 8-9 cup chicken bone broth
- 4-5 cup tomatoes, peeled, seeded, and chopped
- 2 cup dry lentils
- ¼ cup fresh parsley, chopped

Directions:

1. Heat the olive oil over medium-high heat in a large soup pan and cook the turkey for about 5 minutes or until browned.
2. With a slotted spoon, transfer the turkey into a bowl and set it aside.
3. Add the carrot, celery onion, garlic, and dried herbs over medium heat and cook for about 5 minutes in the same pan.
4. Add the potatoes and cook for about 4-5 minutes.
5. Add the cooked turkey, tomatoes, and broth and bring to a boil over high heat.
6. Reduce the heat to low and cook, covered for about 10 minutes.
7. Add the lentils and cook, covered for about 40 minutes.
8. Stir in black pepper and remove from the heat.
9. Serve hot with the garnishing of parsley.

Nutrition Per Serving:

- Calories: 531
- Carbohydrates: 52g
- Protein: 34g
- Fat: 21g
- Sugar: 5.8g
- Sodium: 266mg

- Fiber: 8.7g

282. Thanksgiving Dinner Chili

Preparation Time: 15 minutes
Cooking Time: 45 minutes
Servings: 6

Ingredients:

- 2 tbsp. olive oil
- 1 red bell pepper, seeded and chopped
- 1 onion, chopped
- 2 garlic cloves, chopped
- 1 lb. lean ground turkey
- 2 cup water
- 3 cup tomatoes, chopped finely
- 1 tsp. ground cumin
- 1 (15-oz.) cans black beans, rinsed and drained
- ½ tsp. ground cinnamon
- 1 (15-oz.) can red kidney beans, rinsed and drained
- ¼ cup scallion greens, chopped

Directions:

1. Heat the olive oil over medium-low heat and sauté bell pepper, onion, and garlic for about 5 minutes in a large Dutch oven.
2. Add the turkey and cook for about 5-6 minutes, breaking up the chunks with a wooden spoon.
3. Add the tomatoes, water, and spices and bring to a boil over high heat.
4. Reduce the heat to medium-low and stir in beans and corn.

5. Simmer, covered for about 30 minutes, stirring occasionally.
6. Serve hot with the topping of scallion greens.

Nutrition Per Serving:

- Calories: 315
- Carbohydrates: 23.3g
- Protein: 21g
- Fat: 15.3g
- Sugar: 5g
- Sodium: 319mg
- Fiber: 7.5g

283. Meatless Monday Chili

Preparation Time: 15 minutes
Cooking Time: 1 hour 25 minutes
Servings: 4

Ingredients:

- 2 tbsp. avocado oil
- 1 medium onion, chopped
- 1 carrot, peeled and chopped
- 1 small bell pepper, seeded and chopped
- 1 lb. fresh mushrooms, sliced
- 2 garlic cloves, minced
- 2 tsp. dried oregano
- 1 tbsp. red chili powder
- 1 tbsp. ground cumin
- Salt and freshly ground black pepper, to taste
- 8 oz. canned red kidney beans, rinsed and drained
- 8 oz. canned white kidney beans, rinsed and drained

- 2 cup tomatoes, peeled, seeded, and chopped finely
- 1½ cup homemade vegetable broth

Directions:

1. Heat the oil over medium-low heat in a large Dutch oven and cook the onions, carrot, and bell pepper for about 10 minutes, stirring frequently.
2. Increase the heat to medium-high.
3. Stir in the mushrooms and garlic and cook for about 5-6 minutes, stirring frequently.
4. Add the oregano, spices, salt, and black pepper and cook for about 1-2 minutes.
5. Stir in the beans, tomatoes, and broth and bring to a boil.
6. Reduce the heat to low and simmer, covered for about 1 hour, stirring occasionally.
7. Serve hot.

Nutrition Per Serving:

- Calories: 223
- Carbohydrates: 28.3g
- Protein: 11g
- Fat: 8.6g
- Sugar: 9g
- Sodium: 570mg
- Fiber: 9.04g

284. Beans Trio Chili

Preparation Time: 15 minutes
Cooking Time: 1 hour
Servings: 6

Ingredients:

- 2 tbsp. olive oil
- 1 green bell pepper, seeded and chopped
- 2 celery stalks, chopped
- 1 scallion, chopped
- 3 garlic cloves, minced
- 1 tsp. dried oregano, crushed
- 1 tbsp. red chili powder
- 2 tsp. ground cumin
- 1 tsp. red pepper flakes, crushed
- 1 tsp. ground turmeric
- 1 tsp. onion powder
- 1 tsp. garlic powder
- Salt and freshly ground black pepper, to taste
- 4½ cup tomatoes, peeled, seeded, and chopped finely
- 4 cup water
- 1 (16-oz.) can red kidney beans, rinsed and drained
- 1 (16-oz.) can cannellini beans, rinsed and drained
- ½ of (16-oz.) can black beans, rinsed and drained

Directions:

1. Heat the oil over medium heat in a large pan and cook the celery, bell peppers, garlic, and scallion for about 8-10 minutes, stirring frequently.

2. Add the black pepper, oregano, salt, spices, water, and tomatoes and bring to a boil.
3. Simmer for about 20 minutes.
4. Stir in the beans and simmer for about 30 minutes.
5. Serve hot.

Nutrition Per Serving:

- Calories: 222
- Carbohydrates: 30g
- Protein: 10g
- Fat: 6.3g
- Sugar: 6.5g
- Sodium: 365 mg
- Fiber: 10.9 g

285. Fragrant Vegetarian Curry

Preparation Time: 15 minutes
Cooking Time: 1½ hours
Servings: 8

Ingredients:

- 8 cup water
- ½ tsp. ground turmeric
- 1 cup brown lentils
- 1 cup red lentils
- 1 tbsp. olive oil
- 1 large white onion, chopped
- 3 garlic cloves, minced
- 2 large tomatoes, peeled, seeded, and chopped
- 1½ tbsp. curry powder
- ¼ tsp. ground cloves
- 2 tsp. ground cumin

- 3 carrots, peeled and chopped
- 3 cup pumpkin, peeled, seeded, and cubed into 1-inch size
- 1 granny smith apple, cored and chopped
- 2 cup fresh spinach, chopped
- Salt and freshly ground black pepper, to taste

Directions:

1. In a large pan, add the water, turmeric, and lentils over high heat and bring to a boil.
2. Reduce the heat to medium-low and simmer, covered for about 30 minutes.
3. Drain the lentils, reserving 2½ cup of the cooking liquid.
4. Meanwhile, heat the oil over medium heat in another large pan and sauté the onion for about 2-3 minutes.
5. Add in the garlic and sauté for about 1 minute.
6. Add the tomatoes and cook for about 5 minutes.
7. Stir in the curry powder and spices and cook for about 1 minute.
8. Add the carrots, potatoes, pumpkin, cooked lentils, and reserved cooking liquid and bring to a gentle boil.
9. Reduce the heat to medium-low and simmer, covered for about 40-45 minutes or until the desired doneness of the vegetables.
10. Stir in the apple and spinach and simmer for about 15 minutes.
11. Stir in the salt and black pepper and remove from the heat.
12. Serve hot.

Nutrition Per Serving:

- Calories: 239
- Carbohydrates: 42g
- Protein: 13.6g
- Fat: 2.9g
- Sugar: 6.7g
- Sodium: 129 mg
- Fiber: 8.17g

286. Omega-3 Rich Dinner Meal

Preparation Time: 15 minutes
Cooking Time: 40 minutes
Servings: 4

Ingredients:

For Lentils:

- ½ lb. French green lentils
- 2 tbsp. extra-virgin olive oil
- 2 cup yellow onions, chopped
- 2 cup scallions, chopped
- 1 tsp. fresh parsley, chopped
- Salt and freshly ground black pepper, to taste
- 1 tbsp. garlic, minced
- 1½ cup carrots, peeled and chopped
- 1½ cup celery stalks, chopped
- 1 large tomato, peeled, seeded, and crushed finely
- 1½ cup chicken bone broth
- 2 tbsp. balsamic vinegar

For Salmon:

- 2 (8-oz.) skinless salmon fillets
- 2 tbsp. extra-virgin olive oil
- Salt and freshly ground black pepper, to taste

Directions:

1. In a heat-proof bowl, soak the lentils in boiling water for 15 minutes.
2. Drain the lentils completely.
3. Heat the oil over medium heat in a Dutch oven and cook the onions, scallions, parsley, salt, and black pepper for about 10 minutes, stirring frequently.
4. Add the garlic and cook for about 2 more minutes.
5. Add the drained lentils, carrots, celery, crushed tomato, and broth and bring to a boil.
6. Reduce the heat to low and simmer, covered for about 20-25 minutes.
7. Stir in the vinegar, salt, and black pepper and remove from the heat.
8. Meanwhile, for salmon: preheat your oven to 450 degrees F.
9. Rub the salmon fillets with oil and then season with salt and black pepper generously.
10. Heat an oven-proof sauté pan over medium heat and cook the salmon fillets for about 2minutes, without stirring.
11. Flip the fillets and immediately transfer the pan into the oven.
12. Bake for about 5-7 minutes or until the desired doneness of salmon.
13. Remove from the oven and place the salmon fillets onto a cutting board.
14. Cut each fillet into 2 portions.
15. Divide the lentil mixture onto serving plates and top each with 1 salmon fillet.

16. Serve hot.

Nutrition Per Serving:

- Calories: 707
- Carbohydrates: 45 g
- Protein: 43 g
- Fat: 22 g
- Sugar: 6.4 g
- Sodium: 354 mg
- Fiber: 11.6 g

287. Skillet Gnocchi with Chard White Beans

Preparation Time: 10 minutes
Cooking Time: 30 minutes
Servings: 6

Ingredients:

- 1 tablespoon extra-virgin olive oil
- 1 (16 ounces) package shelf-stable gnocchi
- 1 teaspoon extra-virgin olive oil
- 1 medium yellow onion, thinly sliced
- 4 garlic cloves, minced
- 1/2 cup water
- 6 cups chopped chard leaves or spinach
- 1 can diced tomatoes with Italian seasonings
- 1 (15 ounces) can white beans, rinsed
- 1/4 teaspoon freshly ground pepper
- 1/2 cup shredded part-skim Mozzarella cheese
- 1/4 cup finely shredded Parmesan cheese

Directions:

1. On medium heat, heat 1 tablespoon of oil in a big non-stick pan. Add and cook the gnocchi while frequently stirring for 5-7 minutes until it begins to brown and plump; move to a bowl.
2. Add the onion and the remaining teaspoon of oil into the pan.
3. On medium heat, cook and stir for 2 minutes. Mix in water and garlic; cover. Cook for 4-6 minutes until the onion is soft; put the chard or spinach in. Cook and stir for 1-2 minutes until it begins to wilt.
4. Mix in pepper, beans, and tomatoes; simmer. Combine in the gnocchi, then scatter Parmesan and Mozzarella; cover.
5. Cook for about 3 minutes until the sauce bubbles, and the cheese melts.

Nutrition Per Serving:

- Calories: 301
- Sodium: 734 mg
- Carbs: 46 g
- Cholesterol: 7.4 mg
- Protein: 13 g

Fat: 6.6 g

288. Spaghetti Genovese

Preparation Time: 10 minutes
Cooking Time: 20 minutes
Servings: 5

Ingredients:

- 2 cups packed baby spinach

- 8 ounces whole-wheat spaghetti
- 1 cup thinly sliced new or baby potatoes (about 4 ounces)
- 1-pound green beans
- 1/2 cup prepared pesto
- 1 teaspoon freshly ground pepper
- 1/2 teaspoon salt

Directions:

1. Boil a big pot of water on medium-high heat. Put in the spinach and cook for about 45 seconds, just until it wilts.
2. Move the spinach to a blender using a fine sieve or a slotted spoon.
3. Bring the water back to a boil and put in potatoes and spaghetti.
4. Cook for 6-7 minutes until they are almost soft, only stirring 1-2 times.
5. Put in green beans and cook for another 3-4 minutes until they become soft.
6. When the vegetables and spaghetti are almost cooked, carefully take out 1 cup of the cooking liquid.
7. Pour 1/2 cup of the liquid into the blender; place in salt, pepper, and pesto. Merge until smooth; stop to scrape down the sides if you want.
8. Strain the vegetables and the spaghetti, set back to the pot; add the pesto mixture and stir. Set the heat and cook while gently stirring the pasta for 1-2 minutes until it is hot and the sauce is thickened. If you want a thinner sauce, you can add in more cooking liquid.

Nutrition Per Serving:

- Calories: 333
- Saturated Fat: 1.6 g
- Cholesterol: 25 mg
- Fat: 12 g
- Carbs: 44 g
- Sugar: 3 g
- Protein: 11 g
- Sodium: 310 mg
- Fiber: 8 g

289. Spiced Sweet Potato Wedges

Preparation Time: 10 minutes
Cooking Time: 25-30 minutes
Servings: 4

Ingredients:

- 2 (20 ounces) sweet potatoes, scrubbed
- 1 tablespoon olive oil
- 1 teaspoon packed brown sugar
- 1/4 teaspoon kosher salt
- 1/4 teaspoon smoked paprika
- 1/4 teaspoon black pepper
- 1/4 teaspoon pumpkin pie spice
- 1/4 teaspoon hot chili powder

Directions:

1. Set an oven to preheat at 425ºF. Put a baking tray in the oven to preheat.
2. Halve each sweet potato lengthwise into 8 wedges or 16 wedges in total.
3. Drizzle olive oil on sweet potato wedges in a big bowl, then toss to coat well.

4. In a small bowl, stir the chili powder, pumpkin pie spice, pepper, smoked paprika, kosher salt, and brown sugar.
5. Sprinkle sweet potatoes with the spice mixture, then toss to coat well.
6. On the hot baking tray, lay out the wedges in one layer. Roast until it turns brown and soft, or for 25-30 minutes, flipping the wedges once halfway through the roasting time.

Nutrition Per Serving:

- Calories: 232
- Cholesterol: 0 g
- Saturated Fat: 0.5 g
- Fiber: 6.9 g
- Carbs: 46 g
- Sugar: 10 g
- Protein: 4 g
- Fat: 3.7 g
- Sodium: 246 mg

290. Stetson Chopped Salad

Preparation Time: 10 minutes
Cooking Time: 10 minutes
Servings: 2

Ingredients:

- 3/4 cup water
- 1/2 cup Israeli couscous
- 6 cups baby arugula
- 1 cup fresh corn kernels
- 1 cup halved or quartered cherry tomatoes
- 1 firm-ripe avocado, diced
- 1/4 cup toasted pepitas
- 1/4 cup dried currants
- 1/2 cup chopped fresh basil
- 1/4 cup buttermilk
- 1/4 cup mayonnaise
- 1 tablespoon lemon juice
- 1 small clove garlic, peeled
- 1/4 teaspoon salt
- 1/4 teaspoon ground pepper

Directions:

1. In a small saucepan, set water to a boil. Put in couscous and lower heat to keep a gentle simmer, then cover and cook for 8-10 minutes, until water is absorbed.
2. Move to a fine-mesh sieve and rinse under cold water, then drain well.
3. On a serving plate, spread the arugula. Put the arugula over the currants, pepitas, avocado, tomatoes, corn, and couscous in decorative lines.
4. In a blender or mini food processor, mix pepper, salt, garlic, lemon juice, mayonnaise, buttermilk, and basil, then pulse until smooth. Right before serving, drizzle the salad with the dressing.

Nutrition Per Serving:

- Calories: 533
- Carbs: 52 g
- Sugar: 23 g
- Saturated Fat: 5 g
- Fiber:11 g
- Protein: 12 g
- Fat: 34 g
- Sodium: 516 mg
- Cholesterol: 3.3 mg

291. Stuffed Sweet Potato with Hummus Dressing

Preparation Time: 10 minutes
Cooking Time: 15 minutes
Servings: 1

Ingredients:

- 1 large sweet potato, scrubbed
- 3/4 cup chopped kale
- 1 cup canned black beans, rinsed
- 1/4 cup hummus
- 2 tablespoons water

Directions:

1. Using a fork, stab the sweet potato all over the microwave for 7-10 minutes until completely cooked.
2. Rinse and drain the kale, let the water hold to the leaves. On medium-high heat, cook the kale in a medium saucepan, covered, until it wilts; stir 1-2 times.
3. Put in beans; pour 1-2 tablespoons of water if the pot dries.
4. Cook and occasionally stir without cover for 1-2 minutes until the mixture is steaming.
5. Break and open the sweet potato; add the beans and the kale mixture on top.
6. In a small dish, mix 2 tablespoons of water and hummus. If needed, pour in more water to reach the preferred thickness.
7. Spread the hummus dressing on top of the sweet potato.

Nutrition Per Serving:

- Calories: 472
- Fiber: 22 g
- Cholesterol: 0 g
- Carbs: 85 g
- Sugar: 20 g
- Sodium: 489 mg
- Protein: 21 g
- Fat: 7 g
- Saturated Fat: 1 g

292. Summer Squash White Bean Sauté

Preparation Time: 10 minutes
Cooking Time: 20 minutes
Servings: 4

Ingredients:

- 1 tablespoon olive oil
- 1 medium onion, halved and sliced
- 2 garlic cloves, minced
- 1 medium zucchini, halved lengthwise and sliced
- 1 medium yellow summer squash, halved lengthwise and sliced
- 1 tablespoon chopped fresh oregano
- 1/4 teaspoon salt
- 1/4 teaspoon ground pepper
- 1 (15-19 ounces) canned cannellini or great northern beans, rinsed
- 2 medium tomatoes
- 1 tablespoon red-wine vinegar
- 1/3 cup finely shredded Parmesan cheese

Directions:

1. In a big non-stick skillet, heat oil over medium heat. Add garlic and onion. Cook while stirring for 3 minutes until starting to get tender.
2. Add pepper, salt, oregano, summer squash, and zucchini; mix to blend.
3. Lower the heat to low; put a cover on and cook for 3-5 minutes until the vegetables are tender-crisp, stirring 1 time.
4. Mix in vinegar, tomatoes, and beans; raise the heat to be medium and cook for 2 minutes until heated.
5. Take away from the heat and sprinkle Parmesan cheese.

Nutrition Per Serving:

- Calories: 183
- Cholesterol: 4.8 mg
- Protein: 9.5 g
- Fat: 6.7 g
- Saturated Fat: 1.7 g
- Sugar: 5 g
- Sodium: 303 mg
- Fiber: 6.6 g
- Carbs: 22.8 g

293. Sweet Savory Hummus Plate

Preparation Time: 10 minutes
Cooking Time: 0 minutes
Servings: 4

Ingredients:

- 3/4 cup white bean dip
- 1 cup green beans, stem ends trimmed
- 8 mini bell peppers
- 20 Castelvetrano olives
- 8 small watermelon wedges or 2 cups cubed watermelon
- 1 cup red grapes
- 20 gluten-free crackers
- 1/2 cup salted roasted pepitas
- 8 coconut-date balls

Directions:

1. Separate the items equally into 4 plates.
2. Serve with hard cider if desired.

Nutrition Per Serving:

- Calories: 654
- Cholesterol: 0 g
- Protein: 14 g
- Fat: 30 g
- Fiber: 11 g
- Sugar: 39 g
- Saturated Fat: 3 g
- Sodium: 568 mg
- Carbs: 84 mg

294. Halibut and Quinoa Mix

Preparation Time: 10 minutes
Cooking Time: 12 minutes
Servings: 4

Ingredients:

- 4 halibut fillets, boneless
- 2 tablespoons olive oil
- 1 teaspoon rosemary, dried
- 2 teaspoons cumin, ground

- 1 tablespoons coriander, ground
- 2 teaspoons cinnamon powder
- 2 teaspoons oregano, dried
- A pinch of salt and black pepper
- 2 cups quinoa, cooked
- 1 cup cherry tomatoes, halved
- 1 avocado, peeled, pitted, and sliced
- 1 cucumber, cubed
- ½ cup black olives, pitted and sliced
- Juice of 1 lemon

Directions:

1. Combine the fish with the rosemary, cumin, coriander, cinnamon, oregano, salt, and pepper in a bowl and toss.
2. Heat a pan with the oil over medium heat, add the fish, and sear for 2 minutes on each side.
3. Introduce the pan in the oven and bake the fish at 425 degrees F for 7 minutes.
4. Meanwhile, mix the quinoa with the remaining ingredients in a bowl, toss, and divide between plates.
5. Add the fish next to the quinoa mix and serve right away.

Nutrition Per Serving:

- Calories: 471
- Fat: 22 g
- Fiber: 7.7 g
- Carbs: 29 g
- Protein: 41 g

295. Lemon and Dates Barramundi

Preparation Time: 10 minutes
Cooking Time: 12 minutes
Servings: 2

Ingredients:

- 2 barramundi fillets, boneless
- 1 shallot, sliced
- 4 lemon slices
- Juice of ½ lemon
- Zest of 1 lemon, grated
- 2 tablespoons olive oil
- 6 ounces baby spinach
- ¼ cup almonds, chopped
- 4 dates, pitted and chopped
- ¼ cup parsley, chopped
- Salt and black pepper to the taste

Directions:

1. Season the fish with salt and pepper and arrange on 2 parchment paper pieces.
2. Top the fish with the lemon slices, drizzle the lemon juice, and then top with the other ingredients except for the oil.
3. Drizzle 1 tablespoon of oil over each fish mix, wrap the parchment paper around the fish shaping into packets, and arrange them on a baking sheet.
4. Bake at 400 degrees F for 12 minutes, cool the mix a bit, unfold, divide everything between plates and serve.

Nutrition Per Serving:

- Calories: 506
- Fat: 23 g

- Fiber: 8 g
- Carbs: 47 g
- Protein: 37 g

296. Catfish Fillets and Rice

Preparation Time: 10 minutes
Cooking Time: 55 minutes
Servings: 2

Ingredients:

- 2 catfish fillets, boneless
- 2 tablespoons Italian seasoning
- 2 tablespoons olive oil
- For the rice:
- 1 cup brown rice
- 2 tablespoons olive oil
- 1 and ½ cups water
- ½ cup green bell pepper, chopped
- 2 garlic cloves, minced
- ½ cup white onion, chopped
- 2 teaspoons Cajun seasoning
- ½ teaspoon garlic powder
- Salt and black pepper to the taste

Directions:

1. Heat a pot with 2 tablespoons of oil over medium heat, add the onion, garlic, garlic powder, salt, and pepper and sauté for 5 minutes.
2. Add the rice, water, bell pepper, and the seasoning, bring to a simmer, and cook over medium heat for 40 minutes.
3. Heat a pan with 2 tablespoons of oil over medium heat, add the fish and the Italian seasoning, and cook for 5 minutes on each side.
4. Divide the rice between plates, add the fish on top and serve.

Nutrition Per Serving:

- Calories: 593
- Fat: 21 g
- Fiber: 4.9 g
- Carbs: 77 g
- Protein: 25 g

Chapter 14

HIGH-FIBER (SNACKS)

297. Trail Mix Cookies

Preparation Time: 10 minutes

Cooking Time: 10 minutes

Servings: 60

Ingredients:

- 3/4 cup (165 g) unsalted butter
- 3/4 cup (150 g) sugar
- 1 egg
- 1 teaspoon vanilla extract
- 2 cups whole-wheat pastry flour
- 1 teaspoon baking soda
- 1 teaspoon cinnamon
- 1/4 teaspoon nutmeg
- 3/4 cup (175 ml) skim milk
- 1 ¾ cup (140 g) quick-cooking oats
- 1 ½ cup (200 g) trail mix

Directions:

1. Cream the butter and sugar. Add egg and vanilla; beat well. Stir the dry ingredients.

2. Attach them to the mixture alternately with milk, mixing well.

3. Stir in oats and the trail mix. Set by tablespoons on a baking sheet covered with non-stick vegetable oil spray.

4. Bake at 400ºF (200ºC, gas mark 6) until lightly browned, 8-10 minutes.

Nutrition Per Serving:

- Calories: 70.9
- Fat: 3.51 g
- Carbs: 8 g
- Sugar: 2 g
- Fiber: .07 g
- Protein: 1.5 g
- Sodium: 10.5 mg

298. White Chocolate-Cranberry Cookies

Preparation Time: 10 minutes
Cooking Time: 10 minutes
Servings: 36

Ingredients:

- 1/2 cup (112 g) shortening
- 1 cup (225 g) brown sugar
- 1 egg
- 1 teaspoon vanilla extract
- 13/4 cups (210 g) whole-wheat pastry flour
- 1 teaspoon baking soda
- 1/4 cup (60 ml) buttermilk
- 1/2 cup (87 g) white chocolate chips
- 1/2 cup (60 g) dried cranberries

Directions:

1. Beat the shortening until light. Add sugar and beat until fluffy.

2. Beat in the egg and vanilla.

3. Stir the dry ingredients. Attach them to a mixture alternately with buttermilk.

4. Beat until smooth. Stir in chips and cranberries.

5. Drop about 2 inches (5 cm) apart on a baking sheet coated with non-stick vegetable oil spray.

6. Bake at 375ºF (190ºC, gas mark 5) 8-10 minutes, until lightly browned.

Nutrition Per Serving:

- Calories: 361
- Fat: 10 g
- Saturated Fat: 2 g
- Cholesterol: 0 g
- Sodium: 139 mg
- Fiber: 14 g

299. Oatmeal Sunflower Bread

Preparation Time: 10 minutes
Cooking Time: 20 minutes
Servings: 12

Ingredients:

- 1 cup (235 ml) water
- 1/4 cup (85 g) honey
- 2 tablespoons (28 g) unsalted butter
- 3 cups (411 g) bread flour
- 1/2 cup (40 g) quick-cooking oats
- 2 tablespoons nonfat dry milk powder
- 2 teaspoons yeast

- 1 tablespoon vital wheat gluten
- 1/2 cup (72 g) unsalted shelled sunflower seeds

Directions:

1. Set all ingredients except the sunflower seeds in a bread machine in order specified by the manufacturer. A process on a large white loaf cycle.
2. Add the sunflower seeds at the beep or 5 minutes before the end of kneading.

Nutrition Per Serving:

- Calories: 217
- Fat: 5.6 g
- Carbs: 35 g
- Sugar: 6.8 g
- Fiber: 1.9 g
- Protein: 6.7 g
- Sodium: 9.5 mg

300. Maple Oatmeal Bread

Preparation Time: 10 minutes
Cooking Time: 20 minutes
Servings: 12

Ingredients:

- 1 ¾ teaspoon yeast
- 1 cup (157 ml) warm water
- 2 ½ cups (342 g) bread flour
- 1/2 cup flour
- 1 cup (27 g) rolled oats
- 1 cup (80 ml) maple syrup
- 1/4 cup (17 g) non-fat dry milk

- 2 tablespoons (28 g) unsalted butter, room temperature

Directions:

1. Add all ingredients to the bread machine in the order specified by the manufacturer.
2. A process on a sweet bread or whole-wheat cycle.

Nutrition Per Serving:

- Calories: 221
- Carbs: 44 g
- Sugar: 16 g
- Fat: 2.5 g
- Fiber: 1.1 g
- Cholesterol: 5.3 mg
- Protein: 4.8 g

301. German Dark Bread

Preparation Time: 10 minutes
Cooking Time: 20 minutes
Servings: 12

Ingredients:

- 1 cup (235 ml) water
- 1/4 cup (85 g) molasses
- 1 tablespoon unsalted butter
- 2 cups (274 g) bread flour
- 1 ¼ cup (160 g) rye flour
- 2 tablespoons cocoa powder
- 1 ½ teaspoon yeast
- 1 tablespoon vital wheat gluten

Directions:

1. Set all ingredients in the bread machine in order specified by the manufacturer. A process on a whole-wheat cycle.

Nutrition Per Serving:

- Calories: 162
- Fat: 1.6 g
- Protein: 4.8 g
- Fiber: 2.4 g
- Cholesterol: 0 g
- Carbs: 32 g
- Sodium: 4.36 mg

302. Onion and Garlic Wheat Bread

Preparation Time: 10 minutes
Cooking Time: 20 minutes
Servings: 12

Ingredients:

- 1/2 cup (80 g) finely chopped onion
- 1/2 teaspoon finely chopped garlic
- 1 tablespoon sugar
- 1/2 cup whole-wheat flour
- 2 ½ cups (342 g) bread flour
- 1 ½ tablespoon nonfat dry milk
- 1 ½ teaspoon yeast
- 3/4 cup (175 ml) water
- 1 ½ tablespoon (21 g) unsalted butter

Directions:

1. Set all ingredients in the bread machine in order specified by the manufacturer. A process on a white bread cycle.

Nutrition Per Serving:

- Calories: 144
- Fat: 2 g
- Carbs: 26 g
- Sugar: 1.9 g
- Fiber: 1.5 g
- Protein: 4.39 g

303. Chocolate Peanut Cookies

Preparation Time: 10 minutes
Cooking Time: 2-3 minutes
Servings: 6

Ingredients:

- 1 ounce (45 g) chocolate candy bar
- 4 tablespoons (64 g) crunchy peanut butter
- 1 cup (60 g) lightly sweetened bran cereal, such as Fiber One

Directions:

1. Dissolve the chocolate bar and peanut butter in the microwave until smooth, checking at 30-second intervals. Be careful not to burn.
2. Set to mix the melted chocolate and peanut butter.
3. Add cereal and gently toss until coated.
4. Drop on waxed paper or foil, making 6 cookies. Freeze for 30 minutes.
5. Put in resealable plastic bags and refrigerate.

Nutrition Per Serving:

- Calories: 193
- Cholesterol: 5 g
- Protein: 10 g
- Fat: 6 g
- Saturated Fat: 2 g
- Sugar: 7 g
- Sodium: 599 mg
- Fiber: 7 g
- Carbs: 25 g

304. Whole-wheat–Chocolate Chip Cookies

Preparation Time: 10 minutes
Cooking Time: 10 minutes
Servings: 48

Ingredients:

- 1 cup (225 g) unsalted butter
- 1/4 cup (64 g) peanut butter
- 1 cup (340 g) honey
- 2 eggs
- 1 ½ cup whole-wheat pastry flour
- 1 teaspoon baking soda
- 2 cups (160 g) rolled oats
- 2 cups (350 g) chocolate chips
- 1 cup (110 g) chopped pecans

Directions:

1. Cream together the first 4 ingredients.
2. Add the next 5 ingredients and mix well.
3. Add enough flour for a stiff dough.
4. Drop by teaspoons on a baking sheet.

5. Bake at 375°F (190°C, gas mark 5) for 10 minutes.

Nutrition Per Serving:

- Calories: 143
- Fat: 8.7 g
- Sodium: 10.14 mg
- Carbs: 16 g
- Sugar: 10 g
- Protein: 2.04 g
- Saturated Fat: 1 g
- Fiber: 1.57 g
- Cholesterol: 0 g

305. Good-for-You Chocolate Chip Cookies

Preparation Time: 10 minutes
Cooking Time: 10 minutes
Servings: 36

Ingredients:

- 1/4 cup (55 g) unsalted butter
- 1 cup (150 g) packed brown sugar
- 1/4 cup (85 g) honey
- 1 egg
- 1 teaspoon vanilla extract
- 1/4 cup (60 ml) skim milk
- 1 teaspoon baking soda
- 1/2 teaspoon baking powder
- 1 cup (82 g) granola
- 3/4 cup quick-cooking oats
- 2 cups whole-wheat pastry flour
- 1 cup (175 g) chocolate chips

Directions:

1. Cream the butter and brown sugar.
2. Mix in honey, egg, vanilla, and milk, then baking soda and baking powder.
3. Add granola, oats, and flour. Mix all ingredients.
4. Stir in chocolate chips.
5. Place on a non-stick baking sheet in teaspoons.
6. Bake at 325°F (170°C, gas mark 3) for 10 minutes.

Nutrition Per Serving:

- Calories: 100
- Total Fat: 3.3 g
- Fiber: 1.5 g
- Protein: 1.8 g
- Carbs: 17 g
- Sodium: 12.5 g
- Sugar: 9 g

306. Oat and Wheat Cookies

Preparation Time: 10 minutes
Cooking Time: 12-15 minutes
Servings: 4

Ingredients:

- 3/4 cup (165 g) unsalted butter
- 1/2 cup (130 g) peanut butter
- 1 cup (150 g) brown sugar
- 1 ¼ cup (150 g) whole-wheat pastry flour
- 1 teaspoon baking soda
- 1 ¼ cup (100 g) rolled oats

Directions:

1. Mix all ingredients.
2. Set by rounded teaspoons onto an ungreased baking sheet.
3. Bake at 375ºF (190ºC, gas mark 5) for 10-12 minutes or until golden brown.
4. Let rest on the baking sheet for 1 minute and then cool on racks.

Nutrition Per Serving:

- Calories: 865
- Fat: 52 g
- Fiber: 9 g
- Carbs: 88 g
- Sugar: 41 g
- Protein: 15.9 g
- Sodium: 155 mg

307. Oatmeal Spice Cookies

Preparation Time: 10 minutes
Cooking Time: 30 minutes
Servings: 48

Ingredients:

- 1 cup (145 g) raisins
- 1 cup (235 ml) water
- 1/2 cup (112 g) unsalted butter, softened
- 1/4 cup (60 ml) vegetable oil
- 1 ½ cup (300 g) sugar
- 2 eggs
- 1 teaspoon vanilla extract
- 2 ½ cups (300 g) whole-wheat pastry flour
- 1/2 teaspoon baking powder
- 1 teaspoon baking soda
- 2 teaspoons cinnamon

- 1/4 teaspoon nutmeg
- 2 cups (160 g) quick-cooking oats
- 1/2 cup (60 g) chopped walnuts

Nutrition Per Serving:

Calories: 107.3

Sodium: 8.74 mg

Fiber: 1.4 g

Carbs: 15.8 g

Sugar: 8 g

Protein: 1.8 g

Directions:

1. Preheat the oven to 350°F (180°C, gas mark 4).
2. Simmer the raisins and water in a saucepan on low until plump, for approximately 20 minutes.
3. Drain the liquid into the measuring cup and add water to make 1/2 cup of liquid.
4. Cream butter, oil, and sugar.
5. Add eggs and vanilla.
6. Stir in the raisin liquid.
7. Sift the flour and spices; add to the sugar mixture.
8. Add oats, nuts, and raisins.
9. Set by rounded teaspoons onto an ungreased baking sheet.
10. Flatten slightly and then bake for 8-10 minutes or until slightly brown.

28 DAY MEAL PLAN

Day	Breakfast	Lunch	Dinner	Snack
1	Celery Apple Juice	Best Homemade Broth	Carrot Ginger Soup	Roasted Carrot Sticks in a Honey Garlic Marinade
2	Homemade Banana Apple Juice	Minerals Rich Broth	Chicken Bone Broth	Tomato Cashew Pesto
3	Sweet Detox Juice	Clean Testing Broth	Homemade Beef Stock	Catalan Style Spinach
4	Strawberry Apple Juice	2-Ingredients Gelatin	Sugar-Free Cinnamon Jelly	Apple and Pistachio Salad on Spinach
5	Autumn Energizer Juice	Aromatic Cinnamon Gelatin	Beef with Mushroom and Broccoli	Guacamole
6	Pineapple Ginger Juice	Veggie Lover's Broth	Chicken Tenders with Honey Mustard Sauce	Energy Balls
7	Carrot Orange Juice	Great Lemon Gelatin	Chicken Vegetable Soup	Covered Bananas
8	Breakfast Cereal	New Year's Luncheon Meal	Pan-Seared Scallops with Lemon-Ginger Vinaigrette	Homemade Hummus
9	Sweet Potato Hash with Sausage and Spinach	Entertaining Wraps	Chicken Cutlets	Pina Colada Smoothie

Day	Breakfast	Lunch	Dinner	Snack
10	Coconut Chia Seed Pudding	Flavorful Shrimp Kabobs	Chicken Cacciatore	Papaya-Mango Smoothie
11	Spinach Frittata	Pan-Seared Scallops	Ground Beef Chili with Tomatoes	Diced Fruits
12	Ripe Plantain Bran Muffins	Outdoor Chicken Kabobs	Cod with Ginger and Black Beans	Almond Butter Sandwich
13	Tasty Veggie Omelet	Mediterranean Shrimp Salad	Beef and Bell Pepper Stir-Fry	Applesauce-Avocado Smoothie
14	Super-Tasty Chicken Muffins	Health Conscious People's Salad	Thin-Cut Pork Chops with Mustardy Kale	Gluten-Free Muffins
15	Multigrain Pancakes	Mexican Enchiladas	Rainbow Buddha Bowl with Cashew Tahini Sauce	Trail Mix Cookies
16	Pasta Fritters	Lamb with Carrot and Brussels Sprouts Spaghetti	Sauteed Butternut Squash	Oatmeal Sunflower Bread
17	Toasty Nut Granola	Salmon with Sesame Seeds and Mushrooms	Beans Trio Chili	Chocolate Peanut Cookies
18	Wheat Waffles	High-Fiber Dumplings	Omega-3 Rich Dinner Meal	Whole-wheat–Chocolate Chip Cookies
19	Cinnamon Apple Omelet	Chicken with Asparagus Salad	Spaghetti Genovese	White Chocolate-Cranberry Cookies
20	Vegetables and Fruits Breakfast	Secretly Amazing Salad	Stuffed Sweet Potato with Hummus Dressing	Onion and Garlic Wheat Bread

Day	Breakfast	Lunch	Dinner	Snack
21	Vitamins Packed Green Juice	Leek Quiche with Olives	Sesame Ginger Chicken Salad	German Dark Bread
22	Baked Oatmeal	Stuffed Trout with Mushrooms	Seared Salmon with Pesto Fettuccine	Trail Mix Cookies
23	Oatmeal Raisin Scones	Pork Steaks with Avocado	Vermicelli Puttanesca	Oatmeal Sunflower Bread
24	Bran Applesauce Muffins	Mediterranean Beef Salad	Catfish Fillets and Rice	Whole-wheat– Chocolate Chip Cookies
25	Crunchy Breakfast Topping	Pork Rolls À La Ratatouille	Beans Trio Chili	Onion and Garlic Wheat Bread
26	Healthier Breakfast Juice	Bolognese with Zucchini Noodles	Sauteed Butternut Squash	Chocolate Peanut Cookies
27	Cornmeal Pancakes	Chicken with Chickpeas	Rainbow Buddha Bowl with Cashew Tahini Sauce	German Dark Bread
28	Homestyle Pancake Mix	Lamb Chops with Beans	Spaghetti Genovese	White Chocolate-Cranberry Cookies

INDEX

Printed in Great Britain
by Amazon

81512648R00129